—David Brakke,
Joe R. Engle Chair in the History of Christianity
and professor of history, The Ohio State University

"This collection of diverse perspectives on the formation and
current status of the New Testament canon is an excellent guide
for students in understanding a discourse of growing importance
among biblical scholars. Stan Porter and Ben Laird's introductory
and concluding chapters are exceptional and nicely frame and focus
a series of essays from five scholars of differing faith traditions, East
and West, and their competing perspectives on the global church's
biblical canon(s). The social and historical contexts into which the
canonical process was earthed in antiquity are carefully considered.
But so are the variety of ongoing theological and existential implications that follow from each contributor's reconstruction of what
happened at ground level when the New Testament was formed and
received as the church's Scripture during the early centuries of the
common era. This collection includes a dialogue between the different contributors that sound a range of agreements and disagreements that classrooms and conferences could take up and explore
with new vitality. Like every good textbook, this collection invites
more questions than it provides answers. I highly recommend *Five
Views on the New Testament Canon* as a fluent and balanced introduction to students interested in the historical origins of the New Testament in both East and West; it is that rare introduction that promises
to cue even more consequential questions of the New Testament's
continuing importance in forming Christian faith."

—Robert W. Wall
The Paul T. Walls Professor Emeritus
of Scripture & Wesleyan Studies,
Seattle Pacific University and Seminary

"This volume is a welcome addition to the Viewpoints series, for discussions on the canon of the New Testament have reached an exciting stage, and the five representative views clarify points of agreement and bones of contention between scholars and further the discussion in a useful way. What excites me most is that arguments over the historical origins and development of the canon have led to a fruitful consideration of the ways in which the canon influences the interpretation of the sacred books. The shape of the canon is hermeneutically significant; it makes a difference to how we read this collection of revered writings. In other words, scholars on canon are beginning to ask and answer the important 'So what?' question. What difference does the position of a book in the canon or its place in a mini-collection of canonical books (e.g., the Four Gospels Corpus, the Catholic Epistles) make to how it is read and applied? The fact that the five scholars give different answers does not diminish the importance of what they are saying but only makes it more interesting, for this provides a range of interpretive options for Bible readers to consider."

—Greg Goswell
academic dean, lecturer in Old Testament,
postgraduate coordinator,
Christ College

"Without question, canon formation is one of the most challenging issues in Old and New Testament inquiry today. This is compounded because no one in antiquity preserved this story, and so multiple—often conflicting—interpretations have emerged from engagement with limited surviving primary sources often rooted in perspectives foreign to the sources themselves. The good news is that we now know more than was possible earlier because of careful scholarly research in recent years, including from the contributors to this volume. I applaud their efforts to bring greater clarity to this story and the multiple conflicting perspectives involved in it. I highly recommend this volume to readers."

—Lee Martin McDonald,
Acadia Divinity College, Acadia University

FIVE
VIEWS
ON THE
NEW
TESTAMENT
CANON

STANLEY E. PORTER • BENJAMIN P. LAIRD

EDITORS

JASON DAVID BEDUHN • IAN BOXALL • DARIAN R. LOCKETT
DAVID R. NIENHUIS • GEORGE L. PARSENIOS
CONTRIBUTORS

Five Views on the New Testament Canon
© 2022 by Stanley E. Porter and Benjamin P. Laird

Published by Kregel Academic, an imprint of Kregel Publications, 2450 Oak Industrial Dr. NE, Grand Rapids, MI 49505-6020.

The Greek font, GraecaU, is available from www.linguistsoftware.com/lgku.htm, +1-425-775-1130.

ISBN 978-0-8254-4727-3

Printed in the United States of America

22 23 24 25 26 / 5 4 3 2 1

CONTENTS

FIVE VIEWS ON THE NEW TESTAMENT CANON: MAJOR PROPOSALS

FIVE RESPONSES TO
THE MAJOR PROPOSALS

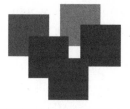

PREFACE

The issue of the formation of the New Testament canon has again become a topic of major discussion. We are pleased with that, because we believe that this is a topic that warrants further exploration. This is not least because there continue to be a wide range of scholarly views on the subject. Because these views are often linked with a variety of theological positions, there are often various and competing interests that insert themselves into the discussion. This volume is an attempt to help sort through many of the issues by providing a means for advocates of some of the various opinions to offer their statements on behalf of these positions and then respond to the proposals of others.

We wish to thank all those who have contributed to this volume in various ways. We first wish to thank our individual contributors. When we contacted each of them, we were not certain of the responses that we would receive. We are pleased that each one has taken his task seriously and offered scholarship of significance in the ongoing debate over the formation of the New Testament canon. We also appreciate their willingness to engage in scholarly debate by offering their essays for the scrutiny of others and their own responding to their colleagues' work. The spirit in which this has been offered has contributed to the enjoyment of working with each author. We also appreciate their timeliness and attention to detail, even though much of the work on this volume occurred during unfortunate circumstances of enduring a global pandemic.

We also wish to thank all our friends at Kregel for their support of this project. From first to last, the people at Kregel have been supportive of the idea and then its execution in this volume. We wish to thank, in particular, Laura Bartlett for her attention to all facets of this project, including details that others might overlook, as well as Robert Hand, who provided excellent guidance throughout the process. We also wish to thank Shawn Vander Lugt for again so expertly managing this book through production.

Each of the editors wishes to thank the other for the opportunity to work together on this project. What began as a chance meeting at one of their doctoral examinations has become a friendship shared over common interests. We look forward to further work together.

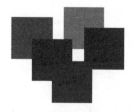

ABBREVIATIONS

ABD	*Anchor Bible Dictionary*
ANF	Ante-Nicene Fathers
BBR	*Bulletin of Biblical Research*
BETL	Bibliotheca Ephemeridum Theologicarum Lovaniensium
BIB	*Biblica*
BMSEC	Baylor-Mohr Siebeck Studies in Early Christianity
BNTC	Black's New Testament Commentaries
BZNW	Beihefte zur Zeitschrift für die neutestamentliche Wissenschaft
CBQ	*Catholic Biblical Quarterly*
EC	*Early Christianity*
EKK	Evangelisch-Katholischer Kommentar zum Neuen Testament
ExAud	*Ex auditu*
FAT	Forschungen zum Alten Testament
HTR	*Harvard Theological Review*
JBL	*Journal of Biblical Literature*
JECS	*Journal of Early Christian Studies*
JETS	*Journal of the Evangelical Theological Society*
JRS	*The Journal of Roman Studies*
JSNTSup	Journal for the Study of the New Testament Supplement Series

JTI	*Journal of Theological Interpretation*
LNTS	Library of New Testament Studies
LSTS	Library of Second Temple Studies
MPER	Mitteilungen aus der Papyrussammlung der Österreichischen Nationalbibliothek
NPNF	The Nicene and Post-Nicene Fathers
PG	Patrologia Graeca
PPSD	Pauline and Patristic Scholars in Debate
RivB	*Rivista biblica italiana*
SBR	Studies of the Bible and Its Reception
SE	*Studia Evangelica*
SP	Sacra Pagina
TENT	Texts and Editions for New Testament Study
TS	*Theological Studies*
VC	*Vigiliae Christianae*

CONTRIBUTORS

Jason David BeDuhn (PhD, Indiana University Bloomington), Northern Arizona University, Flagstaff, Arizona

Ian Boxall (DPhil, University of Oxford), The Catholic University of America, Washington, DC

Benjamin P. Laird (PhD, University of Aberdeen), John W. Rawlings School of Divinity, Liberty University, Lynchburg, Virginia

Darian R. Lockett (PhD, University of St. Andrews), Talbot School of Theology, Biola University, La Mirada, California

David R. Nienhuis (PhD, University of Aberdeen), Seattle Pacific University and Seattle Pacific Seminary, Seattle, Washington

George L. Parsenios (PhD, Yale University), Holy Cross Greek Orthodox School of Theology, Brookline, Massachusetts

Stanley E. Porter (PhD, University of Sheffield), McMaster Divinity College, Hamilton, Ontario

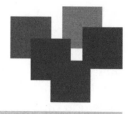

AN INTRODUCTION TO THE STUDY OF THE NEW TESTAMENT CANON

Stanley E. Porter and Benjamin P. Laird

Within a fairly short time of their formation as a recognizable group, Christians began using written texts for a variety of purposes. These texts provided a record of developments within the early church, served as a central medium for the proclamation of their message, and offered a means of providing necessary instruction and exhortation. The use of written works in Christian communities may not seem especially remarkable today, but we must not overlook what they indicate about the roots of Christianity and the literary environment in which they originated. Jesus is not known to have composed any written documents, and only a small percentage of early Christians were literate or had the means to purchase works of literature. Despite these factors, early Christians are known to have composed and circulated a large body of writings. This is clearly attested by a considerable number of writings—both canonical and noncanonical—that have survived from the early centuries of the Christian era. Christianity was, and continues to be, a movement known for its emphasis on written testimony and instruction.

The fact that written texts played such an important function in early Christianity may not seem that profound or significant to those living today, given that the majority of the world's major religions now recognize the authority of a specific collection of writings. To varying degrees, Muslims, Jews, Hindus, and Buddhists, to name just some of the more prominent religions in the modern world, commonly recognize a body of religious writings as authoritative scripture. Outside of Judaism, however, the prominent role of written texts would have been unusual in the first-century Greco-Roman world. Unlike many Greeks and Romans, whose religious experience was often limited to prescribed cultic practices and public gatherings, Christians were known for the emphasis they placed on the public reading and study of religious writings and for the formative role that these texts served in their teaching and doctrine.

Because literacy rates in the first-century Mediterranean world are known to have been relatively low, it might be assumed that the use of Scripture was largely limited to theologians, church leaders, and perhaps a small number of other educated individuals who were fortunate enough to have access to these writings. As we examine the practices associated with early Christian worship, however, and as we consider the ways in which ancient literature was read in public settings, the plausibility of this conclusion begins to diminish. As Harry Gamble helpfully explains, "It may seem paradoxical to say both that Christianity placed a high value on texts and that most Christians were unable to read, but in the ancient world this was no contradiction. In Greco-Roman society the illiterate had access to literacy in a variety of public settings."[1]

---

1.   Harry Y. Gamble, *Books and Readers in the Early Church* (New Haven, CT: Yale University Press, 1995), 8.

One interesting reference to the role of Scripture in the life of the early church appears in the extant writings of the second-century apologist Justin Martyr. At the end of his monumental work known as the *First Apology*, Justin famously describes some of the primary activities that took place when Christians gathered together, one of which was the public reading of Scripture: "And on the day called Sunday, all who live in cities or in the country gather together to one place, and the memoirs of the apostles or the writings of the prophets are read, as long as time permits; then, when the reader has ceased, the president verbally instructs, and exhorts to the imitation of these good things."[2] Of note in this brief description is Justin's assertion that the reading of Scripture was a common practice during public gatherings of Christians. While many Christians would not have owned private copies of the Scriptures or even had the ability to read them, Justin's description would suggest that those who routinely took part in a gathering of the local church would have acquired a familiarity with the content of these writings through the common exercise of public reading.[3] It is also noteworthy that Justin refers not only to "the prophets," a general reference to the writings contained in the Old Testament, but also to the "memoirs of the apostles," a clear reference to the New Testament Gospels. This would suggest not

---

2. *1 Apol.* 67 (ANF 01). A similar statement may be found in Tertullian's *Apology* (*Apol.* 39).

3. For additional insight pertaining to the role of public reading in early Christian gatherings, see Margaret Ellen Lee and Bernard Brandon Scott, *Sound Mapping the New Testament* (Salem, OR: Polebridge, 2009); Brian J. Wright, *Communal Reading in the Time of Jesus: A Window into Early Christian Reading Practices* (Minneapolis: Fortress, 2017); Paul Borgman and Kelley James Clark, *Written to Be Heard: Recovering the Messages of the Gospels* (Grand Rapids: Eerdmans, 2019). However, we must also remember that there were those who could read these texts. Over the course of time, a system of manuscript markings was developed to guide readers. These are known as ekphonetic notation and are found on numerous ancient biblical manuscripts, especially those used liturgically. Such notation is often not included in editions of ancient manuscripts. For some major exceptions, see Stanley E. Porter and Wendy J. Porter, *New Testament Greek Papyri and Parchments. New Editions: Texts, Plates*, 2 vols., MPER 29, 30 (Berlin: de Gruyter, 2008), esp. nos. 24 and 40.

only that the public reading of Scripture was common during Christian gatherings, but that it included the ancient Jewish writings as well as a diverse collection of freshly composed Christian works.

The use of Scripture, of course, was not an aberration during a unique period of Christian history. For nearly two millennia, the New Testament writings have served as an important foundation of the church's doctrine, shaped the church's mission, and provided inspiration to countless readers. It is, in fact, no exaggeration to conclude that the New Testament has been the most influential collection of writings—religious or otherwise—since the time they were composed some two millennia ago. Despite the profound influence that the New Testament writings have played in shaping the church's doctrine and teaching and the affection that they continue to receive today, several of the events and factors that played a role in the formation of the New Testament canon remain a matter of dispute, as does the canon's theological basis and hermeneutical significance. Many contemporary readers have serious questions regarding the historical factors that led to the origin of the New Testament—questions that often have very practical implications for one's understanding of Christianity. How do we know that the correct books were selected? Who was responsible for determining what material was included? What makes one writing more authoritative than another? Was the concept of a "canon" of agreed-upon authoritative writings merely a later invention? Was this process designed to suppress certain forms of Christianity that were viewed as unacceptable? These are just a few of the types of important questions that linger in the minds of many today.

It does not take much imagination to appreciate the significance of these types of questions for one's understanding of the Christian faith. Depending on one's perspective, the writings contained in the New Testament might be regarded as the authoritative and trustworthy witness to the person and work of Jesus Christ or as simply the extant records of one version of

Christianity that rose to prominence at some point during the post-apostolic period. This book is designed to provide a variety of perspectives on important questions such as those raised above. Whether one is a student formally studying the New Testament for the first time or has engaged in serious study of the background and origins of the New Testament for many years, our hope is that the present volume will provide useful information and insight that will enable readers to become familiar with the major issues in the canon debate and how they are addressed by scholars from various backgrounds. More will be said later in this introduction about the objectives and content of this volume. It will be helpful to begin, however, with a brief survey of scholarship relating to the New Testament canon and the major issues that are often disputed.

A Brief History of Prior Discussion of the New Testament Canon

The subject of the New Testament canon has elicited significant interest in recent scholarship, resulting in the publication of numerous works that attempt to lay out the major parameters of the discussion. This has not always been the case, however, as scholars took up the subject of the canon's formation only infrequently during the eighteenth and early nineteenth century and rarely at all before then. As Bruce Metzger explains,

> Throughout the Middle Ages questions were seldom raised as to the number and identity of the books comprising the canon of the New Testament. Even during the period of the Renaissance and Reformation, despite occasional discussions (such as those by Erasmus and Cajetan) concerning the authorship of the Epistle to the Hebrews, several of the Catholic Epistles, and the Book or Revelation, no one dared seriously to dispute their canonicity.[4]

---

4.   Bruce M. Metzger, *The Canon of the New Testament: Its Origin, Development, and Significance* (Oxford: Clarendon, 1987), 11.

Through the sixteenth century, the canon's status was largely unquestioned, despite several lingering questions regarding the authorship and background of several of the canonical writings. The legitimacy of the canon was largely taken for granted and was not a subject of significant scholarly curiosity or inquiry. However, as scholars during the Enlightenment and post-Enlightenment periods began to focus more intently on issues relating to the historical background of the individual canonical writings, questions relating to the canon's formation and legitimacy began to be pursued with greater rigor. This was to be expected, of course, as challenges to the traditional view of the authorship and dating of the biblical writings have natural implications for one's understanding of the formation of the New Testament canon.

From roughly the seventeenth century until the middle of the nineteenth century, the study of the canon proceeded mostly in fits and starts. During this time, scholars began to explore various aspects of the canon's development and produced a variety of scholarly works, albeit much less frequently than works on the canon are typically produced today.[5] It was during the middle of the nineteenth century that scholarship relating to the formation of the canon began to increase in earnest. Since this time, a number of articles, monographs, and other scholarly works have been published on virtually all aspects of the canon. These works seem to have appeared in three major waves before the present resurgence, which we will briefly outline below. Our objective here is not to provide an exhaustive history of research relating to the New Testament canon but rather to account for the seminal works that have shaped scholarly discussion. We fully recognize that, in addition to what we mention here, other scholarly works on canon have

---

5.   For an overview of the scholarship related to the New Testament canon prior to the twentieth century, see Metzger, *The Canon of the New Testament*, 11–24.

been published since the mid-nineteenth century. Nevertheless, it is worth noting some of the enduring works in the field.[6]

Works to note from the middle of the nineteenth century
include the English scholar Brooke Foss Westcott's surprisingly
thorough historical study that attaches appendices with much of
the evidence still considered in discussions of canon.[7] Westcott's
work on canon, which went through seven editions over forty
years, is still worth consulting, even if it is usually neglected in
contemporary debate, as it provides a historically grounded argument for early canon formation by a theologically oriented New
Testament scholar. The German scholar Heinrich Holtzmann
wrote a similar kind of book at about the same time, in which he
argues for a historically grounded Protestant (Lutheran) view of
the canon in distinction to a Roman Catholic view that emphasized tradition.[8] Their work was followed by the more progressive historical-critical scholarship of the Alsatian scholar Edouard
Reuss, who argues for a later date of canonical formation and
acceptance, in his thorough history from the earliest Greek
manuscripts to the nineteenth century.[9]

A second major wave of scholarship on the canon took
place near the end of the nineteenth century and into the early
twentieth century. During these years, several notable works on
the New Testament canon were published by some of the most
enduring figures in the discussion. The most thorough but in
some ways most problematic treatment of the New Testament

---

6. For additional treatment of scholarship on the canon produced during the
    twentieth century, see Harry Y. Gamble, "The New Testament Canon: Recent
    Research and the Status Quaestionis," in *The Canon Debate*, eds. Lee Martin
    McDonald and James A. Sanders (Peabody, MA: Hendrickson, 2002), 267–94;
    Metzger, *The Canon of the New Testament*, 25–36.

7. Brooke Foss Westcott, *A General Survey of the History of the Canon of the New
    Testament*, 7th ed. (London: Macmillan, 1896).

8. Heinrich Julius Holtzmann, *Kanon und Tradition: Ein Beitrag zur neueren
    Dogmengeschichte und Symbolik* (Ludwigsburg: Ferdinand Riehm, 1859).

9. Edouard Reuss, *Histoire de canon des écritures saintes dans l'église Chrétienne*
    (Strasbourg: Treuttel et Wurtz, 1863); ET of 2nd ed. of 1863: *History of the Canon
    of the Holy Scriptures in the Christian Church*, trans. David Hunter (Edinburgh:
    James Gemmell, 1884).

canon was written by the German scholar Theodor Zahn,[10] who provides extensive documentation of sources in very full footnotes throughout. His work was instrumental in formulating some of the enduring theories regarding canon formation such as the early use of the canonical writings in Christian worship, but he is inconsistent regarding the date of canon formation. He apparently wanted to argue for an early, pre-Marcionite form of an incipient canon but recognized that there was still flux even past 200 CE. He was promptly attacked for his conclusions regarding the significance of 200 CE by Adolf Harnack, who argued for a later date than Zahn, with both of them responding to the possible influence of Marcion.[11] Not to be outdone, the French Roman Catholic scholar Alfred Loisy, writing at approximately the same time as Zahn, published a thorough and in some ways equivalent treatment of the topic in French, just years before he was excommunicated by the Roman Catholic church for his modernist views, not least his elevation of critical biblical scholarship over the traditions and dogma associated with Catholicism.[12] With respect to the biblical writings, Loisy criticizes the conviction that some works were of divine origin, describing this belief as "naïve," "inconceivable," and "artificial and fragile."[13] Further contributions to the discussion were made by the German scholar Hans Lietzmann, who succeeded Harnack at Berlin, in a short volume that recognizes

---

10. Theodor Zahn, *Geschichte des Neutestamentlichen Kanons*, 2 vols. (Erlangen: Deichert, 1888–1892). Zahn wrote a shorter summary of his view in Zahn, *Grundriss der Geschichte des Neutestamentlichen Kanons: Eine Ergänzung zu der Einleitung in das Neue Testament* (Leipzig: Deichert, 1904). The first volume of Zahn's work is critically and insightfully reviewed by Alfred Plummer, "Zahn on the New Testament Canon," *Classical Review* 3 (1892): 410–12.

11. Adolf Harnack, *Das Neue Testament um das Jahr 200* (Freiburg: J. C. B. Mohr, 1889); ET: *The Origin of the New Testament and the Most Important Consequences of the New Creation*, trans. J. R. Wilkinson (New York: Macmillan, 1925).

12. Alfred Loisy, *Histoire du canon du Nouveau Testament* (Paris: J. Maisonneuve, 1891); ET: *The Origins of the New Testament*, trans. L. P. Jacks (London: Allen and Unwin, 1950).

13. Loisy, *The Origins of the New Testament*, 10–11.

the continuing difficulties of the canonical question,[14] and by Caspar René Gregory who treats both canon and text (although canon in 290 pages).[15] A similar though much abbreviated work was written by the Scottish classicist Alexander Souter, who also provides forty pages of documents pertinent to the discussion of canon (most untranslated from their original sources).[16]

One of the frequent elements of the first two waves of discussion of the New Testament canon—besides their often exhaustive recounting and treatment of the early documentary sources—is their attention to canon formation and its importance up to and including the sixteenth century or so, a feature that is often not treated at length, and sometimes at all, in the later discussions. Nevertheless, we see that regardless of the orientation of the author and the nature of their conclusions, similar issues regarding history, theology, the role of the church and tradition, and the importance of various forms of evidence, among others, continue to emerge in discussion of the New Testament canon.

A third surge in studies of the New Testament canon took place in the 1960s and lasted until the 1980s. One of the first significant works on canon published during this period was that of the German church historian Hans Campenhausen.[17] This thorough and well-documented treatment of the New Testament canon reflects a new trend in canon studies in that it is only concerned to treat in detail the period up to Origen. During the 1980s, the work by William Farmer and Denis Farkasfalvy combines the interests and approaches of a Protestant (Methodist) and a Roman Catholic, with their emphases

---

14. Hans Lietzmann, *Wie wurden die Bücher des Neuen Testaments heilige Schrift? Fünf Vorträge*, Lebensfragen (Tübingen: Mohr Siebeck, 1907).

15. Caspar René Gregory, *Canon and Text of the New Testament* (Edinburgh: T&T Clark, 1907), esp. 5–295.

16. Alexander Souter, *Text and Canon of the New Testament*, 2nd ed. (London: Duckworth, 1954).

17. Hans Campenhausen, *Die Entstehung der christlichen Bibel* (Tübingen: Mohr Siebeck, 1968); ET: *The Formation of the Christian Bible*, trans. J. A. Baker (London: A&C Black, 1972).

upon the early church and the church fathers.[18] This period may conveniently be closed by noting the book on canon by Metzger, who recognizes the relatively neglected study of canon.[19] Just a year later, F. F. Bruce published his book on the biblical canon, which focuses mostly upon the New Testament writings.[20] The works of Metzger and Bruce are notable for their evaluation of a variety of historical witnesses to the early state of the canon, their consideration of several factors that may have prompted the formation and recognition of the canon, and their discussion of various theological matters that had previously received only scant attention.[21]

Scholarly engagement with the subject of the canon has continued steadily since the 1990s. Since this time, a number of journal articles, essays, and specialized studies on various aspects of the canon have been published. As a general observation, works produced since the 1990s on the entirety of the canon have been written for a more popular audience, while the more scholarly works have tended to focus on particular aspects of the canon's formation such as a particular canonical subcollection, the reception of the New Testament writings in the extant works of historical figures (e.g., Papias or Irenaeus), or the significance of a particular witness to the early state of the canon such as the Muratorian Fragment, the *Diatessaron*, or the canon of Marcion.

Subjects that have received a greater degree of attention in recent years include the emergence of the various canonical subcollections (e.g., the fourfold Gospel, the Pauline corpus,

---

18. William R. Farmer and Denis M. Farkasfalvy, *The Formation of the New Testament Canon: An Ecumenical Approach* (New York: Paulist, 1983).
19. Metzger, *The Canon of the New Testament*.
20. F. F. Bruce, *The Canon of Scripture* (Glasgow: Chapter House; Downers Grove, IL: InterVarsity Press, 1988), 115–251.
21. Additional works of note published during the 1960s through the 1980s include C. F. D. Moule, *The Birth of the New Testament*, BNTC (London: A&C Black, 1962); Robert M. Grant, *The Formation of the New Testament* (New York: Harper, 1965); Harry Y. Gamble, *The New Testament Canon: Its Making and Meaning* (Philadelphia: Fortress, 1985). Moule's volume was revised in subsequent editions in 1966 and 1981.

and the Catholic Epistles) and the insight that our knowledge of ancient literary conventions may provide for how collections of writings were typically assembled, distributed, and reproduced. Unlike the seminal works of the past that focused primarily or even exclusively on historical matters, many contemporary scholars have expressed significant interest in hermeneutical questions related to the canon, many of which are taken up by the contributors of this volume.

Although a substantial number of scholarly works have been published over the last three decades on the reception of certain canonical writings, one or more early witnesses to the canon, and a number of additional subjects, we may briefly highlight three volumes published since the 1990s that have contributed to the study of the New Testament canon as a whole. Lee Martin McDonald's 2007 publication of *The Biblical Canon* covers the entire canon and devotes roughly two hundred pages and several appendices to the New Testament writings.[22] McDonald has published additional works on the New Testament canon, many of which expand upon the content of this volume. A second volume is Tomas Bokedal's 2014 monograph that seeks to "draw the reader's attention to historical dimensions of the canon and its interpretive possibilities for our time."[23] While recognizing that the formation of the canon was a historical process, Bokedal places attention on the theological significance of the canon and textual features that point to its normative function in the life of the church. A third work is Edmon Gallagher and John Meade's study of early canonical lists.[24] A number of earlier authors cited above include such lists, but this volume provides a thorough treatment of the lists

---

22. Lee Martin McDonald, *The Formation of the Biblical Canon: Its Origin, Transmission, and Authority* (Peabody, MA: Hendrickson, 2007). This volume builds upon two prior editions, the second of which was published in 1995.
23. Tomas Bokedal, *The Formation and Significance of the Christian Biblical Canon: A Study in Text, Ritual and Interpretation* (London: Bloomsbury, 2014), xiii.
24. Edmon L. Gallagher and John D. Meade, *The Biblical Canon Lists from Early Christianity: Texts and Analysis* (Oxford: Oxford University Press, 2017).

found in the writings of church fathers, biblical manuscripts, and other sources, all with English translations.

Major Issues in the Canon Debate

Despite a proliferation of scholarly publications that have been produced over the last two centuries on virtually every facet of the New Testament canon, scholars often disagree over fundamental questions relating to the canon's formation as well as a variety of theological and hermeneutical matters. Before presenting various perspectives on the canon, it is helpful first to offer a brief overview of some major points of contention.

The historical questions regarding the canon are numerous and wide-ranging. While we cannot discuss or even identify each of the historical questions that have been debated in recent decades, we may briefly mention four disputed subjects that are central to the debate over the canon's composition and early formation. These are: (1) the biblical authors' self-understanding, (2) the major factors which prompted the formation of the canon, (3) the process involved in the canon's formation, and (4) the question of authorship and apostolic authority.

We will briefly treat each of these issues in order. (1) There is significant disagreement regarding the sense in which the biblical authors understood the nature of their own writings. When an author such as Paul composed an epistle, did he anticipate that it would be regarded as Scripture or even as part of a larger body of writings that would be read by Christians in future centuries, or did he simply seek to address matters of immediate concern with no thought of its future use? To state the question differently, if Paul or one of the other authors of the New Testament writings were alive today, would they be surprised to learn that their works were preserved and still being read, or would they express disappointment that they were not being read as often or taken as seriously as they envisioned? The occasional nature of the New Testament writings—for example, Paul wrote his letters to address current issues in local churches—is often emphasized, and rightly so. The biblical authors clearly wrote with identifiable audiences in mind and sought to address matters that they perceived to be relevant to their unique situation and that of their readers. The situation facing the original audience and the circumstances that prompted an author to write are certainly more apparent in some writings than others, yet the occasional nature of the New Testament writings is widely acknowledged. What is more difficult to determine, of course, is what the authors of the New Testament believed about the nature of their work. Did they believe that their writings were of relevance to those who were not among the original recipients? Did they anticipate that their works would be preserved and ultimately read by Christians around the world and treated as authoritative Scripture? By accepting certain writings as canonical Scripture, are modern Christians ascribing certain attributes to the writings that were not anticipated by the original authors? Many would argue that a writing's occasional nature does not preclude its status as authoritative Scripture or its universal relevance today, yet the precise sense in which the authors of the New Testament understood the nature of their writings remains a matter of dispute.

(2) There remains significant debate over the leading factors that prompted the formation of the New Testament canon. Some have suggested that the canon's emergence was a natural and organic process that was the inevitable result of the natural affinity that early Christians shared for the apostolic writings. No single event precipitated the formation of the canon, some have argued, and no organized body or individual was responsible for its establishment or determining its contents. There may not have been widespread agreement relating to the extent of the canon in the first few centuries of the Christian era, but the core elements of the New Testament were widely recognized. According to this perspective, those writings believed to be rooted in the apostolic period were quickly embraced as authoritative Scripture, and because of their elevated status, they eventually came to be recognized as a discrete literary collection.

Not all scholars are convinced, however, that the emergence of the canon was a natural process or even that the concept of canon had emerged during the first few centuries of the Christian movement. Many have concluded that there was no consensus in the early decades of the Christian era on which writings were to be regarded as Scripture and that it was not until the church was faced with significant internal division or some type of external threat that the need for an established body of apostolic writings became apparent. There may have been a basic concept of Scripture among early Christians, it might be argued, but it was not until decades or even centuries later that the concept of a canon emerged. This emergence of a canon, it has been suggested, was likely prompted by the recognition that the church needed an established body of authoritative writings that could be used to suppress theological movements regarded as aberrant and harmful and to more carefully define the beliefs that were to be the essence of the Christian faith. Some have speculated that it was the influence of the second-century heretic Marcion or the threat of Gnostic Christianity during the second century that led the church's leadership to reject some writings and to elevate the status of those now regarded as canonical. Others, on the other hand, have contended that the universal recognition of the canon does not appear to have taken place until the fourth century when the church's leaders sought to unite a diverse network of Christian communities throughout the Roman world around a unified body of doctrine. This effort was a necessary measure to confront various theological controversies such as the one instigated by the subordinationist Christological teaching of Arius that was opposed by the Council of Nicaea in 325 CE.

(3) Scholars differ in the ways in which they account for the actual process of the canon's formation. With such a diverse body of writings composed by various authors, each of whom wrote during a different time, in a unique place, and under different circumstances, it is only natural to ask how the writings of the canon came together and emerged as a single

literary collection recognized by Christians around the world. For some, the process likely had more to do with the reception of the individual writings than with specific circumstances or events that may have made an immediate impact on which writings were included in the collection. It might be argued, for example, that Christian readers naturally gravitated to writings that were regarded as foundational to the faith, theologically sound, and practically significant. As collections of early Christian writings circulated, certain writings were commonly present and remained popular, while the circulation of others was largely limited to certain locations and eventually waned in popularity. By the fourth or fifth century, the writings now contained in the New Testament had stood the test of time, so to speak, and remained widely esteemed for their connection to the apostles, their theological importance, their fidelity to the teaching of Christ and the apostles, and their practical relevance for Christian living.

A similar understanding of the canon's development also affirms that the formation of the canon was a gradual and natural process, but it places more emphasis on the development of various subcollections. As will be discussed further below, most of the canonical writings first circulated as part of one of three or four smaller subcollections of Christian writings. We find evidence, for example, for the early circulation of the fourfold Gospel, the Pauline Epistles, and the Catholic Epistles—the last of which occasionally circulated alongside of Acts—and possibly some of the Johannine writings.[25] Because of the existence of these smaller collections, it might be suggested that the formation of the canon was simply the result of the eventual combination of the smaller collections into a single codex, a process that would have been quite natural at the time.

Others are more inclined to assume that specific events or threats to the church were largely responsible for the formation

---

25. See Stanley E. Porter, *How We Got the New Testament: Text, Transmission, Translation* (Grand Rapids: Baker, 2013), 84–124.

of the canon. As previously noted, the perceived need for a collection of authoritative writings is often thought to have emerged when the church faced various theological controversies and when its leadership sought to unite against certain theological systems of thought deemed aberrant or seen as a threat to the church's unity. It was in response to such threats that the church's leadership actively suppressed and marginalized some writings and elevated the importance of others. Consequently, it may be said that the church's leadership—leadership that was very much tied to the state by the middle of the fourth century—was largely responsible for establishing which writings were to be regarded as authoritative Scripture and for shaping the canonical collection that has been passed down over the centuries. Those who hold to this perspective tend to understand the emergence of the canon more as a consciously planned ecclesial event than as a natural or spontaneous development.

(4) A fourth major historical matter of controversy relates to the subject of authorship and the scope of apostolic literature. As a result of the developments during the Enlightenment period, biblical scholars began to question much more strenuously the authenticity and the traditional view of authorship of numerous writings in the New Testament. Scholars began to challenge, for example, the tradition that the Gospels were written by Matthew, Mark, Luke, and John and the authenticity of several of the epistles ascribed to authors such as Paul, Peter, and John. Unwilling to take anything for granted and equipped with new methodological approaches to the study of ancient texts, scholars began to scrutinize the language and content of each writing and to ascertain what the content of each work might reveal about the historical context in which it was written. These studies often concluded that the New Testament canon includes several inauthentic writings produced during the late first and even as late as the mid-second centuries. The nineteenth-century German theologian F. C. Baur, for example, famously argued

that the authentic epistles in the Pauline letter corpus were limited to Romans, 1–2 Corinthians, and Galatians, a collection which he referred to as the *Hauptbriefe* (the primary or main letters). Many other scholars embraced similar positions (or, in some cases, even more extreme ones), concluding that several of the canonical epistles were written by the companions of the apostles or by their later admirers who sought to evoke the apostles' authority to combat theological controversies or simply to contextualize the teaching of the apostles for subsequent generations of Christians. Many concluded, for example, that the Pastoral Epistles were written long after Paul's lifetime, as late as the mid-second century, to combat the rise of Gnostic Christianity or the teachings of Marcion.

It is not difficult to recognize the ways in which one's viewpoint on the authorship of the New Testament writings will invariably influence one's understanding of the formation of the canon or perspective on its contemporary relevance. To return to the Pauline letter corpus, the determination that several of the epistles attributed to Paul are later pseudepigraphal works will naturally demand that one embrace the position that this collection did not emerge until several decades after Paul's lifetime, perhaps even as late as the mid-second century, or that new writings such as Ephesians, Colossians, 2 Thessalonians, and the Pastorals continued to be added to the collection at various points after Paul's martyrdom. As this example effectively illustrates, scholarly perspectives on the emergence of the canon are often shaped less by the earliest and most relevant historical witnesses to the canon and more by critical assessments of the authorship of the individual writings. One would be hard-pressed to find evidence in the historical sources, for example, that the authenticity of Ephesians or Colossians was seriously questioned in the early church or that these writings only began to circulate as part of the Pauline corpus some years after the collection emerged. When these writings are determined to have been written years after the lifetime of Paul, however, theories that hold to a later emergence of the corpus or its gradual expansion in subsequent decades become more attractive and even necessary.

In addition to these significant historical issues, scholars have offered a variety of perspectives on diverse theological matters pertaining to the canon. This may be seen, for example, in how scholars have articulated the basis of the canon's authority. Now that the extent of the canon has been widely recognized, do the canonical writings remain authoritative for Christians living today? If so, what is the basis of this authority? Do the works of the New Testament bear authority because of their intrinsic nature, because of their apostolic origins, because they were deemed authoritative by the church at a particular point in time, or simply because God in his providence led the church to make use of them? These types of questions have been answered in a variety of ways and continue to be debated.

As noted above, it is commonly thought that the church's leadership was largely responsible for establishing and shaping the canon of Scripture. This viewpoint often leads to the related conclusion that the authority of the canonical writings—whether real or perceived—is based upon its reception by the early church. Contrary to what some might expect, those who point to the reception of a writing as the basis of its authority often hold differing perspectives on the significance of authorship. For some, the human hand behind the composition of the writings is inconsequential. Whether a writing was composed by the apostle Peter in the first century or an unknown Christian writer in the early second century, a writing such as 2 Peter should be recognized as authoritative because of its reception by the church. Interestingly, this type of reasoning may be observed among those who hold very different viewpoints about authorship and the role of inspiration. Some may argue, for example, that the New Testament contains several pseudepigraphal writings but that the pseudepigraphal nature of a work does not negate its authoritative status. What matters is that God in his providence saw fit to include these writings in the biblical canon and that they bear witness to divine truths. On the other hand, those who deny the presence of pseudepigraphal works in the canon might affirm the authority of an anonymous work such as Hebrews based on the conviction that God has likewise led the church to embrace it as authoritative Scripture. In sum, many hold that each of the writings of the canon, regardless of the human author, has been effectively used to inform, inspire, and encourage God's people and should not be rejected or relegated to secondary status simply because of a particular judgment about the circumstances surrounding its composition.

Not all who attribute the canon's perceived authority to its reception by the church agree that the New Testament writings continue to bear authority today. According to some scholars, there is a notable difference between perceived and actual authority. The church may have recognized certain writings as canonical, but this does not change the nature of the writings or make them any more authoritative today. Why should the canonical writings be recognized as authoritative by modern readers simply because they were recognized as such by Christians during a particular time in history? According to this line of thinking, canonicity is merely a historical designation that is incapable of altering the inherent nature of human writings. The writings produced by early Christians, whether or not they were ultimately recognized as canonical, are human compositions that are little more than expressions of personal perspectives on matters of religious interest. They describe notable events, reflect on various theological subjects, and offer instruction on pertinent matters facing the church during a particular time, but those who penned these works were certainly not flawless and often treated these subjects in a manner that reveals their personal biases, antiquated thinking, and unrefined thought. Contemporary readers may resonate with the content of the canonical writings and find its instruction to be a helpful guide for living the Christian faith in modern contexts, but this does not change the fact that these writings are merely human reflections on ancient events and matters of theological interest. That certain writings came to be recognized as canonical Scripture may be observed as a matter of historical fact, but this historical development should not be confused with actual or intrinsic authority.

A far different explanation of the authority of the writings is shared by those who affirm the divine inspiration of the canonical writings and/or the authority of certain writers. Rather than attributing the authority of the canonical writings to their early reception by the church—a reception marked primarily by the widespread use of writings in public worship—or to a particular ecclesiastical body at some point in church history, others have argued that the authority of the writings should be based upon their status as inspired Scripture. According to this perspective, the church simply affirmed or recognized the writings that could be traced back to the apostles and their close companions and bore the characteristics of divine inspiration—characteristics such as catholicity and orthodoxy. According to this perspective, the recognition of a writing's authority is not to be confused with the basis of its authority. The New Testament writings remain authoritative today, it might be argued, because they were inspired by the Holy Spirit, not because they were received by the church in general or recognized by an ecclesial body during a particular time in church history. As Michael Kruger has contended, "Books do not become canonical—they are canonical because they are the books God has given as a permanent guide for his church. Thus, from this perspective, it is the existence of the canonical books that is determinative, not their function or reception."[26] One of the challenges to this perspective, of course, is determining how one is to determine which writings were in fact inspired. Is this a subjective opinion based upon one's evaluation of a writing's content? Is it an inadvertent recognition of the church's authority given that it equates the inspired writings with those the

---

26. Michael J. Kruger, *The Question of Canon: Challenging the Status Quo in the New Testament Debate* (Downers Grove, IL: InterVarsity, 2013), 40.

church received? Alternatively, is it based on the identity of the human authors, a viewpoint that makes one's critical assessment of the historical background of the writings determinative? In sum, if inspiration is to be regarded as the basis of a writing's authority, how is this to be assessed? By weighing its content, by its historical reception, or by its human authorship?

Having discussed several of the major historical and theological issues that feature prominently in canon studies, we may finally observe that scholars often disagree about the possible hermeneutical significance of the canon. For some, one's reading of the New Testament is to be informed by the way the canonical writings are arranged and structured and by various intertextual features that are present throughout the text. Those who hold to this perspective often emphasize that the canonical structure of the New Testament did not arbitrarily develop and that readers should approach the text with an awareness of what the placement of a given writing may reveal about its canonical function, that is, the way it is designed to complement or provide balance to the other writings. According to this perspective, the New Testament is not to be read as an assortment of disparate writings with little connection to one another, but as part of a coherent story of redemptive history.

Scholars are drawn to canonical readings of the New Testament for a variety of reasons. For some, the canonical reading of Scripture is appropriate, even demanded, in view of the way the writings have been preserved. Because God led the church not only to recognize a specific collection of writings but to preserve them in a particular form, the form should not be overlooked or regarded as something of mere historical interest. Others seem drawn to a canonical interpretation of the New Testament for the practical reason that it elevates the importance of certain writings that historical-critical scholars have relegated to secondary status. For scholars such as Brevard Childs, a canonical reading of Scripture is a necessary antidote to the unfortunate consequences of biblical scholarship during the nineteenth and twentieth centuries that determined that certain writings were inauthentic or products of the post-apostolic church.[27] Critical scholars may be correct in their judgment that certain writings are inauthentic, Childs and others have suggested, but misguided in relegating them to secondary status. A work's significance is to be measured not by its ability to withstand the judgments of historians but by the contribution it makes to the canon as a whole and its use in the life of the church. Rather than obscure relics of antiquity, the canonical writings have been preserved and treasured by the church for two millennia. As an illustration of how a canonical reading might shape one's perspective on the significant role of the writings deemed inauthentic by critical scholars, consider Childs' perspective on the Pastoral Epistles. In his work on the Pauline letter corpus, Childs suggested that these writings are designed to demonstrate to readers how the teachings of "Paul" were to be understood and applied in their contemporary context.[28] While Childs did not affirm the authenticity of the Pastorals, he nonetheless recognized the notable contribution that they make in providing clarity regarding the church's application of the Pauline writings in later contexts. As readers will observe in the chapters that follow, some of the contributors to this volume hold strongly to the necessity of a canonical approach to the New Testament but disagree on various subjects such as the role of the church in the canonical process and the historical background of the individual writings.

Another matter that seems to be unsettled among those who advocate a canonical interpretation is the extent to which the doctrine of inspiration applies to the canonical process. Should inspiration be limited to the composition of the texts, or might it also apply to the formation of the canon or even the

---

27. The same concern has also led many to embrace a so-called theological interpretation of Scripture (TIS). For this reason, many of those associated with the theological interpretation movement have been drawn to a canonical reading of Scripture.

28. Brevard S. Childs, *The Church's Guide for Reading Paul: The Canonical Shaping of the Pauline Corpus* (Grand Rapids: Eerdmans, 2008), 69–75.

arrangement of the material? At what point does inspiration end and human activity begin? Also, what is the relationship between inspiration and divine providence? Might it be possible to attribute certain aspects of the formation of the canon to inspiration and others to providence?

Despite some modern adherents, not all scholars are convinced of the legitimacy or even of the benefit of reading Scripture in a canonical manner. Such scholars might object that the original readers would not have had access to the broader canon and would, quite naturally, have read the writings independently and without the influence or even the awareness of a larger body of writings. Are we to suppose that early Christians were somehow disadvantaged by their inability to read the writings they received in their proper canonical context? Were the original readers of 1 Peter, for example, incapable of fully understanding and benefitting from this epistle without access to the other Catholic Epistles? Some might also object that discrepancies in how the writings were arranged and presented in different times and in different locations call canonical approaches to the reading of Scripture into question. If a canonical interpretation is to be recognized, which specific canonical arrangement is to be preferred? The extant biblical manuscripts attest to a noticeable degree of divergence in the way the individual writings were presented and arranged. Some manuscripts, for example, place the Catholic Epistles immediately after Acts, while others place them after the Pauline Epistles.[29] There are also differences in how the writings within a given subcollection are arranged. This is most apparent in the witnesses to the Pauline Epistles and Catholic Epistles. With regard to the Pauline Epistles, it has been observed that the writings were initially arranged on the basis of length. The only notable exception to this,

---

29. See Stanley E. Porter, "The Early Church and Today's Church: Insights from the Book of Acts," *McMaster Journal of Theology and Ministry* 17 (2015–2016): 72–100, esp. 73–75.

of course, is Hebrews. As the textual witnesses indicate, however, the placement of Hebrews at the end of the corpus was a later development that took place several centuries after the Pauline corpus first began to circulate.

In sum, many scholars remain reluctant to embrace canonical approaches to the study of the New Testament out of concern that the canonical features of the New Testament are later developments in church history that provide little assistance in understanding the original message of the biblical writers or how the canonical writings would have been understood by their readers. Proponents, of course, remain convinced that a canonical reading is demanded by the way the writings have been preserved and handed down over the centuries by the church, that some of the canonical features of the New Testament emerged prior to the post-apostolic period, and that a canonical reading provides a helpful correction to what they regard as the unfortunate neglect of certain writings.

What This Volume Aims to Accomplish

As we have observed, scholars continue to debate several significant questions relating to the canon, such as the precise circumstances that prompted the composition of each writing; the way the writings were collected, edited, distributed, and preserved; the basis of Scripture's authority; and the manner in which the canonical writings are to be interpreted and applied in modern contexts. Given the complex nature of the subject of canon, it is simply not possible for a single volume such as this to provide a comprehensive treatment of all facets of the canon's history or the many theological and hermeneutical subjects to which it relates. There are simply too many subjects to explore and too many perspectives to consider! Rather than attempting to offer a thorough overview of the history of the canon or focus on a particular aspect of its history, our objective in this volume is to provide readers with a unique opportunity to evaluate a variety of perspectives on the more foundational questions relating to the study of canon.

We have invited five biblical scholars with expertise in the New Testament canon who come from different backgrounds and hold divergent theological persuasions to provide their perspective on three fundamental aspects of the canon: (1) the historical factors that led to the formation and recognition of an authoritative collection of Christian writings, (2) the basis of the canon's authority, and (3) the hermeneutical implications of the canon. In addition to offering in a single chapter their unique perspectives on the foundational historical, theological, and hermeneutical issues that relate to the canon, each contributor has been invited to write a response chapter in which they will evaluate and reflect upon the ways their colleagues have addressed these questions. Following the response chapters, we will conclude the volume with thoughts on the overall contribution of the volume, the state of canon studies, and matters that warrant further scholarly attention. Our hope is that the volume will provide readers with a better sense of how scholars from different backgrounds address key questions relating to the canon and where there may be general agreement or disagreement. We anticipate that many readers will be surprised to learn that certain perspectives that they have taken for granted regarding the nature, function, and emergence of the canon have not been embraced as widely as they had imagined. We further anticipate that many readers will be confronted with viewpoints and perspectives that they have not seriously considered and that they will be encouraged to carefully examine the merits of their own positions and to engage in further research and reflection.

As noted above, the five contributors to this volume come from different backgrounds and hold unique perspectives on the key questions related to the canon. The first two contributors represent differing evangelical perspectives. Darian Lockett, professor of New Testament at Talbot Theological Seminary, represents a "conservative evangelical" perspective, while David Nienhuis, professor of New Testament and associate dean of academic programs at Seattle Pacific University, represents what we have described as a "progressive evangelical" perspective. Because there are a variety of perspectives on canon within the evangelical tradition, we have determined that it would be helpful to invite two contributors to represent two of the ways in which evangelical scholars understand the subject of canon. While evangelicals typically share a high view of Scripture and recognize its centrality in the life of the church, not all scholars within this tradition agree over matters such as the nature of Scripture, the background of the individual writings, or the role of the church in establishing the canon.

The third major essay presented in this volume represents what might be described as a "liberal Protestant" perspective and will be presented by Jason BeDuhn, professor of the comparative study of religions at Northern Arizona University. BeDuhn, while not affiliated with a particular Protestant tradition, presents a viewpoint held by many non-evangelical Protestants as well as some historians who do not belong to a particular religious tradition. Those who fit broadly within this camp tend to view the development of the canon primarily or even exclusively as a historical event. Rather than looking to the canon as a collection of divinely inspired writings that were recognized because of their inherent authority, those within this broad camp often emphasize the human nature of the writings and attribute the emergence of the canon to various theological controversies that took place in early Christianity or to some other perceived threat that prompted the leaders of the church to form the canon. Whether the canon emerged in response to Gnosticism or the teachings of Marcion in the second century or in response to the major theological controversies that took place in subsequent centuries, it is often assumed that the concept of a canon emerged during a time in which a collection of authoritative writings was deemed necessary for the church to contend against some perceived theological threat. A common viewpoint among many non-evangelical scholars is that the writings that are recognized as canonical today are simply those that were recognized by the "winners" of these conflicts. Along with this viewpoint it is also commonly thought that the writings contained in the New Testament do not bear inherent authority and that a writing's authoritative status is something that has been ascribed to it by the leadership of the church. Each of the writings in the New Testament is first and foremost a human document that offers reflections on theological and religious matters. These writings may certainly address significant theological truths and bear testimony to the teaching and work of Christ, but the writings themselves are not to be regarded as infallible.

The final two contributors come from backgrounds that may not be as familiar to many of our readers who live in the West or who belong to various Protestant traditions. The fourth major essay treats the canon from a Roman Catholic perspective and is presented by Ian Boxall, associate professor of New Testament at The Catholic University of America. Boxall's essay provides insight into the way various ecclesiastical bodies have recognized the New Testament canon and how one from a Catholic background might understand the basis of the New Testament's authority and its relationship to the church. Finally, George Parsenios, academic dean and professor of New Testament at Holy Cross Greek Orthodox School of Theology, will present an Orthodox perspective on the New Testament canon. Like the previous contributor, Parsenios offers readers the opportunity to explore the subject of canon from a perspective that is not as widely known to many readers living in a North American context, especially those from Protestant backgrounds.

Having briefly described the five perspectives that are offered in this volume, it may be helpful to offer a brief word of clarification. While the volume presents five distinct perspectives on three fundamental aspects of the study of canon, we recognize that there are far more than five perspectives on the subject. There is no single Roman Catholic, Orthodox, Protestant, or even evangelical perspective. Scholars within each of these traditions often account for the extant historical evidence much differently and have differing understandings of the various hermeneutical and theological matters that often emerge in discussion of the canon. In fact, it would not be all that difficult to present at least five different viewpoints on the canon from scholars within each of the traditions represented in this volume! For this reason, we have intentionally used the indefinite article "a" in the title of the five main chapters. Rather than including "*the* Roman Catholic Perspective on the New Testament Canon," for example, this volume simply presents "*a* Roman Catholic Perspective." With this word of clarification, we trust that the presentations contained in this volume and the responses offered by each of the contributors will provide a helpful introduction to the various ways in which the major issues relating to the New Testament canon have been understood and that they will generate further thought and dialogue on this most important and consequential collection of writings.

A CONSERVATIVE EVANGELICAL PERSPECTIVE ON THE NEW TESTAMENT CANON

Darian R. Lockett

In his instruction to the church at Thessalonica, the apostle Paul referred to the apostolic tradition he both received and passed on: "stand firm and hold to the traditions that you were taught by us, either by our spoken word or by our letter" (2 Thess. 2:15). Paul describes the origin of the transmission of apostolic teaching as "spoken word" (oral) and "letter" (written epistles or Gospel narratives). Whereas originally spoken, the written record of apostolic tradition emerged in a context where the spread of the Christian message demanded a more permanent medium that extended the verbal apostolic teaching through space and time. As the immediacy and authority of the oral tradition was threatened by the impending death of the eyewitnesses, there was increasing need to record and transmit the apostolic tradition in a more permanent form.

The historical account of how the apostolic tradition was first composed and then subsequently copied, transmitted, arranged, and collected into a final (canonical) form is difficult to reconstruct completely with the surviving materials. Scholars must draw from a limited pool of evidence consisting of comments from early church leaders, canon lists, manuscripts, and so on. From these overlapping, yet fragmentary, sources one can present a plausible and coherent (though partial) account of how the New Testament came to its present canonical form. As beneficial as it may be to ascertain the precise manner in which the canon was formed, it should be recognized that the study of canon is not of mere historical significance. Often overlooked is the fact that the historical process that resulted in the canonization of the New Testament has direct theological and hermeneutical implications. In fact, how one understands the historical process of canonization directly relates to one's understanding of the theological nature and authority of Scripture and to the way one interprets Scripture. In light of these observations, this chapter will give an account of the historical process of canonization of the New Testament as well as the theological and hermeneutical implications of the canon.

In this chapter, I will offer a "conservative evangelical perspective" on the New Testament canon. The distinctive of this perspective, in my view, is the early dating of the New Testament canon, the theological conviction of an authoritative and inspired text recognized (rather than created) by the church, and the historical and hermeneutical importance of authorial intention. These historical, theological, and hermeneutical convictions influence how "conservative evangelicals" understand the origins and significance of the New Testament canon and thus constitute a particular "perspective." It is important to note at the outset that I do not assume that all of my views expressed here represent those of all "conservative evangelicals." With this in mind, I look forward to conversation with the other perspectives represented in this book, as well as with other "conservative evangelicals" regarding the importance of canon and the ways in which it influences one's interpretation of the New Testament.

The Historical Formation of the New Testament Canon

Much of the debate regarding the origin of the New Testament canon centers around one fundamental issue: how to define the term "canon."[1] For some, the term canon refers only to a fixed list of texts. With this understanding, one can only speak of a New Testament canon once there is an agreed upon list of twenty-seven books. Others argue that the term canon should be understood as a norm or rule and that it is simply a way of describing texts that functioned authoritatively much earlier in the apostolic period. There will be more to say regarding the definition of canon, but first it is necessary to describe its historical formation. The discussion of the origins of the New Testament canon traditionally leads to three positions, and it will be helpful to set out these three positions as a starting point.

Origins of the New Testament Canon

The first two positions grew out of a well-known debate between Theodor Zahn and Adolf Harnack at the turn of the twentieth century.[2] In his exhaustive two-volume study of the canon, Zahn argued for an early origin of the New Testament.[3] For Zahn, the New Testament canon developed

---

1. Stephen B. Chapman argues that "the fundamental question of definition must be reexamined prior to any discussion about the dates of canon formation." Stephen B. Chapman, "The Canon Debate: What It Is and Why It Matters," *JTI* 4 (2010): 273–94 (277). See also John Barton, *Holy Writings, Sacred Text: The Canon in Early Christianity* (Louisville: Westminster John Knox Press, 1997), 11–14; and Lee Martin McDonald and James A. Sanders, "Introduction," in *The Canon Debate*, eds. Lee Martin McDonald and James A. Sanders (Peabody, MA: Hendrickson, 2002), 3–17 (see esp. 8–15).
2. The debate was described at the time by Heinrich Seesemann as the "Harnack-Zahnscher-Streit" (see Seesemann, "Der Harnack-Zahnsche Streit," *Mitteilungen und Nachrichten für die evangelische Kirche in Rußland* 45 [1899]: 201–16).
3. Theodor Zahn, *Geschichte des neutestamentlichen Kanons*, 2 vols. (Erlangen: Deichert, 1888–1892); see also his summary of conclusions, Zahn, *Grundriss der Geschichte des neutestamentlichen Kanons* (Leipzig: Deichert, 1904).

spontaneously within the first generation of Christian tradition and was "not something forced on the Church by internal or external pressures."[4] He exhaustively traced the reception of New Testament texts in patristic sources, supposing that the manner in which they were used and the frequency with which they appeared reveals that they had achieved normative and authoritative status. Another key factor Zahn traced was the use of New Testament texts in public worship. Taken together, Zahn was convinced that the early citations of the New Testament writings in early Christian literature and the use of these texts in Christian worship were indicative of an early process of canonization.

Unlike those who argued that the church's response to Marcion provided the catalyst for the formation of the New Testament canon, Zahn reasoned that Marcion actually *received* a functioning canonical collection from the church, a collection which he then revised for his purposes.[5] Thus, for Zahn, the New Testament writings functioned as canon well before the time of Marcion, that is, before the mid-second century.[6] Rather than an ecclesiastical decision to consolidate power or as a reaction to heterodox pressures, the formation of the New Testament canon, in Zahn's estimation, was a broad development which came about spontaneously and without the need of an official decision as the church received and use these texts.

Though not questioning Zahn's evidence *per se*, Adolf Harnack challenged his interpretation of the evidence,

---

4.   Barton, *Holy Writings, Sacred Text*, 3.
5.   The "New Testament of about 200," Zahn argues, "was not the result of a revolution occurring 150–170, but of a broad development which was many-sided." Theodor Zahn, "Canon of Scripture," in *New Schaff-Herzog Encyclopedia of Religious Knowledge*, ed. Samuel Jackson (New York: Funk and Wagnalls, 1908), 2:393–99 (395).
6.   Zahn acknowledges that early church fathers did not refer to this collection as the New Testament *per se*, but that "there was in existence a collection of writings from the early period of the church, which was read in the service of the congregation as the now scriptural Word of God and of the Lord Jesus Christ." Theodor Zahn, "The Permanent Value of the New Testament Canon for the Church," *The Lutheran Church Review* 19 (1900): 3–36 (5).

specifically calling into question the significance of early citation in the patristic sources.[7] Harnack pointed out that Zahn
had failed in his analysis of the early fathers to distinguish
between the mere use of a text and the treatment of a text as
Scripture. For Harnack, when considering patristic citations, a
text must be cited specifically as Scripture in order to establish
its recognition as canonical—a kind of citation not found prior
to the second century. Unconvinced that the mere reading of
a text in public worship indicated anything about its canonical
status, Harnack argued that the New Testament canon formed
only when Christian writings came to be used alongside of
the Old Testament Scriptures.[8] Thus for Harnack, the origin
of the New Testament canon can be fixed sometime in the
latter half of the second century. In contrast to Zahn, Harnack
was persuaded that the canon was born out of apologetic and
polemical pressures. The major catalyst for the finalization
of the canon, he suggested, was the church's reaction against
heterodox movements such as Marcionism. Harnack's views
were widely embraced and became the default position for most
of the twentieth century. Scholars such as Hans Campenhausen adapted and strengthened his theories, emphasizing that
the critical period for the New Testament canon was the late
second century and that reaction to Marcion played a significant role in prompting this development.

In the late twentieth century, two central essays by Albert
Sundberg challenged the Harnack consensus.[9] Insisting on a
higher degree of terminological clarity, Sundberg argued for

---

7.   See the sixth appendix in Adolf Harnack's *The Origin of the New Testament and the
     Most Important Consequences of the New Testament Creation*, trans. John Wilkinson
     (London: Williams & Norgate, 1925), 218–29.

8.   Rather than "the public [reading] of the separate works," it is the "setting of
     a new collection of sacred writings on a level with the Old Testament" that
     indicates canon for Harnack (*Origin of the New Testament*, 228). See also Hans
     Campenhausen, *Formation of the Christian Bible* (Philadelphia: Fortress, 1971), 103.

9.   Albert C. Sundberg, "Toward a Revised History of the New Testament Canon,"
     SE 4 (1968): 452–61 and Sundberg, "Canon Muratori: A Fourth Century List,"
     HTR 66 (1973): 1–41.

a sharp distinction between canon and Scripture. In his estimation, the failure to distinguish between these two concepts inevitably results in lack of precision regarding the origins of the New Testament canon.[10] According to his perspective, the term "canon" must refer specifically to a closed and definitively fixed list of texts. In agreement with Sundberg's view, Harry Gamble argues that it is a misconception to "speak of an 'open canon,' or 'core canon,' or a 'developing canon.'"[11] In other words, it would be inappropriate to recognize the establishment of the New Testament canon prior to the time in which there is evidence of a closed and established list of recognized New Testament texts. The simple fact that many early church figures cited texts as Scripture is irrelevant, Sundberg contends, because labeling a text as Scripture says nothing of whether that text was part of a closed list of texts or canon—this evidence is thus ruled out by definition. Therefore, because fixed lists of New Testament texts only appear in the fourth and early fifth centuries, it is misguided to speak of a New Testament canon prior to this time.

A second contribution made by Sundberg was his challenge of the early dating of the Muratorian Fragment.[12] Traditionally dated to the late second or early third century (and to a Roman provenance), the somewhat enigmatic Muratorian Fragment served as support for an earlier date for the New Testament canon. Sundberg argued that the Fragment originated later in

---

10. Sundberg "Revised History," 453–54.
11. Harry Y. Gamble, "The New Testament Canon: Recent Research and the Status Quaestionis," in *The Canon Debate*, eds. Lee Martin McDonald and James A. Sanders (Peabody, MA: Hendrickson, 2002), 267–94 (269).
12. An often-discussed witness to the early state of the New Testament canon, the Muratorian Fragment is a seventh- or eighth-century Latin manuscript. It contains a list of New Testament writings that is thought to have originated much earlier. The list cites each of the New Testament books with the exception of Hebrews, James, 1–2 Peter, and one of the Johannine Epistles (reference is made to only two). Although Matthew and Mark are not cited by name in the extant manuscript, they are almost certainly to have been cited in the original given that the list refers to Luke as the third Gospel and John as the fourth.

the fourth century and that it was of an eastern provenance.[13] For Sundberg, this is further evidence that one can only speak of a New Testament canon in the late fourth to early fifth century when evidence first appears for a fixed list of texts described as authoritative Scripture. Like Harnack, Sundberg concludes that motivation for the establishment of an exclusive list of canonical texts was polemical or apologetic. Bishops, synods, and councils (extrinsic powers) moved to finalize the canon with the objective of consolidating their ecclesiastical power and influence.

It is important to note that among these views there is very little disagreement regarding the actual evidence. As Michael Holmes observes, for "all their definitional differences, however, none of the three really disagrees about the basic facts or evidence."[14] The differences are more often over definitions of terms and the interpretation of that evidence. John Barton helpfully points out that "much in the progressively later dating of 'canonization' from Zahn through Harnack to Sundberg is generated simply by an ever-increasing narrowness of definition for the term canon."[15] With such pressures placed upon the definition of canon, it is necessary to consider whether one should define canon in narrow or broad terms and whether canon and Scripture should be viewed as distinct or overlapping concepts.

Definition of Canon

As noted above, "canon" can typically be defined in two ways: either as rule (or norm) or as a fixed list. In an influential article,

---

13. For discussion regarding the controversy over the dating of the Muratorian Fragment, see Geoffrey Hahneman, *The Muratorian Fragment and the Development of the Canon* (Oxford: Clarendon, 1992); Hahneman, "The Muratorian Fragment and the Origins of the New Testament Canon," in *The Canon Debate*, eds. Lee Martin McDonald and James A. Sanders (Peabody, MA: Hendrickson, 2002), 405–15; Joseph Verheyden, "The Canon Muratori," in *The Biblical Canons*, eds. Jean-Marie Auwers and Henk Jan de Jonge, BETL 163 (Leuven: Leuven University Press, 2003), 487–556.

14. Michael Holmes, "The Biblical Canon," in *The Oxford Handbook of Early Christian Studies*, eds. Susan Harvey and David Hunter (Oxford: Oxford University Press, 2008), 406–26 (408).

15. Barton, *Holy Writings, Sacred Texts*, 11–12.

Gerald Sheppard labelled these as canon 1 (norm) and canon 2 (fixed list) and demonstrated that both senses share an equally historical warrant.[16] He demonstrates that the term was used in reference to a rule or norm (canon 1), that is, as an authoritative set of teachings that shaped the early Christian community. This canon or "rule of faith" functioned as a guiding principle for belief and practice (*norma normans*, "norming norm") for early Christian communities. By contrast, the understanding of canon as a fixed list (canon 2) defines canon as an exclusive collection and places emphasis upon the delimitation of texts (*norma normata*, "normative norm").

Canon as a fixed list or closed corpus by definition is a later phenomenon, which only comes at the end of a process of textual exclusion. Thus, the closed-corpus definition of canon demands that one foreclose any discussion of a New Testament canon until the late fourth century at the earliest. Geoffrey Hahneman's comment, agreeing with Sundberg, is representative of this view:

> To speak of a Christian "canon" of scriptures is an anachronism before the second half of the fourth century because it is only after that time that Christian writers begin to employ the word [canon] for a list of books counted as accepted scriptures.[17]

The closed-corpus definition (canon 2) focuses on textual delimitation as the definitive moment in canon formation. This defining moment, as Eugene Ulrich explains, "represents a conscious, retrospective, official judgment."[18]

---

16. Gerald T. Sheppard, "Canon," in *Encyclopaedia of Religion*, ed. Mircea Eliade, 16 vols. (New York: Macmillan, 1987), 3:62–69.
17. Hahneman, "Muratorian Fragment," 406.
18. Eugene Ulrich, "Notion and Definition of Canon," in *The Canon Debate*, eds. Lee Martin McDonald and James A. Sanders (Peabody, MA: Hendrickson, 2002), 21–35 (32).

This official judgment marked the closing of the canon and took place as a result of the will and actions of certain individuals and institutions. As Gamble argues,

> emphasis on the sharp distinctions furnished by *lists* tends to represent canonization more as *a process of exclusion* than of inclusion, *thus emphasizing polemical and apologetic moves*. This view also stresses the role of ecclesiastical authorities—bishops, synods, and councils—and downplays the importance of second-century controversies with heterodox movements.[19]

Thus, the motivation for an official New Testament canon consisted mainly of apologetic and institutional pressures rather than a reception of these texts based upon an appreciation and understanding of their inner logic.

It is not clear to me that canon should be understood strictly as the closure of a fixed list of writings. In fact, one might argue that there never was a particular "conscious, retrospective, official judgment" regarding the closure of the New Testament canon. Stephen B. Chapman reasons that, rather than a "minor point, this concession actually goes to the heart of the methodology employed, for why should one adopt as proper a definition of 'canon' that does not ever appear to have existed in reality?"[20] In other words, if one cannot point to a "conscious, retrospective, official judgment" regarding the closing of the New Testament canon in reality, then why should one insist on the closed-corpus definition of canon? Perhaps the absence of such a definitive and official closure suggests that the closed-corpus definition is implausible. However, John Poirier disagrees with this conclusion. He insists that Chapman's objection is guilty of category confusion, arguing that "if 'canon' denotes the idea

---

19. Gamble, "New Testament Canon," 271 (emphasis added).
20. Stephen B. Chapman, "The Old Testament Canon and Its Authority for the Christian Church," *ExAud* 19 (2003): 125–48 (136). Chapman argues that Ulrich is "forced to concede that an officially complete and absolute listing of the canon *never really took place at all* in either Jewish or Christian tradition" (emphasis original).

of closure, then it does so regardless of whether everyone agrees when and where that closure is."[21] The fact that Catholics and Protestants do not agree on *one specific closure* of the canon is not evidence against the conviction of both Catholics and Protestants that the canon is in fact closed and that it should be defined that way.

Though one should heed Poirier's concern, there is a further category confusion lurking here. According to Tomas Bokedal, there was a complex set of notions attached to canon. He suggests that the concept of canon as a definitive list arose in the Eastern church near the middle of the fourth century, yet when taken over in the Latin West, this meaning of canon quickly shifted. "A new meaning of the word arose, namely 'canon' as representing, not a list of authoritative books, but the biblical books themselves (*canon as the book[s] of the Bible*)."[22] Bokedal continues,

> The differences between the authoritative collection of New Testament writings of these early editions (canon as the Old and the New Testaments) as compared to the canon of the New Testament as defined in the latter half of the fourth century (canon as regional list of Old and New Testament writings) should not be exaggerated, as Eusebius' and Origen's notion of ἐνδιάθηκος ["canonical"] . . . indicates.[23]

The use of "canonical" in Eusebius and Origen indicates that there was consciousness of a growing collection of Scripture before there ever was a closed list of twenty-seven New Testament texts. As a result, the exclusively closed-corpus definition of canon seems unlikely.

Furthermore, an insistence upon the closed-corpus definition of canon risks emphasizing the moment of definitive

---

21. John C. Poirier, "An Ontological Definition of 'Canon'?" *BBR* 24 (2014): 457–66 (463).

22. Tomas Bokedal, *The Formation and Significance of the Christian Biblical Canon: A Study in Text, Ritual and Interpretation* (London: Bloomsbury, 2014), 67.

23. Bokedal, *Formation and Significance*, 67.

closure at the expense of the process of canonical development. That is, it has the tendency to stress the one, final, and official closure of the canon, while effectively obscuring the fact that several mini- or subclosures occurred earlier in the process of canonization. For example, well before there was a final twenty-seven-book New Testament, it is clear that the four Gospels circulated as an authoritative canonical subcollection. The same is true of a collection of Paul's letters. The formation, circulation, and function of these subcollections demonstrates the early development of the New Testament canon (late first or early second century), while also suggesting that the concept of canon be understood as both a rule and norm as well as a definitive list (in this case, a list that fills out the subcollections).

Thus, I find it more reasonable to take the broad view of canon and to understand that, though distinct, Scripture and canon constitute overlapping concepts. This does justice to the very early development of subcollections that eventually make up the New Testament canon and enables us to examine the entire sweep of canonical development from composition to canonization. Thus, in my estimation, Brevard Childs is correct in arguing that

> the formation of the canon was not a late extrinsic validation of a corpus of writings, but involved a series of decisions deeply affecting the shape of the books. Although it is possible to distinguish different phases within the canonical process—the term canonization would then be reserved for the final fixing of the limits of scripture—the earlier decisions were not qualitatively different from the later.[24]

The pressures that led to the formation of the Old and New Testaments were not exerted from the outside and were not manipulative of the texts themselves. The term "canon" cannot

---

24. Brevard S. Childs, *Introduction to the Old Testament as Scripture* (Philadelphia: Fortress, 1979), 59.

"be reserved for the final fixing of the limits of scripture." What
Childs is emphasizing here is that the texts themselves bore the
characteristics of authority and canonical connection.

An Early New Testament Canon: Subcollections

It strikes me that it is reasonable to recover Theodor Zahn's
perspective on the early emergence of the New Testament
canon, especially if we understand the early development of
subcollections as a crucial part of that process.[25] The actual
historical development of the New Testament canon was generally characterized by the formation of subcollections, that is,
smaller units of writings (e.g., the four Gospels and the Pauline
Epistles) that circulated independently prior to their incorporation into the larger canon.[26] Jens Schröter notes that whereas the
"two most important collections, which stand at the beginning
of the emergence of the New Testament" are "the four Gospels
and the Letters of Paul," at a later time "Acts and the Catholic
Letters," developed as well.[27] Though perhaps the least recognized canonical subcollection of the New Testament, there is
a growing body of literature that argues the Catholic Epistles

---

25. An initial argument in support of Zahn's interpretation of the evidence might be
    formed like this. First, the criticism that Zahn failed to distinguish between various
    ways early patristic sources cited the canonical texts is misleading. Generally,
    patristic references are notoriously difficult because they often quote sources in
    an authoritative way, yet without clear citation markers or explicitly indicating
    the source was Scripture. That these markers are absent does not constitute clear
    evidence that these texts were not used as canonical Scripture. Second, though
    Harnack criticized Zahn's emphasis upon use in public worship, the reading of
    texts in public worship has been reconsidered in recent research as being much
    more significant than Harnack thought. I am thinking of the now growing
    discussion of material culture and the public use of texts. See especially Brian J.
    Wright, *Communal Reading in the Time of Jesus: A Window into Early Christian Reading
    Practices* (Minneapolis: Fortress, 2017) and Tomas Bokedal's discussion of public
    reading and canon in Chapter 7 of *Formation and Significance* (237–78).
26. See David Trobisch's discussion of the various "collection units" of the New
    Testament and their canonical significance. *First Edition of the New Testament*
    (Oxford: Oxford University Press, 2000).
27. Jens Schröter, *From Jesus to the New Testament: Early Christian Theology and the
    Origin of the New Testament Canon*, trans. Wayne Coppins, BMSEC (Waco, TX:
    Baylor University Press, 2013), 273.

collection of James, 1–2 Peter, 1–3 John, and Jude was a coherent letter collection which formed toward the latter part of the canonical process.[28]

In light of the emergence of various subcollections, it is helpful to understand the development of the New Testament canon as "a collection of collections."[29] In other words, it is not the case that individual books came into the New Testament canon on their own (Revelation, perhaps, is the exception). Evidence from patristic citation and the manuscript tradition indicates that the four Gospels and the Pauline corpus were received and recognized as distinct collections early in the canonical process. In fact, Larry Hurtado noted it is "remarkable how early these collections of writings appear."[30] With respect to the fourfold Gospel, Hurtado notes that "recent studies agree in pushing back [their] likely origin . . . to the earliest years of the second century."[31] Hurtado surveys several early second-century dates for the origin of the fourfold Gospel noting a range from 100 to 150 CE. With respect to the Pauline corpus, Hurtado notes

---

28. See, especially, Karl-Wilhelm Niebuhr, "Exegese im kanonischen Zusammenhang: Überlegungen zur theologischen Relevanz der Gestalt des neutestamentlichen Kanons," in *The Biblical Canons*, eds. Jean-Marie Auwers and Henk Jan de Jonge, BETL 163 (Leuven: Leuven University Press, 2003), 557–84; Jacques Schlosser, "Le Corpus Épîtres des Catholiques," in *The Catholic Epistles and the Tradition*, ed. Jacques Schlosser, BETL 176 (Leuven: Leuven University Press, 2004), 43–71; David R. Nienhuis, *Not by Paul Alone: The Formation of the Catholic Epistle Collection and the Christian Canon* (Waco, TX: Baylor University Press, 2007); Enrico Norelli, "Sulle origini della raccolta delle Lettere Cattoliche," *RivB* 4 (2011): 453–521; and Darian R. Lockett, *Letters from the Pillar Apostles: The Formation of the Catholic Epistles as a Canonical Collection* (Eugene, OR: Pickwick, 2017).

29. Gamble, "New Testament Canon," 275. Likewise, Larry Hurtado argues that the formation of the New Testament in the second century is "a collection of prior collections." Larry W. Hurtado, "The New Testament in the Second Century: Text, Collections and Canon," in *Transmission and Reception: New Testament Textual-Critical and Exegetical Studies*, eds. Jeff Childres and David Parker, Text and Studies: Contributions to Biblical and Patristic Literature 4 (Piscataway, NJ: Gorgias, 2006), 3–27 (21).

30. Hurtado, "The New Testament in the Second Century," 20.

31. Hurtado, "The New Testament in the Second Century," 20. Hurtado interacts with several scholars who have argued that the emergence of the fourfold Gospel should be dated to the early second century (20–21).

"the evidence points back at least as early."[32] He argues that "Marcion's exclusivist claims for his ten-letter Pauline collection sometime around 140 CE probably presupposes a widespread circulation of Pauline letter-collections already by that point."[33] Furthermore, Hurtado notes that by 200 CE "there was an 'apostolikon' category of Christian scriptures, comprising a Pauline collection plus letters attributed to other apostolic figures (esp. 1–2 John, 1 Peter, James)."[34]

Bokedal offers further evidence for the early emergence of New Testament subcollections. One aspect of his important work focuses on how the codex form contributed to the shaping of the final twenty-seven-book form of the New Testament canon. The codex form, Bokedal argues,

> seems to have contributed by delimiting and closing the major three or four part-collections making up the New Testament. That is, in particular the fourfold Gospel, and the *Corpus Paulinum*, but also the so-called Praxapostolos (Acts and the Catholic Letters) and the Apocalypse. In scholarly discussion on the canon this organization of the NT material, in three or four closed collections/codices, has been largely neglected.[35]

Bokedal argues that "the *Corpus Paulinum* and the fourfold Gospel . . . may be at hand as early as ca. AD 60–140 and 100–180, respectively."[36] These dates are in keeping with Zahn's pre-Marcion dating and, along with Hurtado's observations,

---

32. Hurtado, "The New Testament in the Second Century," 21.
33. Hurtado, "The New Testament in the Second Century," 21. Stanley Porter, following some of the evidence offered by Trobisch, suggests that Paul's letter collection could originate from the mid-second century (if not perhaps as early as the late first century). See Stanley E. Porter, *How We Got the New Testament: Text, Transmission, Translation* (Grand Rapids: Baker, 2013), 110; Porter, "When and How Was the Pauline Canon Compiled? An Assessment of Theories," in *The Pauline Canon*, ed. Stanley E. Porter, Pauline Studies 1 (Atlanta: SBL Press, 2009), 95–127.
34. Hurtado, "The New Testament in the Second Century," 21.
35. Bokedal, *Formation and Significance*, 151.
36. Bokedal, *Formation and Significance*, 151. See the helpful bibliography supporting these dates provided on 151, n.108.

support an early dating for the development of major sections of the eventual New Testament canon.

In the debate on the canonization of the New Testament, the focus should not exclusively be on the listing of a fixed twenty-seven-book collection. As Bokedal argues, "It seems historically accurate to discuss the Four-Gospel codex, the *Corpus Paulinum*, the Praxapostolos and the Book of Revelation one at a time."[37] It seems clear that the majority of the texts that were eventually included into the New Testament canon were collected into one of four subcollections which, from an early time, were themselves fixed collections functioning as authoritative Scripture in early Christian communities. Therefore, it is reasonable to argue for the early development of the New Testament canon.

The Authority and Inspiration of New Testament Writings

As suggested above, the development of the New Testament canon was not due to an external force imposed by institutional pressures, nor was it motivated by political or apologetic concerns. As Childs explains, the canonization of the New Testament was not "a late, ecclesiastical activity, external to the biblical literature itself, which was subsequently imposed on those writings." To the contrary, a "canonical consciousness" may be observed "deep within the New Testament literature itself."[38] Put simply, the recognized authority and inspiration of the texts that were eventually collected into the New Testament was not something that was granted by the church but was, rather, an intrinsic property of those texts that was recognized by the church. The church's reception of the New Testament canon may therefore be understood as an act of confession and worship.

---

37. Bokedal, *Formation and Significance*, 151.
38. Brevard S. Childs, *The New Testament as Canon: An Introduction* (London: SCM, 1984), 21.

Authority

As Zahn noted, the growing recognition of the authority of these texts can be traced through their citation by early church fathers and their public reading (often alongside the Old Testament) in Christian worship. While the church's recognition of the canonical writings was marked by certain historical events, these events did not in themselves confer or grant to the texts their authority as Scripture. In other words, it cannot be said that the church formed the New Testament canon via institutional pressure or apologetic reaction, nor did the church somehow authorize the New Testament canon by means of the church's performance or use of the texts to form disciples of Jesus. Rather, as John Webster notes, "Scripture's authority *within* the church is a function of Scripture's authority *over* the church."[39] Because Scripture's authority "stands *over* the church," Webster rightly concludes that "the church is not competent to confer authority on Holy Scripture."[40] Instead the church recognized (or confessed) the authority of these texts such that the Christian church can be "said to have *inherited* a scriptural canon."[41]

The church's inheritance of the New Testament canon indicates that from the very beginning, from the composition of the apostolic writings, it had authority in the churches where they were known. As suggested above, it seems clear that in the very least, the fourfold Gospel and the Pauline corpus achieved recognized authority by the late first and early second century, with other subcollections recognized soon thereafter. As the history of the early church reveals, the canonical writings were frequently read in the public gatherings of early Christians, often alongside the writings of the Old Testament. Though the exact place and time cannot be fixed, the writings that eventually became the New Testament were "spontaneously"

---

39. John Webster, *Holy Scripture: A Dogmatic Sketch* (Cambridge: Cambridge University Press, 2003), 56 (emphasis original).

40. Webster, *Holy Scripture*, 53.

41. Chapman, "Old Testament Canon, 140 (emphasis original).

(Zahn's word) and "automatically" (Herman Bavinck's word) received as Scripture without any formal or institutional judgment needed.[42]

The divine origin of the New Testament writings naturally led to the early recognition of their authority. As Bavinck explains,

> The canonicity of the Bible books is rooted in their existence. They have authority of themselves, by their own right, because they exist. It is the Spirit of the Lord who guided the authors in writing them and the church in acknowledging them.[43]

Bavinck's reflections echo Calvin's affirmation of the *autopistia* (αὐτοπιστία) or self-authenticating nature of Scripture, what might be described as the self-confirmation of the Scriptures through the testimony of the Holy Spirit.[44] This, for Calvin, is because if "the teaching of the prophets and apostles is the foundation, this must have had authority before the church began to exist."[45]

The historical process that gave rise to the recognition of the canon does not stand in contradiction to the unique theological nature of Scripture's *quiddity* or essence. As Webster explains, the interpretation of the New Testament "will only prove fruitful if grounded in a theological account of what Scripture *is*."[46] As Kevin Vanhoozer further observes, "The canon has a 'natural history,' but we cannot fully explain the ontology of the canon in terms of this-worldly causality only."[47] To

---

42. See Herman Bavinck, *Reformed Dogmatics*, vol. 1, *Prolegomena*, ed. John Bolt, trans. John Vriend (Grand Rapids: Baker, 2003), 401.

43. Bavinck, *Reformed Dogmatics*, 401.

44. John Calvin, *Institutes of the Christian Religion*, I.vii.1, 2, 5, ed. John T. McNeill, trans. Ford Lewis Battles (Philadelphia: Westminster, 1960), 74–75, 80.

45. Calvin, *Institutes*, I.vii.2.

46. John Webster, *Domain of the Word: Scripture and Theological Reason* (London: T&T Clark, 2012), 32–33 (emphasis added).

47. Kevin J. Vanhoozer, "Holy Scripture," in *Christian Dogmatics: Reformed Theology for the Church Catholic*, eds. Michael Allen and Scott R. Swain (Grand Rapids: Baker, 2016), 30–56 (49).

identify a theological causality of the canon is to affirm that the New Testament canon, along with the Old Testament, is God's triune self-communication. Thus, Webster rightly argues that the New Testament canon is "Christ's active, communicative presence in the Spirit's power though the commissioned apostolic testimony."[48]

Whereas the canonical writings were widely recognized as authoritative Scripture by the early church, the basis of Scripture's authority ultimately derives from God himself. Stated simply, God's authority stands behind these texts. While God used human authors to reveal himself to his people, Scripture is ultimately of divine origin and therefore bears God's authority. For this reason, Paul expressed his gratitude that the Thessalonian believers, "received the word of God . . . not as the word of men, but as what it really is, the word of God" (1 Thess. 2:13). Because the texts that became the New Testament canon are God's words, they were received and confessed by the church as canon.

Inspiration

Because the New Testament canon was received by the church "as what it really is," namely the Word of God, these texts bear the character of God's authoritative communication. Paul describes Scripture or canon as God's authoritative communication in this way: "All Scripture is breathed out by God [θεόπνευστος]" (2 Tim. 3:16) and likewise, Peter argues that "men spoke from God as they were carried along by the Holy Spirit" (2 Peter 1:21). The acknowledgment that God's authority authorizes the New Testament canon, as recognized by the early church, implies verbal inspiration and divine authorship of these texts. Inspiration is the confession of divine-human action in the production of the Scriptures.

---

48. Webster, *Holy Scripture*, 59. Also John Webster, "The Dogmatic Location of the Canon," in *Word and Church: Essays in Christian Dogmatics* (Edinburgh: T&T Clark, 2001), 9–46.

With respect to the verbal inspiration of Scripture, Vanhoozer argues that God "leads the human authors to say the right words not through a mechanical or coercive process but by working with and through their created personalities, histories, and intelligence."[49] Similarly, Webster considers inspiration as a kind of sanctification, "not a unilateral cognitive force but a compound act in which the creator and reconciler takes creatures and their powers, acts and products into his service."[50] God's self-communication comes through the text by means of human authors, yet in such a way that there is no competition or conflict between human and divine author. Human agents "were carried along by the Holy Spirit," which in turn produced a text that what is inspired or "breathed out" by God—both human involvement and textual end-product are necessary components of inspiration.[51]

In claiming inspiration for the New Testament there need not be a denial of the historical development of the canon. Rather, the divine-human reality behind the origin of the canon is affirmed. For Chapman, taking both the development of the New Testament canon and inspiration into account results in understanding the "divine-human encounter as occurring over a lengthier period of time and as including more people than just one author alone."[52] That is to say, in recognition of God's providence, Chapman extends inspiration to the entire process of New Testament canonization. To anticipate a particular kind of objection to Chapman's claim, one could argue that if the entire canonical process is inspired, this would imply that the canon continues to develop in the hands of the church such that Scripture's authority over the

---

49. Vanhoozer, "Holy Scripture," 48. See also Bavinck, *Reformed Dogmatics*, 430–39.
50. Webster, *Domain of the Word*, ix.
51. For a discussion of the difficulties of equating inspiration only with human authors see the insightful essay by Stephen B. Chapman, "Reclaiming Inspiration for the Bible," in *Canon and Biblical Interpretation*, eds. Craig Bartholomew et al. (Grand Rapids: Zondervan, 2006), 167–206.
52. Chapman, "Reclaiming Inspiration for the Bible," 172.

church is called into question. However, this is not necessary. Chapman argues that the final form of the New Testament canon actually fixes the apostolic witness which the church receives and confesses.[53]

Whereas I am sympathetic to Chapman's thesis, it might be more cautious to claim that providence rather than inspiration *per se* is the way to talk about God's superintending of the process of collection, arrangement, and final canonization of the New Testament. The doctrine of inspiration is usually focused upon God's providential guiding of Scripture's composition. Thus, inspiration is a divine-human word-making event. Chapman is correct that the canonical process is equally theological because it is a kind of divine-human canon-making event. Therefore, just as the authors of Scripture were "carried along by the Holy Spirit," in a sense one can say that God "breathed out" the canon. However, rather than extending the doctrine of inspiration to include canonization, it seems the doctrine of providence covers this concern; yet it would be worth further theological reflection on whether canon might be construed as a dogmatic sibling of inspiration and illumination. In the end, the work of writing, collecting, arranging, and transmitting the texts that became the New Testament was guided by God's providence. The New Testament canon, therefore, is the authoritative and inspired Word of God.

---

53. Chapman notes this very concern as articulated by Carl Henry, yet responds with the approach of Brevard Childs: "Childs has been quite emphatic about the need to honor 'the decisive role to the prophets and apostles.' For Childs, one of the main features of the canon is that it fixes the prophetic-apostolic witness necessary for the church to remember its identity." The only difference is that Childs argued that the prophetic-apostolic witness "continues to develop and deepen over time, a process reflected in the history of the biblical literature itself, until that witness is acknowledged by the community of faith to be complete" ("Reclaiming Inspiration for the Bible," 179–80). Though not advocating for the authority of canonical collections, Michael A. Grisanti argues for the place of textual updating in the final canonical form in "Inspiration, Inerrancy, and the OT Canon: The Place of Textual Updating in an Inerrant View of Scripture," *JETS* 44 (2001): 577–98.

The Hermeneutical Significance of the Canon

Having explored the historical process by which the canon was recognized and the basis of its authority, we may now consider the possible significance of the canon's final form. For some, the historical and theological subjects relating to the study of canon are unrelated and bear little significance to how Scripture should be read and interpreted. As we will soon discover, however, there are significant hermeneutical implications to our understanding of the historical and theological dimensions of the canon. Regarding the historical and theological character of the canon, Chapman writes, "The church's concept of a canon lay precisely at the fault line between history and theology."[54] A similar point is made by Schröter: "historical-critical interpretation of the New Testament texts and a theology of the New Testament do *not* exclude each other—and neither should they be dissolved into each other—but stand in a tension-filled dynamic in relation to each other."[55] Rather than pitting historical description against theological significance, it is the fundamental role of canon that allows for taking up both together in interpretation.

The Two-Testaments Canon

Before considering some of the notable ways in which the shape and form of the New Testament canon might influence interpretation, we must first recognize that the Christian canon is fundamentally a two-testament reality. I will argue below for the specific canonical characteristics of the New Testament that must be borne in mind for interpretation, but it must first be acknowledged that the New Testament does not stand alone as Christian Scripture. As Childs argues, "Biblical theology is by definition theological reflection on both the Old and New

---

54. Chapman, "Reclaiming Inspiration for the Bible," 167. Childs has noted, "The canonical form marks not only the place from which exegesis begins, but also the place at which it ends" (*New Testament as Canon*, 48).
55. Schröter, *From Jesus to the New Testament*, 330 (emphasis original).

Testament."[56] Interpretation that considers both the historical and theological nature of Scripture will require reflection
on the two Testaments as separate yet necessarily connected
witnesses. Writing from a Jewish perspective, Jon Levenson has
helpfully argued that

> Christian exegesis requires that the Hebrew Bible be read ulti-
> mately in a literary context that includes the New Testament. . . .
> Christian theology cannot tolerate exegesis that leaves the two
> Testaments independent of each other. . . . But the two antholo-
> gies cannot be collapsed into one, either, lest the newness of the
> New Testament be lost.[57]

The importance of recognizing a close canonical relationship
between the two Testaments has long been acknowledged.
But what is the basis for this, and why is it relevant? To pose
these questions differently, in what sense are the two Testaments related and how might a canonical reading of the Bible
inform our understanding of a particular passage or the relationship between the canonical writings? Though much could
be said regarding these questions, Chapman's comments mark
out important hermeneutical and theological territory:

> By establishing the canonical format of Christian Scripture as one
> Bible in two testaments, the Church simultaneously proclaimed
> both that the Old Testament *had* a "Christian" witness *and* that
> its "pre-Christian" form had lasting theological significance.
> Of central importance, as Adolf von Harnack once observed,
> was that the Christian church recognized the authority of the
> Old Testament *as it was*, without the interpolation of Christian

---

56. Brevard S. Childs, *Biblical Theology: A Proposal* (Minneapolis: Fortress, 2002),
     13. Christopher Seitz notes the same in *The Character of Christian Scripture: The
     Significance of a Two-Testament Bible* (Grand Rapids: Baker, 2011), 96.
57. Jon Levenson, *The Hebrew Bible, the Old Testament, and Historical Criticism*
     (Louisville: Westminster John Knox Press, 1993), 9.

> commentary into the biblical text, the interspersing of Old and
> New Testament books or some other editorial strategy.[58]

First, Chapman notes that the Old Testament canon functions
as Christian Scripture without the need of Christian commentary or redaction. The canonical form of the Old Testament
itself has lasting theological significance. Second, he insists that
it is precisely in its original canonical form that the Old Testament functions as Christian Scripture and serves as a witness
to the reality of Jesus Christ. Therefore, canonical interpretation first insists that the Christian Bible consists of two normative Testaments bearing authoritative (yet different) testimony
to the same Lord, Jesus Christ. Canonical interpretation will
always keep these two witnesses together.

Collection and Arrangement

In addition to the importance of recognizing the existence of
the two Testaments of Scripture and their close relationship to
one another, we may briefly consider some of the specific ways
in which the reality of the New Testament canon influences
interpretation: collection and arrangement.

It may first be observed that the act of collection itself
suggests a kind of hermeneutical rubric at work in the New
Testament canon. Perhaps this can be demonstrated by considering various ways of reconstructing what texts belong in
the New Testament. What books should be collected in the
New Testament canon according to historical-critical reconstruction? This question is too large to cover with any kind of
adequacy here, but for the sake of illustration, we might ask
why the Gospel of John should be recognized as canonical
Scripture and not a writing such as the *Gospel of Thomas*. Based
on a particular historical reconstruction of the sayings of Jesus,
some might conclude that *Thomas* should be included in the

---

58. Stephen B. Chapman, *1 Samuel as Christian Scripture: A Theological Commentary*
     (Grand Rapids: Eerdmans, 2016), 6.

collection and John left out. As another example, it might be asked why the Apocalypse of John should be included in the canon and not the *Apocalypse of Peter*. Scholars do not always agree on fundamental matters relating to a text's origin such as authorship, dating, and provenance. The point here is that if guided by historical-critical concerns alone, the collection of texts we call the New Testament may look quite different depending on how the evidence is assessed.

Those who approach the study of canon from a historical-critical perspective often presume that the specific content of the canonical collection was influenced by the church and is therefore hermeneutically suspect. Adolf Harnack, for example, argued, "Canonization works like whitewash; it hides the original colors and obliterates all the contours," hiding "the true origin and significance of the works."[59] For Harnack, one must keep historical-critical reading distinct from whatever later canonical meaning the church added to the New Testament texts. It is interesting to note that the historical-critical perspective would likely claim neutrality regarding any kind of final collection of these texts. And such neutrality, it is claimed, would prove a more objective starting point for interpretation. However, when the boundaries of the canonical New Testament are stripped away, another default collection emerges—a collection selected by the underlying logic of historical reconstruction. I would argue that collection (whether based on historical-critical or canonical considerations) inevitably influences interpretation and that the theological logic that shapes the canonical collation of New Testament texts is necessary for correct interpretation.

A second observation is that the arrangement of the New Testament has a bearing upon the inter-canonical connections that may be observed both within the New Testament canon and between writings contained in the Old and New Testaments. If historical-critical concerns alone are pursued, the

---

59. Harnack, *Origins of the New Testament*, 140–41.

manner in which the canonical writings relate to one another would differ in various ways from how they relate to each other in the established form of the biblical canon. Take the Gospels as an example. Though Matthew is usually listed as the first Gospel in the canon, historical reconstruction argues for the priority of Mark based on various theological, historical, and linguistic observations and arguments. The logic that guides this ordering is a historical reconstruction based on theories of literary dependence, rather than the canonical association between Matthew and the Old Testament. This historical reconstruction (Mark as the first Gospel) tells us something about the history of composition, but the canonical arrangement (Matthew as the first Gospel) emphasizes the potential connections between the opening of Matthew's Gospel, including Jesus's genealogy, and the end of the Old Testament.

We may also point to the example of Luke-Acts. Whereas in traditional historical-critical reconstruction it is common to read Luke and Acts as a two-part history of early Christianity, the Gospel of Luke had circulated in the early church as part of the fourfold Gospel. This arrangement is clearly seen in the manuscript evidence as virtually all of the fragments indicate that Luke was collected and circulated with the other Gospels rather than as a two-volume collection that included Acts.[60] In an attempt to justify the historical-critical reconstruction noted above, some scholars have argued that the early church broke the unity of Luke-Acts apart in order to create a fourfold Gospel collection.[61] Because no extant manuscripts appear to place Luke and Acts together as a literary collection, it would be difficult to conclude that the early church ever made such a binding association that would need to be broken in the first

---

60. See Schröter's chapter on Acts and the formation of the New Testament in *From Jesus to the New Testament* (273–304).

61. Surprisingly Robert W. Wall, "The Acts of the Apostles in Canonical Context," in *The New Testament as Canon: A Reader in Canonical Criticism*, by Robert W. Wall and Eugene E. Lemcio, JSNTSup 76 (Sheffield: Sheffield Academic, 1992), 110–28, esp. 114.

place. As a result, reading Luke and Acts as a single canonical unit may be said to obscure the canonical association of Luke with the other Gospels. Interestingly enough, the early church recognized Luke as the author of both Luke and Acts, yet authorship was not the controlling logic for associating Luke with the other Gospels to form the fourfold Gospel collection. Rather, the logic that recognized and led to the fourfold Gospel collection was the historical and theological witness to the life and message of Jesus.

One final example from the Catholic Epistles will help illustrate the difference between the canonical and historical-critical relationship of the New Testament writings. According to the logic of historical-critical reconstruction, the Gospel of John, the three epistles of John, and the book of Revelation might be read together as "Johannine literature." This associa-tion, of course, is based upon the traditional recognition that each of these writings is related with respect to their author-ship. Similar to the Gospel of Luke, however, the Gospel of John appears to have been read in the early church as part of the fourfold Gospel rather than as part of a set of Johannine writ-ings. The early church generally recognized common author-ship by John, but this did not lead to the "common sense" association of a Johannine corpus. In fact, there is no plausible evidence in the manuscript tradition that a so-called "Johan-nine corpus" ever circulated.[62] What we find instead is that the Gospel of John was associated with the other Gospels, while Revelation was placed at the end of the New Testament, func-tioning as a fitting climax to the canon rather than simply one of several writings that circulated as part of a Johannine corpus. In the end, the letters of John, being separated from the Gospels and Revelation, found a rich set of associations with the other Catholic Epistles. Perhaps the witness of the pillar apostles in Jerusalem reinforced the association between James, Peter, and

---

62. Contra Charles E. Hill, *The Johannine Corpus in the Early Church* (Oxford: Oxford University Press, 2006), 455–56.

John in the Catholic Epistles collection—an association that is even referred to by Paul in Galatians 2:9.

Each of these examples demonstrates that the manner in which the canonical writings were collected and associated with each other often influences interpretation. I am not arguing that we should never analyze Luke and Acts together, or that we should never consider the stylistic similarities between the Johannine texts—these are legitimate exegetical exercises that bear interpretive fruit. However, I am suggesting that whereas historical associations are important and useful, the canonical collection of the New Testament and the associations it generates should take precedence in interpretation. Perhaps two images might help further illustrate the crucial role that collection and association play in interpretation.

The function that canonical collection plays in interpretation can be illuminated by an analogy to a mosaic work of art. The image created in a mosaic depends on the collection and expert arrangement of a number of tesserae, or tiles. Often the tesserae consist of a variety of different materials and colors and, though often cut into very small pieces, frequently consist of different shapes. Though the work is made up of the individual tesserae, all the individual pieces must be seen together as a collection in order for the final image to come into focus—in fact it is only as a carefully curated collection that the image appears at all. This is the point famously made by Irenaeus regarding the heretical misinterpretation (or twisting) of Scripture by the Valentinian Gnostics (*Adv. haer.* 1.7.1). Without the logic of canonical collection and ordering, one can take the tesserae of Scripture (the individual passages) and construct an image of a dog or fox, when the real image is of the king. Interpreting the individual texts on their own is simply insufficient for a right understanding of Scripture—they must be interpreted within the authoritative collection of the canon. The canonical logic of collection guides interpretation by clarifying the limits (extent) of Scripture while establishing a fundamental biblical unity that provides the appropriate context for locating a text's meaning.

A different analogy might highlight the interpretive importance of textual association in the New Testament canon. In the examples above, it is clear that the New Testament canon intentionally associates particular texts with each other. Luke is framed within the fourfold Gospel collection and is therefore associated with the other Gospels, especially the Synoptic Gospels. Or again, the letters of John are placed within the Catholic Epistles collection and associated with the letters of the pillar apostles of James, Peter, and Jude rather than within a smaller collection of "Johannine literature." Just as the gravitational pull between planets in a solar system exerts influence over each planet's particular orbit around the sun, so too does the association between New Testament writings (both in subcollections as well as within the twenty-seven-book New Testament) influence interpretation. Both the scope and arrangement of the canon influence the manner in which the individual writings relate to one another as well as the unique contribution that each writing offers.[63] The fact that James, a letter to the "twelve tribes in the diaspora," is associated with 1 Peter, addressed to "elect exiles in the diaspora," for example, influences how both texts are interpreted. Understood in this light, the canon functions as the authoritative context in which these texts are interpreted.

Recontextualization

The unique contexts created by the canonical collections might be described as a kind of authoritative recontextualization of the New Testament texts. For methodological clarity, a hermeneutical process is often laid out in a number of steps. Typically, after determining the original meaning of the text through grammatical-historical analysis (usually

---

63. Both the image of a mosaic and that of planetary orbit come from Timothy J. Stone, *The Compilational History of the Megilloth: Canon, Contoured Intertextuality and Meaning in the Writings*, FAT 59 (Tübingen: Mohr Siebeck, 2013), 7, 211.

described as the determination of the original intention of the historical author), the text is then recontextualized for the modern hearer. This recontextualization is understood in terms of the application or contemporary significance of the text. Importantly, the recognition that the individual writings were first collected and circulated in specific subcollections (e.g., the fourfold Gospel and the Pauline corpus) and were later formed into a twenty-seven-book collection is to accept that the individual writings have been recontextualized for modern readers. Though the text must still be applied to the modern context, this canonical recontextualization, as it were, serves as an authoritative or apostolic reorienting of these individual texts to the canonical whole. As Levenson observes,

> The fact of canon also challenges the most basic presupposition of historical criticism, that a book must be understood *only within the context in which it was produced*. The very existence of a canon *testifies to the reality of recontextualization*: an artifact may survive the circumstances that brought it into being. . . . Indeed, it can outlive the culture in which it was produced.[64]

In his discussion of the process of recontextualization, Levenson highlights the theological function of canonical interpretation, noting that the texts collected in the New Testament canon continue to speak beyond their original historical situations of composition to later readers. To be clear, the study of the historical background and content of the individual New Testament texts makes an important contribution to our understanding of their meaning and modern relevance.[65] However, it

---

64. Levenson, *The Hebrew Bible*, 123 (emphasis added).
65. Levenson himself acknowledges this, arguing that the "original culture continues to inform the text. . . . [And] Because the Bible can never be altogether disengaged from the culture of its authors, historical criticism is necessary." Levenson, *The Hebrew Bible*, 123.

must also be recognized that the New Testament was received and confessed by the early church as a canonical collection (or as a small number of subcollections) and that it is within this context that the individual writings speak to us today. It may therefore be recognized that the texts of Scripture have undergone what might be described as an authoritative recontextualization; they have been collected, arranged, and placed in a particular manner within the New Testament canon at a time subsequent to their composition. To rightly understand the meaning of the New Testament, therefore, each text must be interpreted in light of the entire collection.

Central to the canonical approach is the recognition that canon does not obscure meaning, nor is it contrary or anachronistic to the meaning of the text. To the contrary, it plays a role in elucidating the meaning of the text and the coherence of God's self-revelation. To state it differently, the canonical recontextualization of the texts within the New Testament constitutes their (present) natural context of meaning and interpretation for the church. Because this recontextualization was initiated very early (within the living memory of the apostles), it should be considered authoritative and not quickly dismissed as a later development.

Conclusion

The historical process of canonization and the theological nature of the New Testament are both necessary for right interpretation. I have attempted to demonstrate how the early origin of the New Testament canon, especially understood as the development of very early subcollections, is in keeping with the particular theological persuasion that the canon is the authoritative and inspired Word of God. In the last section above, my goal has been to articulate some of the hermeneutical consequences and benefits that derive from such a view of the canon's history and theology.

As I have emphasized, acknowledgment of the canonical nature of the New Testament clarifies rather than obscures the meaning of Scripture given that the historical and theological characteristics of the New Testament find their right balance in a canonical approach to interpretation. Such an approach must be careful to avoid pitting canonization against composition or defining canon by appealing to the church's use or performance of the text. I would suggest that a canonical approach guides interpretation of the New Testament by enabling the interpreter to recognize that Scripture is in essence a unified two-testament witness to Christ.

A PROGRESSIVE EVANGELICAL PERSPECTIVE ON THE NEW TESTAMENT CANON

David R. Nienhuis

The editors of this volume have asked us to share our perspectives on the New Testament canon by addressing three primary questions, the first historical (what factors precipitated the establishment and recognition of the New Testament canon?), the second theological (should the New Testament writings be regarded as more authoritative than other early Christian writings, and if so, what serves as the basis for this authority?), and the third hermeneutical (what are the hermeneutical implications that derive from one's perspective on canonicity?).[1]

---

1. I must begin by confessing that I have no real idea what a "progressive evangelical" actually is! Presumably I was chosen to represent this particular "view" because my prior work on the topic reveals me to be someone who holds a high view of Scripture (in common with Protestant evangelicals) while articulating that view in a manner that is noticeably different from the conservatism(s) of mainstream American evangelicalism. While some might consider me both "progressive" and "evangelical," I prefer to think of myself as a disciple of the Lord Jesus whose

Excellent and important questions, all three. But the ordering of such queries is not without significance. Indeed, the priority we give to these questions will have an effect on how we answer those that follow.

The sequence of questions as presented follows the orthodoxy of modern biblical scholarship, which gives privileged place to historiography in the task of interpreting Scripture. The story of the rise of biblical studies as an academic discipline is far too long to tell here;[2] suffice it to say that the European Renaissance impulse to seek abiding truth in ancient sources (*Ad fontes!*; "to the sources") became a reforming tool in the hands of those who wished to constrain the range of interpretive options against institutional corruption on the one hand and an increasingly fractious Protestant movement on the other. By beginning with historical investigation, one could (it was supposed) constrain the range of interpretive options by grounding Christian reading of the Bible in the only truths that could be (supposedly) claimed with certainty—that is, the truth unearthed by experts in emerging historical sciences like archeology, chronology, paleography, and philology—hence the continued focus on *origins* in modern academic study of the Bible. Regardless of political or ecclesial orientation, most of us have been taught that responsible exegesis must begin with a reconstruction of the original situation of the author and audience, and an analysis of a reconstructed original text. Doing so, we are assured, will enable us to arrive closer to an understanding of the original intent of its authors and the original meaning

---

practice of Christianity includes being a theologian of the Triune God's One, Holy, Catholic, and Apostolic Church. Thus, the reader should understand that this essay is not written to provide a defense (much less a definition) of a particular, intentionally held ecclesial perspective called "progressive evangelicalism." I write as one formed by a Protestant Christianity of a Wesleyan-Anglican stripe that has been sharpened through sustained interaction not only with Roman Catholic and Orthodox scholars, but also with countless laypeople who turn in faith to the Bible day in and out in order to hear a sustaining word from the Lord.

2.   Treatments abound, but an excellent example is Michael Legaspi, *The Death of Scripture and the Rise of Biblical Studies* (Oxford: Oxford University Press, 2011).

derived by its first hearers.[3] In such a context it makes sense that a description of one's view of the canon would likewise begin with the historical question: *What factors precipitated the establishment and recognition of the New Testament canon?* By beginning with a portrait of the persons, events, and processes that brought about the canon's ancient emergence, we might hope to arrive at an "accurate" understanding of what the canon actually is, that is, its nature and intended function.

To be clear, I have no quarrel with historical analysis of the Bible. Indeed, the texts of the biblical canon are *ancient* texts, so it should come as no surprise that interpretive insights forged by the tools of historical methodologies have again and again been utilized profitably to help us hear the Bible's message more clearly. Nevertheless, several problems emerge for those of us who receive the Bible as Holy Scripture when we pursue an investigation of the nature and function of the biblical canon by prioritizing historical reconstruction. I would therefore like to begin this essay on my view of the New Testament canon by making the case that our approach to the task must begin on a different footing.

The problems that emerge when we prioritize historical matters in our approach to the biblical canon come in the form of a series of forced contrasts. First, prioritizing historical reconstruction leads us inevitably to draw a contrast between the "informed" scholarly reader and the "uninformed" lay reader. To arrive at a right reading, it is supposed, one must take the Bible out of the hands of everyday Christians, who know little to nothing of the Bible's historical origins, and out of the context of the church that has carried and tended this text since its inception, and place it instead in the authoritative hands of the scholarly expert, who studies it in the context of the modern university, who alone wields the requisite tools of

---

3.   Criticisms of this naïve historical positivism abound. For a helpful analysis, see Part I of Jens Schröter's helpful study, *From Jesus to the New Testament: Early Christian Theology and the Origin of the New Testament Canon*, trans. Wayne Coppins, BMSEC (Waco, TX: Baylor University Press, 2013), 9–70.

historical and linguistic analysis, and who reveals these insights in the hallowed context of the university classroom. This must happen, presumably, because an error occurred in the canonization process: it resulted in the canonization of biblical *texts* without the canonization of historical *contexts*—information about those texts that, it is supposed, *must* be ascertained in order to make right sense of the Bible's message.

The divergence created by this overdetermined distinction between scholar and layperson is mirrored in a second contrast. While expressions of Christian faith often direct believers to the Bible as the authoritative "Word of God," a study of its formation reveals a history of canonization that was enmeshed in a protracted and complicated process of human decision-making about which texts should be received as canonical. A glimpse into this ancient process often widens the gulf between scholar and layperson, the latter of whom would quite naturally struggle to understand how it is that God's holy Word could come to us through a human process, subject as we all are to errors of ignorance and bias resulting from human sinfulness and finitude.

What is required—and indeed what is typically lacking in historical accounts of canonization—is a careful theological articulation of the relation between human and divine agency in history. Indeed, what is needed is a clear-eyed, good-faith historical accounting of how we arrived at a closed canon, no matter how profane the process (what some German scholars might label *Historie*), viewed through the theological confessions of the community that continues to receive that canon as a sacred vessel bearing the self-communication of the Triune God (what might be called *Geschichte*).[4] That is to say, one must articulate how the human history played out "from below"

---

4.   The distinction was articulated earlier by Martin Kähler and is taken up by Brevard S. Childs in *The Church's Guide to Reading Paul: The Canonical Shaping of the Pauline Corpus* (Grand Rapids: Eerdmans, 2008).

while making a coherent theological case for understanding God's involvement "from above."[5]

Keeping these two orientations in honest balance has proven to be a tricky business in Western modernity, given its forced bifurcation between objective and subjective poles of knowing. More "conservative" treatments of the canonical process tend to lapse into apologetics in an attempt to defend the authority of Scripture against presentations of its canonical history that emphasize intricate human involvement in a manner they perceive as threatening to its divinely rooted authority. Thus, they often uncritically blur *Historie* and *Geschichte*, carefully sifting the historical evidence and smudging the human fingerprints in order to keep their particular doctrine of Scripture pristine.[6] More "liberal" narrations of the process, by contrast, often insist on a sharp separation of the two under the presumption that theological commitments only get in the way of ascertaining the "real" truth of the matter, which is of course the truth as it is reconstructed by the professional historian who is (supposedly) able to operate unencumbered by the imposition of a religious filter.

For those of us who read the Bible as Scripture (whether scholar *or* layperson), what is needed is an honest articulation of this history that is informed throughout by a theology of canonization. But this careful theological work does not often happen, and as a result a third contrast has emerged. Informed by the reconstructed history of composition and canonization, many a modern Bible scholar discovers still other errors when surveying the product of the ancient canonization process: not only did the canonizing community fail to include important information about the text's historical contexts, it also constructed a canon

---

5. This is how my colleague Robert W. Wall and I articulate the difference in our book *Reading the Epistles of James, Peter, John and Jude as Scripture: The Shaping and Shape of a Canonical Collection* (Grand Rapids: Eerdmans, 2013).

6. In German scholarship, the term *Historie* has become widely associated with the objective facts that relate to historical events and developments, while the term *Geschichte* is often used to describe the subjective interpretation of these events.

that is misordered, with books that are frequently mislabeled. Examples abound. Though the fourfold Gospel begins with the Gospel according to Matthew, historical-linguistic analysis has led scholars to conclude that Mark is the earliest Gospel and thus must be studied first. The Gospel according to John must be pulled out of its canonical setting in order to be read alongside the letters that bear his name (and perhaps also the Revelation to John) to form a new canonical subcollection called "Johannine literature." Pulling John out of its canonical placement allows us to restore the Gospel according to Luke to its proper place alongside its sequel, the Acts of the Apostles. The letters of the apostle Paul must be reorganized as well: not only are they presented in the wrong sequence (1 Thessalonians may be the earliest), it turns out that they do not all actually come from the hand of Paul and should therefore be divided into two subcollections, one set labeled "authentic" and the other labeled "deutero-Pauline." I could say more, but suffice it to say that a historical analysis of canonization devoid of theological understanding has resulted in the formation of a new canon—a "scholar's canon" that is reconstructed according to the conventions of modern biblical studies.

What holds so many modern biblical scholars back from approaching the canon theologically? Again, the story is too long to tell in full, but the roadblock emerged, at least in part, as an unintended result of the Protestant emphasis on Scripture as the sole authority in theological reflection. The "back to the sources" impulse that fueled so much of Reformation-era polemics cast the Bible as the one and only trustworthy source of knowledge about God for Christian doctrinal tradition. This resulted in locating the Bible in a particular place within the larger theological task. In particular, the Bible has come to be viewed by many as a resource for *doing* theology, but not as an artifact that is itself entirely theological in nature and function.[7]

---

7.   This is one of the primary points underscored by John Webster in his masterpiece *Holy Scripture: A Dogmatic Sketch* (Cambridge: Cambridge University Press, 2003), and profitably taken up by Daniel Castelo and Robert W. Wall in *The Marks of Scripture: Rethinking the Nature of the Bible* (Grand Rapids: Baker, 2019).

As I will elaborate below, the biblical canon is not simply a repository of divine revelation, dispensed at a particular historical moment and encapsulated in textual form to be taken up and used by individuals who subsequently create Christian theological tradition. While there is certainly a distinction that must be made between the biblical texts and subsequent products of Christian tradition (more on that below), a sharp separation between Bible and theology obscures the fact that the biblical canon is itself thoroughly theological: its authors and editors are themselves theologians, not disinterested historical observers or mute secretaries writing by dictation. The titles and sequence of its books indicate that theological convictions were given priority over historical processes; its contents do not simply provide the divine revelatory bricks which later thinkers use to construct human theological buildings, but are themselves a creaturely construction of a particular theo-logic—an artifact, designed of God's providence, using human hands, for the purpose of transforming readers into holy hearers made fit for divine actions.

The results of the separation between the study of the Bible and theological reflection have been disastrous for scholar and layperson alike. We see it in the academy, where the biblical studies guild continues to operate mostly independently of theology (whether systematic, practical, historical, constructive, or philosophical), as though they do not ultimately address the same subject matter and can get their work done in isolation and without myopic distortion. We see it when it is affirmed that one can engage in critical historical study of the Bible without believing a word of its message, proceeding as though the requisite tools of the task are simply intellectual and informational but not spiritual or formational—as though

---

Readers familiar with these scholars will immediately recognize the depth of my debt to their insights. Those looking for a helpful survey of Robert W. Wall's decades-long work on a canonical approach to the Bible as Scripture should see his recently published collection, *Studies in Canonical Criticism: Reading the New Testament as Scripture*, LNTS 615 (London: T&T Clark, 2020).

one can engage fruitfully in a study of words *about God* without becoming engaged in a transformational relationship *with God*. We see it also among laypeople who often hold a largely retrospective understanding of God's involvement in the matter, as though the Bible's authority is based on the past inspiration of its authors but not on the present sanctification of its readers— as though one can insist on the divine authority of its words without considering the theological quality of its use, or the spiritual, ecclesial, and social formation of its users. Such thinking leads some to conceive of Scripture's sufficiency to mean that Scripture simply announces its truth without the need for careful theological reflection; one has a Bible from which to quote, and thus one has all that is needed. And we see it whenever the history of canonization is treated without a clear and guiding sense of what that history produced, that is, without a theological understanding of the Bible's nature and purpose.

Again, what is needed is a theology of canonization, one that enables those who approach the Bible as Scripture to understand the Bible's past, present, and future within the much larger scope of God's salvific work. Before we can track the formation of the canon of Christian Scripture, then, we must speak to what Christian faith holds the canon of Scripture actually to be, for our conception of what it is will shape how we make sense of the extremely limited historical evidence available to us. What is required is a theology of Scripture that helps us to make sense of how God could produce a human text through human processes that nevertheless operates toward divine ends. It is to an articulation of that theology that we now turn.

The Theological Nature of the New Testament Canon

While the term itself has a wider application in the Christian tradition, the subject matter of this chapter calls us to speak of "the canon" as a gathering of texts. Of course, one cannot speak meaningfully of a "canon" of gathered texts without elaborating on the sort of *literature* gathered therein, the particular *community* that composed that literature and participated in its gathering, and the intended *ends* to which such texts were gathered in the first place. Thus, what we mean by "the New Testament canon" depends largely on what we mean by a series of other words—words like "holy" and "Scripture" and "church"—because the Bible is the Christian church's canon of Holy Scripture.

And of course, if we are to speak meaningfully of all these other words, we must be far more precise about what we mean by the word that demands central place among them all—that is, the word "God." For the Christian, God is Triune—Father, Son, and Holy Spirit; creator, savior, and sanctifier; one God in three persons. This God's very being is relational and self-giving: the Father pours himself into the Son, the eternal Word; the Son gives himself entirely to the Father in perfect obedience; and the Spirit is the fire of self-giving love that perfects the bond they share. This mutual self-giving is a mutual self-communication of Persons—an eternal, perfect *communion*, the depth of which knows no bounds.

All the actions of this God are characterized by this essential self-giving. As the two "arms" of God operative in the economy of salvation (so Irenaeus), the Word and the Spirit communicate God's being to the creation that is itself brought into being through that Word and Spirit. The Word is God's revelatory self-presentation, the communication of God's loving and sovereign presence in creation, in the words of the prophets and apostles, and most preeminently in the person and work of Jesus, the Word made flesh to whom prophets and apostles give witness. The Spirit is the means by which that communication is delivered and received; the Spirit is the giver of life who proceeds from the Father and the Son to reveal and convict and awaken and hallow God's creation, drawing it fully into the Triune communion, so that the life and work of creation, in all its diversity, may be ordered toward its divinely intended end.

We call this communication "revelation," and this drawing in "sanctification." John Webster aligns the two terms in a

helpful manner by defining sanctification as "the act of God the
Holy Spirit in hallowing creaturely processes, employing them
in *the service of the taking form of revelation* within the history of the
creation."[8] The self-giving God takes hold of the things God
has made and purifies them for divine self-communicative use.
When we identify the texts of the Bible as "Holy Scripture,"
then, we are identifying them as creaturely productions—
human writings, *scriptura*—that are "made holy," set apart for
God's self-revealing and sanctifying purposes. In this way we
can posit a distinction between the Bible, which is merely a
collection of books—*ta biblia*—and Holy Scripture, which is a
transformative place of meeting. Anyone may read the Bible,
given sufficient interest in doing so; those who read the Bible *as
Scripture* do so seeking an encounter with God.

Such a Trinitarian understanding of Scripture avoids the
typical dualisms that plague Western theology, which rightly
distinguishes between creator and creature but struggles to
relate the two in terms of their respective agency in history.
Such is the case also in histories of canonization, which give
priority to either natural (*Historie*) or supernatural (*Geschichte*)
accounts of the process but fail to meaningfully relate the two
within the economy of salvation. Or in conceptions of Scripture which locate the divine center of gravity either in the
created object (the Bible as the inerrant Word, the revelation
itself) or in the experience of the subject (elevating either the
author as uniquely inspired composer, or the reader as uniquely
inspired hearer). Trinitarian thinking enables us to keep our
focus on God as the active agent of revelation and sanctification, who works through created things—author and text and
reader alike—by means of the revealing Word and sanctifying
Spirit. Thus, "no prophecy was ever produced by the will of
man, but men spoke from God as they were carried along by
the Holy Spirit" (2 Peter 1:21). Revelation is *from God,* and the
means of revelation are creaturely. Similarly, "All Scripture is

---

8.   Webster, *Holy Scripture,* 17–18 (emphasis mine).

breathed out by God and profitable for teaching, for reproof, for correction, and for training in righteousness, that the man of God may be complete, equipped for every good work" (2 Tim. 3:16–17). Sanctification comes about *by God's act* of inspiring and gathering human written compositions in order to make them "profitable" for God's sanctifying purpose. Debates over whether to give interpretive priority to the author, the text, or the reader miss the point (clearly, all three play their appointed role), as do sharply drawn distinctions between intrinsic versus communal understandings of canonical authority. All of these tendencies misplace the authoritative center in a creaturely reality and not in the persons and work of the Triune God.

Much more could be said, but we can sum up this unavoidably brief portrait of a Trinitarian understanding of Scripture's nature and function by attempting to answer the question raised by the editors of this volume under the "theology" heading: *Should the New Testament writings be regarded as more authoritative than other early Christian writings? If so, what serves as the basis for this authority?* Given what I have suggested thus far, the answer to the first question has to be yes, the New Testament writings form a distinctive class of authoritative ancient Christian literature identified as *Holy Scripture,* texts that were set apart from other early Christian writings in order to function as a particular instantiation of God's self-communication for the purpose of Christian sanctification. The basis of this authority is of course God alone, whose blessing of these human compositions is made manifest through God's inspiration and use of Holy Scripture in the history of God's people. The history of Scripture's formation is called "canonization," which we are now ready to consider.

The History of Canonization Viewed Theologically

This volume asks, *What factors precipitated the establishment and recognition of the New Testament canon?* The question as stated calls forth a more naturalistic understanding of the process

as observable "from below": we are asked to identify the
"precipitating factors"—presumably the historical events,
movements, and persons—that resulted in the creation of the
New Testament canon. To be sure, the addition of a collection
of texts eventually labeled "New Testament" to the received
Jewish Scriptures did not happen spontaneously but was
a relatively long and deliberate process instigated by a wide
range of precipitating factors. Scholarly analyses of the process
are widely available, and I make no attempt to summarize it all
in detail here. Suffice it to say that though a good deal of the
history remains unknown (and likely unknowable), and while
the precise details of what we might know remain under
debate, the all-too-brief summary that follows can probably
be asserted without much controversy.

We might begin by noting that though we have grown
used to looking here and there for a particular event or crisis
in ancient Christianity that convinced the church of the need
for an additional canon, it can be justifiably argued that the
eventual development of an authoritative collection of Christian writings was an inevitability once Jesus called together a
community and instructed them to go out into the world and
teach others as he had taught them. This teaching was originally passed on primarily by word of mouth but also by the
written word, and these two presentations of the gospel were
overlapping realities. So the missionary Paul, who travels about
the Roman Empire proclaiming the gospel, must keep in touch
with his communities through letters, which he sends along
as textual stand-ins for his own personal presence (e.g., 2 Cor.
10:8–11). In similar fashion, John the elder, who would much
prefer to communicate face-to-face (2 John 12; 3 John 13),
remains confident that his letters can proclaim the gospel and
perform the spiritual work of establishing authentic fellowship
with God and Christian sibling (1 John 1:1–4).

The texts of the New Testament themselves witness to
the fact that the written word took on increased importance
as the original ear- and eye-witnesses began passing away. So

Luke, who was himself neither an ear- nor eye-witness, determined to "investigate everything carefully from the very first" by interviewing the "eyewitnesses and servants of the word" who had gone before in order to produce a trustworthy written Gospel for Theophilus (Luke 1:1–4). So also the final editors of the Gospel according to John must pass on what the beloved disciple had written with their own assurance that his testimony is true (John 21:24). So also Paul, who throughout his ministry needed to send epistolary reminders of his particular proclamation to keep his churches from turning to a different gospel (e.g., Gal. 1:6), is depicted at his death as passing on a standard of sound doctrine to which subsequent teaching must conform (e.g., 1 Tim. 1:10–11; 2 Tim. 2:2; Titus 2:1). So also is the case with Peter, who is depicted at the end of his life as intent on leaving behind a means by which his teaching might be recalled after his death (2 Peter 1:12–15).

The value of these mostly first-century documentary witnesses only intensified with the second-century emergence of alternative, incompatible versions of the gospel. We are by now familiar with the list of names and movements and tendencies—names like Marcion and Montanus; various brands of Gnosticism, including Valentinian and Cerinthian; expressions of Christianity promoted by Jewish believers that marginalized Gentiles, or those promoted by Gentiles that denigrated Jewishness; leaders and associations who claimed Jesus in ways that obscured or denied the truth and implications of the incarnation, or the cross, or the coherence of Christian and Jewish tradition. Each in their own way contributed to an epistemological crisis of contestable faith norms that were best adjudicated by appeal to the available documentary witnesses to the original message. Thus, in the late second century Irenaeus began the third book of his work *Against Heresies* (*Adv. haer.*) by asserting, "The Lord of all gave his apostles authority to proclaim the gospel. . . . Nor have we learned the economy of our salvation from any others. . . . Moreover, in accord with God's will, they later transmitted it to us in writings, to be the future foundation and pillar of our faith."[9] In this manner texts that were initially considered valuable artifacts of the Christian past came increasingly to function also as authoritative Scripture for life in the Christian present.

Still other aspects of this history have been seen to contribute to the eventual closure of the canon. For example, the rapid spread of Christianity throughout the Roman Empire revealed the utility of the codex over the scroll, the former being a far more mobile technology, but which required determinations about which texts would be sown into the binding and which would not. Intermittent persecutions involving the confiscation of Christian books gave rise to increased reflection on which writings could be handed over without spiritual detriment and which must be protected despite pain of loss of life and limb. And the unification of the Christian churches through intercommunication, mutual influence, and ultimately ecumenical councils helped regional Christian communions come to agreements around the distinction between textual canon and confessional creed.

All of the factors I have described thus far are quite defensible from a historical point of view, but they are also broadly a-theistic. One could offer the same sort of explanation for the formation of the Quran, or the Vedas, or the canon of Western literature, or indeed any other grouping of texts deemed authoritative by this or that particular community. That is to say, one can strive to explain the formation of the Bible easily enough using historical tools, but if we are to understand the formation of the Bible as Holy Scripture for the Christian church, much more must be said; indeed, the theological claims I made earlier would suggest that a naturalistic description of the historical factors at work "below" would provide an incomplete answer to the question of the Bible's actual provenance.

---

9.   Preface of *Adv. haer.* 3, as quoted by Robert W. Jenson, *Canon and Creed* (Louisville: Westminster John Knox, 2010), 34.

It must be reiterated that viewing this history theologically—that is, in the keen awareness of a single factor working "above" (and indeed within and through) the various "natural" historical factors—does not somehow render the latter evidence irrelevant or force us to offer up fideistic, ahistorical assertions designed to obscure what appears to have actually happened "on the ground." But a theological understanding of the formation of the Bible as Scripture trains our eyes toward particular elements of the process, such that some features of the history "from below" become more fascinating, and others are simply determined to be less important, or at least less relevant or fruitful. Again, much can and should be said to elucidate this claim, but for the purposes of this short chapter, the following elaboration will have to do.

Viewed theologically, the history of the Bible's canonization is subsumed under the much larger category of God's providential ordering of history within the economy of salvation. It is the particular work of the Holy Spirit to extend the Word throughout creation so that everything God has made may be restored to the divine embrace. Thus, the formation of the Bible is not to be thought of narrowly, as an end unto itself, or even in terms of a discrete process that began with the apostles and ended sometime in the fourth century. It must instead be considered part of the much larger process of God's justification and sanctification of all things. So when we think about all the various developments that resulted in the New Testament canon—the inspiration to write and to read such texts, to gather them together and to share them with others, to translate them when necessary, to gather them into meaningful subcollections, and ultimately to bind them into a single, authoritative canon—we must think of these as particular instantiations of God's much larger work of "preserving, accompanying and ruling creaturely activities, annexing them to his self-revelation."[10] God is not simply producing a book;

---

10. Webster, *Holy Scripture,* 10.

God is saving the world, and the production of this book is one part of the much larger drama of the divine deliverance of creation from the powers of sin and death.

As I described earlier, re-centering the Triune God as the active agent in the economy of salvation has the effect of reconfiguring our understanding of the various creaturely elements involved. Thus, while biblical studies in modernity has focused rather narrowly on the particularities surrounding a proto-canonical text's point of historical origin, a theological approach to canonization will result in the decentralization of this particular moment. Precise reconstructions of the original author and audience are simply less freighted with importance, because the authority of the text is not rooted solely in the context of its historical provenance. As it is, we know very little about who wrote these texts and where they came from; many of the New Testament texts are anonymous, and much of what we claim to know about their authors simply combines the scant historical evidence available to us with trust in the titles and corresponding narratives of origin that have been passed down as part of the *traditum* ("tradition").

And it must be acknowledged that the tradition itself preserved a good deal of patristic witness *against* the notion that a text's authority is grounded solely in matters of authorship. So Origen, reflecting on the letter to the Hebrews, can affirm the text's canonical authority while also noting that the style and composition make it very unlikely that the letter came from Paul's own hand, concluding "who wrote the epistle, in truth God knows."[11] Likewise Jerome, writing at the end of the canonization process in the late fourth century, is happy to pass on to posterity all sorts of doubts about the authorship of particular New Testament texts: he notes that Peter "wrote two epistles which are called Catholic, the second of which, on account of its difference from the first in style, is considered by

---

11.   Quoted by Eusebius in his *Hist. eccl.* 6.25.14 (NPNF).

many not to be his."[12] For his part James "wrote a single epistle, which is reckoned among the seven Catholic Epistles, and even this is claimed by some to have been published by someone else under his name, and gradually as time went on to have gained authority."[13] As for debates over the authorship of the letter to the Hebrews,

> It makes no difference whose it is, since it is from a churchman, and is celebrated in the daily readings of the churches. And if the usage of the Latins does not receive it among the canonical Scriptures, neither indeed by the same liberty do the churches of the Greeks receive the Revelation of John. And yet we receive both, in that we follow by no means the habit of today, but the authority of ancient writers, who for the most part quote each of them.[14]

One notes in these examples that the ultimate determinant of canonical authority is the Spirit's profitable use of a text in the churches and not strict determinations of authorship *per se*. So also Eusebius, in his early-fourth-century *History of the Church* (*Hist. eccl.*), can include all sorts of doubts about the authorship and canonicity of 2 Peter but still acknowledge that "many have thought it valuable and have honored it with a place among the other Scriptures."[15] He says much the same about the letter of James: "Admittedly its authenticity is doubted, since few early writers refer to it, any more than to Jude's, which is also one of the seven called catholic. But the fact remains that these two, like the others, have been regularly used in very many churches."[16] While Eusebius shares this information in order to argue against the unqualified inclusion of these texts in the canon of Scripture, his recognition that believers are *using* these texts regardless of his opinions on their authorship was

---

12. Jerome, *De Viris Illustribus* 1.3.
13. Jerome, *De Viris Illustribus* 2.2.
14. Jerome, *Epistle* 129.3.
15. Eusebius, *Hist. eccl.* 3.3.1.
16. Eusebius, *Hist. eccl.* 2.23.25.

prescient: ultimately the "apostolicity" of a text had less to do with the actual author and more to do with a text's spiritual utility—as the canonical Paul himself insisted when he identified inspired texts as those which are "useful for teaching, for reproof, for correction, and for training in righteousness" (2 Tim. 3:16).[17] The fact that a New Testament text is anonymous or pseudepigraphical or even historically sub-apostolic posed no limitation to the Spirit's capacity to annex such writings for the purpose of God's self-revelation.

Thus, a theological approach to the history of canonization helps us to move beyond a myopic focus on a text's point of composition and a reconstruction of the meaning derived from its first readers. Indeed, the historical evidence itself shows that these texts were preserved *not* simply because of who wrote them or what their first readers thought of them, but because the Spirit used these texts in particular to communicate God's revelatory Word to readers *regardless* of their particular socio-historical locale. The ultimate reception of these books into a larger canonical whole provided them with a *new* authoritative setting, one that displaced the social world of author and first readers in favor of the literary setting of the biblical canon. Thus, a more theological understanding of canonization will address the historical significance and hermeneutical implications of a text's ultimate placement within the New Testament canon rather than focusing solely on its historical point of origin.

One final point must be described before we consider the interpretive implications of the approach I have been outlining. The fact that God's providential ordering of things did not simply result in the emergence of this or that ancient text, but in a well-ordered, spiritually useful *collection* of texts, invites us

---

17.   So Martin Luther's famous claim from the Preface to James and Jude in the Luther Bible: "Whatever does not teach Christ is not apostolic, even though St. Peter or St. Paul does the teaching. Again, whatever preaches Christ would be apostolic, even if Judas, Annas, Pilate and Herod were doing it." Martin Luther, "Preface to the Epistles of St. James and St. Jude," in *The Works of Martin Luther 35: Word and Sacrament 1*, ed. E. Theodore Bachmann (Philadelphia: Fortress, 1960), 396.

to consider anew the question of how and when these ancient writings might rightly be said to have become Scripture. It is often noted that Paul, for instance, did not think he was writing Scripture when he produced his letters. But what is not often given due weight is the manner in which Paul's writings were frequently used to support heresy when gathered into other configurations and taken up by other tradents like Marcion or Valentinus.[18] Irenaeus addresses this problem in his valuable analogy of the mosaic of a king, which is susceptible to someone coming along and removing the jewels and gems and rearranging them into the image of a dog, insisting all the while that *this* was what the original artist intended.[19] In like manner, Paul's teaching was used by some first- and second-century hearers and readers to argue, for instance, that the God revealed by Jesus was a different God than that of the Jews, or that God's graceful justification of our sin rendered Christian obedience entirely unnecessary, or that Paul was alone among the apostles in understanding the true message of Jesus.

We can guard against this dangerous tendency when we recognize that the Spirit did not bequeath to the church individual "Scriptures" to be treated in isolation or mixed and matched at our pleasure, because they are not in fact Scripture on their own: the proto-New Testament texts were not *written* as Scripture *per se* but *became* Scripture as they were gathered together into fruitful relationships with other texts. This process of Scripture's becoming took place over generations of use, as churches worked with texts, under the tutelage of God's Spirit, in a variety of configurations, until a particular set of writings in a particular sequence slowly emerged which proved over time to be the arrangement that produced the greatest

---

18.   "For Paul's letters to be Scripture," writes Jenson, "they would have to be set in a wider apostolic context, to balance their liability to unfortunate interpretation— and we may even think that this continues to be the case." Jenson, *Canon and Creed*, 36. This same conviction drives the primary thesis of my first book, *Not by Paul Alone: The Formation of the Catholic Epistle Collection and the Christian Canon* (Waco, TX: Baylor University Press, 2007).

19.   Irenaeus, *Adv. haer.* 1.8.1.

utility in the Spirit's work of training God's people in righteousness and equipping them for good works.

As an example, we may point to the letters of the Pauline corpus. What we call "the letters of Paul" are in fact a highly edited, carefully stylized collection of materials (some deriving from the hand of Paul, some not) that is designed to communicate the apostolic witness of the "canonical Paul." This collection is introduced by the Acts of the Apostles, which carefully depicts an undeniably Jewish Paul working very much in concert with the larger apostolic band, and is followed up by the Catholic Epistles, which offer explicit counterpoints and correctives to some of Paul's claims, an important role given that some of what he says is "hard to understand" and liable to be "twisted" in ways that lead people to spiritual destruction (2 Peter 3:16). The historical "Paul" must be read in the light of his canonical presentation, or believers may end up in heresy; by extension, Paul's letters cannot be said to be Christian Scripture apart from the Acts and Catholic Epistles that frame his letter collection—and indeed, with the Gospels and Revelation, which provide the interpretive frame for the whole.

The Hermeneutical Implications of a Theological Approach

A number of interpretive implications flow from the approach I have just sketched. I begin with what may be the most obvious benefit of receiving the New Testament texts within their canonical context: because the individual writings do not and in fact cannot stand on their own, no one text needs to bear the weight of providing a faultlessly complete articulation of the gospel. Indeed, no one text could ever do so, because the good news of the gospel, being *God's* revelation, exceeds any one writer's capacity to articulate. Thus the pressure is off for any text to be immaculate: texts may include material that is questionable ("Does not nature itself teach you that if a man wears long hair, it is degrading to him?" 1 Cor. 11:14, NRSV), offensive ("women should be silent in the churches," 1 Cor. 14:34, NRSV), unjust

("Slaves, obey your earthly masters," Eph. 6:5, NRSV), or uncouth ("Cretans are always liars," Titus 1:12); texts may in fact include teachings that the majority of Christians do not affirm today ("it is impossible to restore again to repentance those who have once been enlightened . . . and then have fallen away," Heb. 6:4, 6, NRSV). There is no fault here, because no one text stands alone; where one falters or offends or confuses, another steps in to bolster or counterpoint or correct. In this manner the whole gospel is communicated through the interactions of each constituent part.

Indeed, the New Testament texts are intentionally arranged to form a complementary and mutually correcting whole. The canon's internal diversity is intentional and purposeful. The canonical Paul insists that we are justified by faith (e.g., Gal. 2:16) and even wholly saved by faith (Eph. 2:8), while James insists that we are justified by works and that faith alone cannot save us (James 2:14–26). Readers may strive to harmonize these texts, or engage in all sorts of interpretive gymnastics to insist that they really all share the same theological perspective, but in the end it is readers who do this; the canon does not do it for them.

Of course, the canonical shape *does* provide readers with certain interpretive helps, the most important of which is the sequence in which the texts are presented to the reader.[20] Indeed, canonical sequence is indicative of canonical function. I have already described the intentional shaping and framing of the Pauline witness; as another example, consider the fourfold Gospel. The first book of the four is Matthew, even though Mark was written earliest. While modern scholarship insists that we begin our Gospel study with Mark, the canon begins with Matthew, because no other Gospel is better suited to transition readers out of the Old Testament and into the

---

20. The notion that the sequence of biblical texts bears hermeneutical significance was introduced to me through the work of my colleague Robert W. Wall. I utilized this approach to create the first New Testament introductory textbook to focus on the interlocking, sequential logic of the New Testament books, *A Concise Guide to Reading the New Testament: A Canonical Introduction* (Grand Rapids: Baker, 2018).

New: from its opening genealogy, to its repeated emphasis on Scripture's fulfillment, to its insistence that God's promised salvation always involved the eschatological incorporation of the Gentiles. Among the four, Matthew alone is capable of functioning as the hinge on which the two Testaments swing. Another feature of Matthew's Gospel is its well-organized and relatively optimistic presentation of the call to Christian discipleship. Matthew's organization of Jesus's teaching into five topical sermons provides the reader with a helpful compendium of Christian instruction. And though Jesus's disciples are presented as people of "little faith" (e.g., Matt. 6:30; 8:26), in the end, a little faith is all it takes to move mountains (17:20), to walk on water (14:28–33), and to confess Jesus rightly (16:13–20).

This Gospel is followed up by that of Mark, which repeats so much of Matthew that early interpreters believed it to be little more than an abridgment. Yet Mark follows Matthew as its dark-side mirror-image. Here the disciples do not have "little faith"; they have "no faith" (Mark 4:40). Throughout Mark's account, they do not understand who Jesus is or what he is doing (e.g., 4:13; 6:52; 7:18; 8:17; 9:32), and in the end they flee from the tomb of the risen Lord, "for terror and amazement had seized them; and they said nothing to anyone, for they were afraid" (16:8 NRSV). Thus, while Matthew launches the fourfold Gospel with a clear presentation of the *call* to discipleship, Mark follows up with a rather bleak account of the *cost* of discipleship. Readers are thereby provided a kind of canonical speed bump to slow them down and cause them to reflect more deeply on their own spiritual failure, and their deep dependence on the one who alone is capable of giving his life as a ransom for many (Mark 10:45).

Nevertheless, while the Spirit led the canonizing community to carefully redact a canonical collection that is meaningfully and intentionally ordered, it remains the case that an internally diverse collection of texts unavoidably creates the conditions for interpretive indeterminacy. The fact of their gathering gestures toward coherence and meaning, but the canon does not fully establish its meaning for the reader. Though Christians throughout the centuries have worked to help readers make sense of what they are reading, the canon itself was not published with these interpretive helps; it does not include introductory essays which provide the reader with information about the authors, the writing's historical context, or how one particular writing ought to be understood in light of another. Once again, this is not a fault of the text, but it is a crucially important aspect of its design and intended function. An internally diverse collection of texts resists reduction; it cannot be summed up or boiled down without remainder; it does not allow the reader to sit comfortably with one perspective, one teaching, or one viewpoint. In so doing it enforces the reader's active participation as an interpreter and frustrates the reader's desire for a simpler, more directly consumable portrayal of God and of life in God's world. As Kathryn Tanner poignantly describes it,

> Texts that speak to every time and place are able to do so because of their indeterminacies, irreconciled pluralities, their ambiguities, and absences. . . . They are of continual interest because they always leave their audience with something to do; readers are left with the task of understanding, a desire for sense that the text holds out hope for but refuses in any direct way to appease. In short, such texts are always reaching out to new readers by their failure to give a definitive account of themselves.[21]

Or as Brevard Childs put it in his discussion of the fourfold Gospel,

> The unique feature of the Gospel's shape is that the unity is asserted, but never established in a fixed literary form. According

---

21. Kathryn Tanner, "Scripture as Popular Text," *Modern Theology* 14 (1998): 279–98 (286).

> to the canonical shape the unity must be determined from read-
> ing the four, but no one definitive entrance—neither literary, nor
> historical, nor theological—has been established by the shape
> of the canonical text. Fluidity, therefore, is constitutive of the
> canonical shape of the corpus. . . . The unity of the one Gospel
> lies within its fourfold witness, but each new generation of read-
> ers is challenged to discern that unity. Nowhere is it presupposed
> that the one correct interpretation lies hidden, waiting for the day
> to be finally uncovered. Rather, the richness of the witness to
> the gospel is such that each new reading challenges its hearers to
> reflect theologically on its testimony to the one Lord.[22]

Put directly: the canon is designed to force the reader into the
space in between the texts. This is the case because the Spirit
led the canonizing community to create a Bible that cannot
replace God. It cannot be turned into an idol and worshipped
as perfect, and it is not capable of displacing God's Spirit.
Instead, like John the Baptist, it is designed to prepare the way
for the advent of the Lord's guiding and healing presence. In
this manner the canon is designed to function as a technology
for spiritual formation. It *works on the reader* who abides long
before its mirror—it calls and cajoles, it inspires and frustrates, it smooths and makes rough—in order that the Word
might cleave open a space within the reader for the Spirit to
do her sanctifying work. In this manner the canon of Scripture becomes the vehicle of God's self-communication and the
mediation of God's very presence.

But of course the Lord did not leave us with a textually
indeterminate canon of Scripture alone. Long before there was a
New Testament canon there was a community of believers who
witnessed the Lord's presence and instruction and received the
Spirit for its ongoing comfort and empowerment. This Spirit,
who was sent to teach us and remind us of what Jesus said and

---

22. Brevard S. Childs, *The New Testament as Canon: An Introduction* (Philadelphia:
Fortress, 1994), 155–56.

did (John 14:26), called forth the earliest summary statement of the gospel, "Jesus is Lord" (1 Cor. 12:3; cf. Rom. 10:9, Phil. 2:11). As the church spread and grew and diversified, authoritative confessional elements developed organically alongside the recognition of authoritative scriptural texts, not to displace them but to provide believers with a set of basic agreements about Scripture's message and import. These confessional elements, often collectively called "the rule of faith," developed as an analogy of the canon of Scripture to function as a kind of interpretive lens—in the form of creed and doctrine and song and sacrament—through which the unity of Scripture's message might be profitably communicated to God's people. Yet as my friend Robert W. Wall puts it, these helps provide the reader with an interpretive rule of thumb, not a set of interpretive rules;[23] they are not designed to force Scripture into a set of predetermined boxes, but to provide a kind of trellis of the Spirit on to which the Word might grow and flourish in the life of the believer.

There is no shame at all in acknowledging the need for a rule to guide one's reading of the canon, provided that the rule does not become so grand and overly articulated that it ends up simplifying our reception of the message and thus displaces God's guiding and convicting presence. For this reason, the canon of Scripture in all its wild messiness must always assume a position of priority over any of the clean and precise tools that are brought in to help us read it. Whether those tools come in the form of scholarly historical reconstruction, ecclesial dogmatic proclamation, or the privileging of a particular set of biblical texts to function as a ruling canon within the canon, the Scripture can only function as the living and active Word of God if it is allowed to strike close to the bone, to pierce and divide and judge; it must be allowed to strip away our religious and academic coverings in order to render us exposed before

---

23. Nienhuis and Wall, *Reading the Epistles*, 72.

the eyes of the one to whom we must all render account (Heb. 4:12–13).

In all this we come to see that faithful interpretation of an internally diverse biblical canon is more a matter of inculcating the manners of the Spirit than the methods of the scholar.[24] Readers who approach the Bible as Scripture must do so with the knowledge and expectation that the Spirit intends to use it to grab hold of them, to draw them in, and to sanctify them for God's service. Doing so will empower them to be repentant enough to seek the Lord's help in their reading, patient enough to linger long before the text, wise enough to hold its conflicting viewpoints, disciplined enough to return again and again to its pages, hopeful enough to bear the inevitable frustration, strong enough to weather the Lord's long and painful silences, humble enough to be reminded of truths neglected or overlooked, discerning enough to receive a new and unexpected word, and, through it all, grateful enough to share that word with others, so that in the end, all of creation might be joined together in the life-giving communion of the Triune God of light and love.

---

24. For a far more helpful and concise articulation of this idea, see, e.g., Stephen E. Fowl, *Theological Interpretation of Scripture* (Eugene, OR: Cascade, 2009); for greater elaboration, see Fowl's earlier treatment in the book he coauthored with L. Gregory Jones, *Reading in Communion: Scripture and Ethics in Christian Life* (repr., Eugene, OR: Wipf and Stock, 1998).

A LIBERAL PROTESTANT PERSPECTIVE ON THE NEW TESTAMENT CANON

Jason David BeDuhn

The hallmark of the liberal Protestant view of the Bible is openness to the results of its historical-critical study and willingness to recognize the possible ways in which its findings speak to issues relevant to the contemporary church. If the Bible serves as a major authority for Christian teaching and practice, then using the tools of scholarship to understand it more fully and accurately would seem to be a valuable contribution to the faith. These tools include such fields as linguistics, comparative literature, rhetoric, history, socio-cultural studies, and the comparative study of religion. The collective application of these fields is called the "historical" approach because this way of examining the Bible seeks to establish the meaning of biblical texts in their historical context (both the context in which it was composed and the subsequent history of the transmission, selection, and interpretation of the texts). The approach is "critical" in the sense of being objectively analytical (German *kritische*) rather than apologetic, forming its conclusions on the basis of evidence rather than theological axioms. The work of scholarship is to determine what was (e.g., the meaning of a text or the practice of early Christians), not what should be. Decisions about the possible theological or practical applications of the results of such research are left to faith communities to determine for themselves.

Liberal Protestants selectively take up the advancements made through historical-critical research in order to serve the larger vision and goal of liberal Protestantism: the establishment of a dynamic experience of faith in the modern church like that which may be observed in early Christianity. This is achieved not by reestablishing the social conditions and worldview that were known among Christians two thousand years ago but by generating the equivalent meaning of faith for churches embedded in modern conditions. In this way, liberal Protestant Christianity practices a kind of "dynamic equivalence" translation of the faith, a translation from the terms and tropes and themes and metaphors in which it was expressed in Greco-Roman civilization, to modern equivalents capable of producing the same faith effect in contemporary people. To achieve this objective, it is necessary to understand not just the literal meaning of the words of the Bible but the inner logic and intended effect by which these words functioned in their original context. By doing so, we may then consider the possible meaning that transcends time and place. This type of work is certainly not novel. We find in the New Testament itself a record of this kind of activity, of communities searching for meaning and interpretations of experience that would effectively convey core principles of faith to others. Throughout the biblical writings we find evidence of a dynamic environment of creativity, dialogue, and disagreement in earliest Christianity, characteristics that are also evident in today's churches.

The Hermeneutical Legacy of the Protestant Reformation

During the Protestant Reformation, several Reformers turned to the Bible as a source of authority to counter the authority claimed by the Roman Catholic Church as an institution. But what was the Bible? No ecumenical council had ever declared an official biblical canon. The limits of the canon were only a matter of tradition, varying from one regional form of Christianity to another, and the authority of tradition was precisely what the Reformers wished to combat. Therefore, Reformers such as Martin Luther purged several books from the traditional Catholic Old Testament canon that provided biblical sanction for Catholic doctrines to which they objected. They found justification for these changes by appealing to the Jewish canon, which did not include those books. Luther flirted with the idea of reforming the traditional Catholic New Testament canon in the same way (rejecting Hebrews and James, for instance), but cooler heads among his colleagues prevailed upon him to leave it untouched. Since the Reformers sought to place ultimate authority in *Sola Scriptura*, "Scripture alone," it would be dangerously circular for them to edit the contents of the Bible to suit their beliefs.

For many centuries, access to written texts was limited, and it was not uncommon for individuals to encounter Scripture only through oral proclamation in ecclesiastical settings. This made comparison of one passage to another very difficult. This all began to change, however, during the fifteenth and sixteenth centuries. The freedom to dissent from traditional interpretation won by the Protestant Reformation, combined with the revolution of the printing press, soon created conditions in which individuals discovered all sorts of issues with the Bible that had previously received little attention. Luther could immediately see, for example, that the epistle of James does not appear to agree with Paul's position in his epistle to the Galatians, and in fact could be read as a direct attack against Paul; Paul, on his part, seemed to have had harsh words for James and Peter as leaders of the nascent Christian movement. Even more troubling for many was the way that the four Gospels do not seem to agree with each other in their depictions of Jesus, in the sequence of events in his life, and in many of the details that pertained to these events. Simply put, the New Testament did not seem to speak with one voice on both historical and theological matters.

These discoveries led to the historical-critical study of the Bible in the eighteenth and nineteenth centuries. In the same way that Protestants had examined and called into question some of the claims that the Roman Catholic Church made about its own historical foundations and the documents they used to back up those claims (such as the *Donation of Constantine*), some investigators began to question how and when the New Testament came to be recognized as Christian Scripture. Some Protestant scholars pointed out that even the authorship of some of the books of the New Testament could only be known through the very same set of traditions associated with the Catholic Church from which Protestants sought independence. In this way, liberal Protestants pressed forward with the Reformation, taking it further into the very foundations of Christianity, seeking to discern what could be verified historically and what was merely the product of later tradition.

The Formation of the New Testament Canon from a Historical Perspective

Despite earlier attempts by various Christian groups to define a limited set of valued texts, the watershed moment in the drive toward a Christian canon came with the legalization of the Christian faith by Constantine in the Edict of Milan in 313 CE. For the first time, Christians were able to create stable public institutions and seek a consensus on what form these should take as expressions of the identity and unity of the religion. The move toward an agreed-upon canon of Scriptures received its impetus from this turn of affairs, even if it remained far down the list of priorities of church leaders who were grappling with pressing issues of church doctrine and practice. Eusebius of Caesarea, in his *Church History* (*Hist. eccl.*), reports on the disagreements over canon among his peers—disagreements that remained unresolved throughout his lifetime.

In its prior clandestine period, Christianity existed in many varieties, with different forms of community organization and practice. Some communities were more text-focused than others, and those that did place special value on key texts differed among themselves as to which texts should be given greater prominence and recognition. The majority of these Christian groups used some form of Gospel (or set of Gospels) to provide an account of the life and teachings of Jesus, and many made use of some set of Paul's letters for further guidance in doctrinal and practical developments following Jesus's death and resurrection. Other writings later included in the New Testament canon had nowhere near the level of acceptance and use enjoyed by these foundational texts. So it is reasonable to speak of smaller, tentative proto-canons that later were incorporated into the full New Testament. The reader will note the stress here on *use*: whenever early Christians discussed and debated matters regarding a canon of Scriptures, they were much more concerned about which texts should be used in public gatherings[1] than which texts were "inspired."[2]

In fact, the peculiarities of the New Testament canon can best be explained by its use in early Christian communities. Early Christians had very little need to write anything, living with an eye on an imminent eschaton and organizing their communities primarily through face-to-face encounters. Initially, no one was thinking about creating a collection of Scripture for future generations. When Paul describes the Christian meetings known to him, he makes no mention of

---

1. Lee Martin McDonald, *The Formation of the Biblical Canon* (Peabody, MA: Hendrickson, 1995), 246–49.
2. Inspiration tended to be posited of writings once they had been accepted into the canon on the basis of other criteria.

written texts, scriptural or otherwise.[3] On the other hand, oral accounts of the teachings and example of Jesus naturally formed the core of Christian discourse, material that eventually became the basis of written records that could be read on set occasions. No authority governed such literary productions, however, and they did not bring to a close the ongoing oral tradition, from which additional material could be drawn for the creation of "Gospels" of various kinds. The apocalyptic environment in which Jesus and his followers lived likewise made apocalyptic texts a favorite form of expression. These texts included not only the Apocalypse of John and the *Apocalypse of Peter*, but several other texts with a considerable amount of Jewish content, works that have misleadingly been categorized as "Intertestamental" or "Second Temple" writings. These apocalyptic texts helped early Christians conceptualize and come to terms with the traumatic experiences of their time and to ascertain how the events that were unfolding in their lifetime fit into God's grand design.

Unlike the easily understandable place of Gospel narratives and apocalypses among early Christian writings, the prominent place of letters ("epistles") in the New Testament canon requires further explanation as nothing in prior Jewish tradition prepares the ground for this genre of Scripture. Instead, we must look to the practices of Greco-Roman associations and organizations, and the key role that correspondence played in their formation and operation.[4] While there was little in individual community activities that necessitated the production of written texts, communication across distances proved to be the exception. In many cases, it became necessary for leaders to address individuals, single communities, or an entire circuit of Christian associations

---

3.   Paul does, of course, ask for his letter to be read to the community in 1 Thessalonians 5:27 and Colossians 4:16; but this reflects the typical role of correspondence in the management of voluntary associations in the Roman world, on which see further below.

4.   See Richard S. Ascough, Philip A. Harland, and John S. Kloppenborg, *Associations in the Greco-Roman World: A Sourcebook* (Waco, TX: Baylor University Press, 2012).

through written correspondence. Such letters from an authoritative figure were preserved and prized as charters for the communities to which they were addressed. Any abiding instruction or guidance in them would be cited, while their ephemeral content would be left in place out of respect for the occasion of their composition. Various editorial work on the letters would strive to make them more useful; letter fragments on related subjects might be combined, or the specific addressees might be removed to give a letter general applicability.[5]

As later generations of Christians sought out documents from the earliest years of the movement—the valuation of age being deeply embedded in ancient society—they may have had little else to find besides such letters. This paucity of recoverable material may explain the presence in the later canon of such texts as Jude or 2–3 John, even the point of which can scarcely be discerned in the absence of more information on the contexts in which they were written. Paul's epistles appear to be the earliest Christian texts to survive, and perhaps were the earliest ever written. The Gospels had less sharply defined points of origin, and experienced a more fluid development, either as community documents (note the "we" who speak at the end of the Gospel of John) or as the end products of accumulated sources (note the Gospel of Luke's opening reference to the many other collections of Jesus material that had preceded it). They were probably stabilized in the form we now have them only in the mid-second century CE when they begin to be mentioned as discrete compositions. Indeed, the initiation of discussions of "canon" probably proved the decisive factor in stabilizing the texts and brought an end to the phase of their existence when they were freely redacted.

Already in the mid-second century, Marcion promoted something approximating a canon, consisting of a single account

---

5.   See Nils A. Dahl, "The Particularity of the Pauline Epistles as a Problem in the Ancient Church," in *Neotestamentica et Patristica: Freundesgabe O. Cullmann* (Leiden: Brill, 1962), 261–71.

of the life of Jesus, the *Evangelion,* as well as ten of Paul's epistles.[6] This canon, if one can call it that, had a certain simplicity
and elegance to it. The *Evangelion,* a gospel closely related to
the Gospel of Luke (but needing no such name, since it was
the Gospel used in the community), provided the story of Jesus
without the complication of rival, divergent accounts in other
Gospels alongside of it. Paul's community letters offered practical guidance on operating Christian communities and living
Christian lives, as well as further insights into the meaning of
Jesus's life and death. Writing a half-century after Marcion,
Tertullian understood that the Marcionite proposal regarded
what Christian associations should count as their *instrumentum,* that is, the official documents that served as the charter for
Christian organizations.[7] But the majority of second-century
Christians rejected Marcion's efforts to define such a limited
canon. They preferred a larger variety of texts, each valued for
its unique perspective and insights on the meaning of Christianity.[8] In fact, Christians in the second century continued
producing more books that would become serious contenders for canonical status, including more Gospels, more epistles,
and more apocalypses, all of which would be championed at
one time or another to be important enough to be considered "Scripture." This ongoing production demonstrates that
for these Christians no special or unique authority had been
bestowed as of yet upon any earlier Christian literature.[9]

Responding to Marcion's preference for a single Gospel,
Irenaeus of Lyon insisted that just one was not enough. And
although he knew of several more Gospels of varying worth,
he declared that Christians should recognize the authority of
no more and no less than four: those associated with the names

6.   Jason David BeDuhn, *The First New Testament: Marcion's Scriptural Canon* (Salem,
     OR: Polebridge, 2013); Hans Campenhausen, *The Formation of the Christian Bible*
     (Philadelphia: Augsburg Fortress, 1972), 147–65.
7.   See Harry Y. Gamble, *The New Testament Canon: Its Making and Meaning*
     (Philadelphia: Fortress, 1985), 21.
8.   Campenhausen, *Formation of the Christian Bible,* 167–70.
9.   See Gamble, *New Testament Canon,* 25.

of Matthew, Mark, Luke, and John. His argumentation for why there should be four Gospels, however, probably would not be persuasive to most modern Christians. On one occasion, Irenaeus contended that four was the correct number of Gospels simply because there were four cardinal directions on earth, and four winds, each emanating from one of those directions.[10] There was no other common characteristic that set these four specific Gospels over any of the others. They were not all apostolic compositions, since only Matthew and John had apostolic names associated with them. Mark and Luke were obscure individuals in early Christianity, receiving scant mention as minor coworkers in Paul and Peter's letters, and Mark appearing in a negative light in Acts. Of course, the four names had become attached to the Gospels merely by tradition, the validity of which Irenaeus had no means to confirm. These four Gospels did not agree on how they portrayed Jesus, the sequence in which the major events of his life occurred, or when, where, and with whom he was interacting when he said or did certain things. The Gospel of John posed the greatest problem in this regard, disagreeing fundamentally with the other three Gospels. Irenaeus, however, seemed unaware and unconcerned about these complications.

Irenaeus is, in fact, the earliest surviving Christian writer to identify these four Gospels by the names with which they have been known ever since.[11] Attaching such names to Gospels became necessary once divergent narratives of Christ began to circulate. In the mid-second century, Justin knows of such a multiplicity, which he refers to collectively as the apostles' memoires (*apomnemoneumata*), a designation that explicitly treats them as equivalent to other secular narratives based on memory

---

10. Irenaeus, *Adv. haer.* 3.11.8–9.
11. Half a century earlier, Papias of Hierapolis associates the names of Mark and Matthew with Gospels, but his characterization of Matthew's Gospel as a set of *logoi* (sayings) of Jesus in "Hebrew" (by which Papias may have meant Aramaic) does not correspond with the Gospel of Matthew, which is a narrative composed in Greek; Papias may have been referring to the Q source incorporated into the Gospel of Matthew (and Gospel of Luke), which does match his description.

and reports.[12] Justin's contemporary Papias cites stories about Jesus from the oral tradition that he considered just as valid as, if not more valid than, anything contained in written Gospels.[13] They and other Christian writers of the second century did not quote from Gospels as they did from Jewish Scriptures, that is, with the use of formal expressions of quotation.[14] Instead, they treated the Gospel accounts as raw resources of material from which they could draw and mix information freely, only taking care to be precise with the words of Jesus. This attitude is evident from the earliest stages of Gospel development, when, for instance, the authors of Matthew and Luke freely reworked Mark and their other sources. The same attitude persists through the time of Tatian in the late second century, who, in his creation of the *Diatessaron*, handles in the same manner the four Gospels that would later become canonical. Syrian Christian communities long preferred the *Diatessaron* to the four canonical Gospels, and had the latter imposed on them by force only in the fifth century.

Irenaeus' argument for the four-Gospel collection that would ultimately be recognized as canonical represents the earliest appearance of this idea, circa 190 CE, and comes as a bolt out of the blue.[15] As Harry Gamble remarks, "The evidence shows that the Gospels which eventually became canonical did not attain a clear prominence until late in the second century, and that even then their pre-eminence was neither universal nor exclusive."[16] Irenaeus' contemporary, Serapion of Antioch, for example, found the Christian community of Rhossus in Syria using only (*monon*) the *Gospel of Peter*, and had no problem with the practice until others persuaded him that it contained heretical content, whereupon he wrote to the community to

---

12. See Gamble, *New Testament Canon*, 28–29, and the literature cited there.
13. Eusebius, *Hist. eccl.* 3.39.3–4. See Campenhausen, *Formation of the Christian Bible*, 133.
14. Andrew Gregory and Christopher Tuckett, eds., *Trajectories through the New Testament and the Apostolic Fathers* (Oxford: Oxford University Press, 2005).
15. Campenhausen, *Formation of the Christian Bible*, 188–90.
16. Gamble, *New Testament Canon*, 24.

point out these problematic details.[17] Eusebius, on whom we rely for this story, makes no mention of which Gospel(s) Serapion proposed instead, and it would be anachronistic for us to assume that it was the four that Irenaeus, at the other end of the Roman Empire, was promoting.

The other early Christian writings later taken up into the New Testament canon had an equally tentative emergence in the late second and early third centuries. Irenaeus quotes from Paul, but never speaks of a definitive set of Pauline Epistles and never mentions the epistle to the Hebrews. A generation later, Tertullian has such a definitive set of Pauline Epistles, which he compares to Marcion's shorter set; he also knows the epistle to the Hebrews, which he attributes to Barnabas.[18] Hebrews is included in an early third-century codex of Paul's writings from Egypt, P^{46}, and its Pauline authorship is defended against doubts by Clement of Alexandria (contemporary to Tertullian). On the other hand, the Muratorian Canon, a fragmentary list of uncertain place and date, appears to omit any mention of Hebrews. Among the non-Pauline Epistles (often called the Catholic Epistles), only 1 Peter and 1 John found wide acceptance among early Christians. The Syriac Peshitta canon, introduced in the fifth century and still standard among those Syriac Christians who remained outside the authority of the Greek Orthodox Church, consists of only twenty-two books, omitting 2 Peter, 2 and 3 John, Jude, and Revelation.

Eusebius of Caesarea, writing in the early fourth century, chronicles the ongoing debates of his time over books later included in the Orthodox and Catholic canons (James, Jude, 2 Peter, 2 and 3 John, Revelation) as well as those that eventually would be excluded from them (the *Acts of Paul*, the *Shepherd of Hermas*, the *Apocalypse of Peter*, the *Epistle of Barnabas*, and the *Didache*).[19] He anachronistically reads the canonical tendencies

---

17. Eusebius, *Hist. eccl.* 6.12.2–6.
18. Tertullian, *De pudicitia* 20.
19. Eusebius, *Hist. eccl.* 3.25.1–7.

of his own time back into early Christian sources. To hear him tell it, the writer Clement of Alexandria a century earlier had surveyed and commented on all the books in the running to be included in the canon of Eusebius' day: "even the disputed writings, I mean the epistle of Jude and the remaining Catholic Epistles, and the epistle of Barnabas, and the Apocalypse known as Peter's [and] the epistle to the Hebrews."[20] Yet Eusebius characteristically avoids saying if Clement himself spoke of the books as a canon, or whether these canonical contenders were the only books Clement had discussed and possibly even approved in his now lost *Hypotyposeis*. Other works of Clement that do survive show him citing several other early Christian texts in an equally authoritative manner as he does the books later included in the canon.[21] By selectively reporting on Clement and other earlier sources, Eusebius succeeds in obscuring the fact that they did not think in the same canonical terms as he did, nor limit scriptural authority to the specific texts he considered worthy.

Athanasius of Alexandria's thirty-ninth Festal Letter (*Ep. fest.* 39) of 367 CE bears the honor of containing the first list of the New Testament canon that corresponds with the twenty-seven books now found in the Bibles of most Christians. Of course, it bears this distinction only in hindsight, and by omission of differing New Testament canons found, for instance, in the Syriac Church of the East and the Ethiopian Church. Athanasius' authority was only regional, and different canons continued to be upheld after his time. Only four years earlier, the Council of Laodicea accepted just twenty-six of Athanasius' twenty-seven books as suitable for reading in church, omitting Revelation, as many Bibles did down through the centuries since it was not read from in the liturgy. Recently discovered additional fragments of Athanasius' letter now confirm that he issued his list in the context

---

20. Eusebius, *Hist. eccl.* 6.14.1–2.
21. Campenhausen, *Formation of the Christian Bible*, 294–98.

of competition and conflict with other forms of Christianity in Egypt.[22] Even the region where Athanasius claimed authority, therefore, contained Christian communities that would not recognize his canon. Biblical manuscripts that differed with respect to the material they included continued to be produced during the lifetime of Athanasius and the years that followed. Codex Sinaiticus includes the *Epistle of Barnabas* and the *Shepherd of Hermas*; Codex Alexandrinus contains *1* and *2 Clement*. Athanasius' own appointee as head of the Alexandrian catechetical school, Didymus the Blind, continued to treat the *Shepherd of Hermas*, *Barnabas*, the *Didache*, and *1 Clement* as canonical, despite the fact that Athanasius' canon explicitly excluded them.[23]

In significant ways, therefore, the Protestant Reformation itself brought about an emphasis upon the canon of the Bible as the ultimate authority of the faith to a greater degree than may be observed among early Christians. The abundant signs of slowness, resistance, and indeterminacy in defining the canon in earlier eras serves as a caution against anachronistic views of the role of the New Testament at the historical foundations of Christianity. Consequently, the authority of the writings of the New Testament may come to be seen in a different light, inviting interpretive stances that allow modern readers to engage them in a more dialogic manner.

The Basis of the New Testament's Authority

All Protestants—conservative, evangelical, and liberal—must confront the fact that the New Testament canon is itself a product of the Catholic Church and its leadership (at a time when it was still conjoined to the Orthodox Church). Decisions about which books to include and which to exclude were made based upon the same traditions and institutional authority

---

22. David Brakke, "A New Fragment of Athanasius' Thirty-Ninth *Festal Letter*: Heresy, Apocrypha, and the Canon," *HTR* 103 (2010): 47–66.
23. Bart D. Ehrman, "The New Testament Canon of Didymus the Blind," *VC* 37 (1983): 1–21.

that Protestantism typically questions and challenges. That the Protestant Reformation stopped short of bringing to the New Testament canon the same critique it made of the Old Testament canon and other church traditions represents an anomaly in the history of the movement. Without diverging from this general state of Protestant acceptance of a New Testament created by the Catholic Church in the fourth and later centuries, liberal Protestants qualify the authority of the New Testament in other ways.

For liberal Protestants and many of those who are not affiliated with a particular religious tradition, the books of the New Testament are understood as humanly composed records of the spiritual experiences and insights of key figures and communities within early Christianity. This is how the New Testament texts and authors present themselves,[24] and this is how early Christians such as those of the second century viewed the texts as they copied and used them.[25] Only two of the four Gospel authors—Luke and John—speak about the circumstances in which the works were composed. Neither author, however, speaks of divine inspiration.[26] Luke refers to the work of diligent collection of traditions and of his concern for accuracy (Luke 1:1–4), while John alludes to the process of selection from a multitude of traditions, a process that sought to determine the material that was best suited for his purposes (John 20:30–31). The role of the human author is foregrounded even

---

24. With the exception of the authors of Revelation and other similar works, whose apocalyptic character required a different authorial stance.

25. Robert M. Grant, *The Earliest Lives of Jesus* (New York: Harper, 1961), 14–30.

26. The only book of the New Testament to claim for itself divine inspiration is Revelation—ironically, the book with the most checkered history in the canon. Eusebius reports considerable objections to it as authoritative Scripture from leading figures of the Christian church before him and acknowledges that the dispute continued in his own day (Eusebius, *Hist. eccl.* 7.25.1–27; 3.25.2–4). Revelation is, in fact, absent from many New Testament codices right up to the advent of printing. The reason for its exclusion is no mystery. Readings from Revelation were not included in the cycle of Bible readings in church services, and the book failed one of the standard criteria for this "canonical" status, since it was all but incomprehensible to an audience listening to it read out.

more in the epistles of Paul. These letters often address the ephemeral activities of specific communities and individuals, pass along greetings, and communicate short-term plans. The personal greetings and other ephemeral content of the letters demonstrate that they were written without any consciousness of being received as timeless Scripture.[27] Those who preserved, copied, and read from these writings valued them as the voices of the religion's founders, sources closer to the historical experience of Jesus's mission; they expressly evaluated them in those terms, and display in their scribal work a freedom to edit them for style and content, to "improve" them for greater serviceability to their living Christian communities.

As a result of these considerations, many liberal Protestants, as well as a number of historians who do not associate with a particular religious tradition, commonly base the authority of the New Testament on various historical factors, recognizing them to be records of salvation history or, otherwise stated, accounts of the human encounter with the divine. God reveals himself in the events and experiences described, not in the particular words chosen to describe them. The books of the New Testament are neither verbally inspired nor equally authoritative in all parts. Consequently, authority resides in the human religious experience of the communities and individual authors behind the biblical texts. We can speak of inspiration of the people, rather than the text,[28] particularly when modern biblical scholarship reveals that the texts developed over time and remained fluid, with multiple stages of authorship and redaction. This situation points to the collective "social"

---

27. Paul himself speaks with full self-consciousness of uttering his own personal opinions, with which his correspondents may or may not agree. He differentiates his own opinions from the teachings of Jesus (1 Cor. 7:10–13). He reasons and argues and cites analogies, rather than speaking like a prophet. He hints at wider spiritual knowledge drawn from his own visionary experiences but does not connect his instructions on individual matters to such revelations. "I think that I too have the Spirit" (1 Cor. 7:40) is as far as he goes in characterizing his sense of authority in expressing those opinions.

28. See William Sanday, *Inspiration* (London: Longmans, 1894).

inspiration of the community, the sharing in experiences that were commonly recognized in the texts they accepted into their canon. On the other hand, individual biblical authors may have stood against the community consensus on certain crucial issues in their own time, only to have their insights later gain wide acceptance.[29]

The human composers of the books of the New Testament may have been anointed leaders of early Christian communities, the wisest and most insightful followers of Jesus; nevertheless, we must recognize that as human beings they were fallible. This understanding of their authorship opens the door to critiques of various aspects of their texts that, in the judgment of Christian communities, somehow fall short of Christian ideals. In this respect, one can speak of a *norma normans* ("the norm that norms") embedded within the New Testament by which other parts of the New Testament may be assessed, and in that sense a "canon within the canon." In other words, it is possible and legitimate to identify a core set of biblical teachings that are unquestioned, and to assess other contents of the Bible by them.

All Christians do this to a certain degree in prioritizing the teachings of the New Testament over those of the Old Testament and setting aside large portions of the latter's instructions as time-bound to past circumstances and now obsolete. The books of the New Testament themselves repeatedly promote this stance (e.g., the Gospel of Matthew, the epistles of Paul, and the epistle to the Hebrews). Similarly, the Gospel accounts of Jesus and Acts show shifts and changes in early Christian practices and norms. Jesus initially declares that his mission is not for non-Jews but only for the children of Israel, but to varying degrees the Gospels recognize a change in that policy following Jesus's death and resurrection. Acts records the actual negotiations among Christian leaders about the form that outreach beyond the Jewish people should take. It would be a rare kind of Christian who would today argue on

---

29. John McKenzie, "The Social Character of Inspiration," *CBQ* 24 (1962): 115–24.

the basis of Mark 7:27, "It is not right to take the children's bread and throw it to the dogs," that Christianity is reserved solely for Jews. Even a saying of Jesus can become a dead letter in the biblical text.

Based on such an example, there may be reasons to identify various portions of the New Testament as time-bound relics of the original context that shaped its form and substance. For example, the geocentric universe assumed in the biblical text, with layers of solid-domed skies above which reside the sun, moon, and stars in fixed positions, would not be considered the final word as to the way modern Christians should think of the physical world.[30] But even in what many would regard as the more essential area of moral principles, aspects of the biblical text can be judged to be conditioned by the values of another age and therefore relativized in their authority. For example, the failure of Paul or Peter in their epistles to rebuke the institution of slavery as inherently evil, and instead their commands to enjoin slaves to obedience, seem to fall short of Christian ideals and perhaps reflect a moral compromise with existing social order to which Christian institutions have been all too prone in the past. Likewise, certain attitudes and expectations about women and work expressed in the biblical text need to be understood within the conditions of the Roman Empire of the first century, namely, a highly patriarchal society in which women generally endured various kinds of social restrictions on both their education and mobility. This means that the assumptions biblical authors might bring to question in this area would not hold true in the modern world. As a result, it would be imprudent to inflexibly uphold judgments made on the basis of those time-bound assumptions.

Paul especially has been the prime subject of "canon within the canon" interpretation. His teachings are frequently assessed against Gospel principles taken from the higher authority of

---

30. These are *obiter dicta*, non-binding incidental content of the biblical text; see John Henry Newman, *On the Inspiration of Scripture* (London: Assumption Press, 2014).

the words of Jesus. In his human frailty, Paul may have failed to consistently apply those Gospel principles to all matters that came before him. His encouragement of slaves to be obedient to their masters (Eph. 6:5–8; Col. 3:22–23) and to not even seek their own freedom in orderly and legitimate ways, and of wives to be obedient to their husbands "in everything" (Eph. 5:24; cf. Col. 3:18), seems to fall well short of Jesus's expectation that the higher calling of God supersedes, if necessary, family loyalties and cultural norms. Yet even in Paul such disappointing instructions appear to be momentary lapses, since he often expresses more radical forms of the Gospel: "There is neither Jew nor Greek, there is neither slave nor free, there is no male and female; for you are all one in Christ Jesus" (Gal. 3:28). The recognition that Paul may not be completely consistent in his teaching, that he often tailored his instructions to meet the specific needs of particular communities, and that he even displays possible lapses of judgment, may yield a more satisfactory understanding than trying to invent a system that accounts for his every statement.

Another way that many biblical scholars have sought to solve the apparent contradictions in Paul's epistles is by separating the authentic Pauline writings from those that appear to be pseudepigraphic.[31] In other words, inconsistencies among the Pauline letters that relate to either ideas or terminology have led to arguments that some of the letters are forged, that is, written by an unknown author under Paul's name.[32] There is no question, of course, that writings were forged in the names of most if not all of the early apostles, including Paul (the writing *Third Corinthians* is one such example). Literary forgery was a common phenomenon in the ancient world, whether motives were well-intentioned or malign. Numerous early Christian writers refer to debates over authenticity. The inconsistencies

---

31. Ernst Käsemann, *Essays on New Testament Themes* (London: SCM, 1964), 63–107, 169, 195.

32. Bart D. Ehrman, *Forged: Writing in the Name of God—Why the Bible's Authors Are Not Who We Think They Are* (New York: Harper, 2012).

among the Pauline Epistles are real and cannot be ignored. Read in Greek, some letters show very different vocabulary and style from others. More significantly, even on core matters of faith, such as Christology or eschatology, differing positions may be observed throughout the writings.[33] Based on such an analysis, there is a majority opinion among modern biblical scholars that the authentic Paul is to be found in Romans, 1 and 2 Corinthians, Galatians, Philippians, 1 Thessalonians, and Philemon.[34] For many liberal scholars and historians, therefore, this would constitute the "canon within the canon" of the Pauline Epistles. As a matter of practice, what Paul says in these epistles must take precedence over anything said in Paul's name in the other letters ascribed to him. The task of identifying the authentic instruction of Paul is not limited to determining which writings are authentic or inauthentic, however. Even in the writings universally recognized as authentic, several passages have been flagged as possible interpolations based on a variety of arguments.

Solutions that do not rely on setting aside some epistles as inauthentic potentially have even more radical implications when we consider the widely varying ways these texts discuss core Christian teachings. If Paul was willing to affirm a low Christology in one letter (e.g., Rom. 1:3–4, and, while a pseudonymous writing, 1 Tim. 2:5) and a high Christology in another (e.g., Col. 1:15–17), what does that say about how much importance he placed on that subject, or on being dogmatic in general? If he did not think it important enough to risk alienating one of the communities he addressed by insisting on a definitive understanding of the metaphysical nature of

---

33. Was Jesus only appointed to his super-human status upon his resurrection (Rom. 1:4) or did he preexist as the "firstborn of all creation" (Col. 1:15)? Do we know the specific signs presaging the end times (2 Thessalonians) or does no one know when the end will come (1 Thessalonians)? Do distinctions of ethnicity, social status, and gender no longer matter (Gal. 3:28) or should they be maintained (1 Cor. 7:20–24)?

34. Note that this determination does not resolve all of the apparent contradictions to be found in the Pauline Epistles, including those found in the previous note.

Christ, it suggests that he did not consider it an essential point
of Christian faith. One could in principle adopt any number of
views of Christ's position vis-à-vis God and humankind and
still be a faithful Christian in Paul's eyes. The same could be
said of any of the apparent contradictions between what Paul
says in one of his letters and what he says elsewhere. Paul clearly
tailored his message to his audience, a practice that helps us to
determine what he considered to be the essential, core principles and values of the Christian faith and what he viewed as
negotiable and flexible. In fact, Paul speaks directly about liberty
with regard to differing Christian practices (1 Cor. 8:1–10:33;
Rom. 14:1–23), and we may infer from the differences among
his letters that the same held true for some (even if certainly not
for all) elements of belief.

As mentioned before, the "canon within the canon"
approach usually takes its starting point from the teachings
of Jesus. All other voices in the New Testament are assessed
in light of the dominical sayings and actions. Thus, in certain
ways, liberal Christians are "red letter" Christians. Most liberal
Protestants are Trinitarians, holding to a high Christology,
and therefore will not question the validity and applicability
of Jesus's words in the same way that they might Paul's. Even
for those Christians who are not Trinitarians, Jesus remains
the master. Consequently, they are more likely to call into
question the possible editorial hand of the Gospel writers (and
scribal copyists) in altering the words of Jesus than to attribute
to Jesus himself some Gospel content that seems to be at odds
with the values generally found there. Liberal Protestants tend
to accept the prevailing determination by biblical scholars of
the literary interdependence of the Gospels. Knowing this
relationship enables the modern reader to see how individual
authors altered and made use of their sources, which in turn
helps to elucidate their motives and viewpoints and to identify
places where they may possibly have invented episodes not
found in their sources. Most would not, however, go so far as
the findings of the academic Jesus Seminar. Using very strict

criteria for determining which words and deeds had a high likelihood of going back to the historical Jesus, the members of the seminar concluded that only a very small percentage of the events and sayings recorded in the Gospels may be deemed historically plausible.[35] While the historical Jesus remains an ideal fountainhead of all Christianity, most liberal Protestants recognize and value the role played by the Gospel writers as human recipients of the experience of Christ, witnesses to his impact on his followers, and formulators of compelling portraits of the Jesus of faith. Nonetheless, when a particular passage portrays Jesus speaking or acting in a way that is perceived to be inconsistent with his own teachings, the Gospel authors are typically assumed to be responsible, not Jesus himself.

Recognizing that the identity of many of the biblical authors is only a matter of dubious tradition, many liberal Protestants and historians cannot situate the authority of the New Testament systematically in the identity of the authors of the individual books. Even if such traditions are accepted, one finds that several authors such as Mark, Luke, and Jude are relatively obscure figures. What gives their writings authority over others penned in the name of better-known individuals? Hence, if the books of the New Testament carry authority, it is not due to the identity of their authors but to the character of their contents. For liberal Christians, therefore, the authority of the New Testament rests in its character as a record of primitive Christianity.[36] While most other standards for setting New Testament texts apart from other Christian writings have fallen to the critique of modern biblical studies, there remains

---

35.   Robert W. Funk, Roy W. Hoover, and The Jesus Seminar, *The Five Gospels: The Search for the Authentic Words of Jesus* (San Francisco: Harper, 1997); Robert W. Funk and The Jesus Seminar, *The Acts of Jesus: The Search for the Authentic Deeds of Jesus* (San Francisco: Harper, 1998).

36.   Paul Achtemeier, *The Inspiration of Scripture: Problems and Proposals* (Philadelphia: Westminster Press, 1980), 114–47; Robert Gnuse, *The Authority of the Bible: Theories of Inspiration, Revelation, and the Canon of Scripture* (New York: Paulist, 1985), 102–24.

a general confidence that these texts at least stem from the first century of Christian history, giving them greater authority than later compositions, such as those of the church fathers or, for that matter, such newly discovered sources such as the so-called Gnostic Christian writings from Nag Hammadi. One could fairly characterize this attitude as Protestant in its orientation toward an earliest, ideal expression of the faith, preserved in the New Testament against alterations over time as the religion continued to develop.

Yet liberal Protestants have revived the practice found in early Christian communities of reading noncanonical early Christian literature that brings additional or alternative perspectives to those found within the canon. Biblical research increasingly questions the historical priority of the books later included in the New Testament over other surviving early Christian literature. In some liberal Christian circles, it is occasionally suggested that texts such as the *Gospel of Thomas* be at least experimentally incorporated into Christian study and worship. The same is true of other recently discovered early Christian texts that give greater prominence and voice to women leaders among the first Christians such as Mary Magdalene. Moreover, as historical research increasingly reveals the great diversity that was present even in the earliest period of Christian history, liberal Protestants have been faced with the necessity of laying aside the Protestant ideal of an original, unified, pure form of the faith and the need to adjust their expectations of what constitutes a Christian community coming together in worship.

The Hermeneutical Implications of Canon

The Christian faith emphatically declares itself as the product of events that took place in history. In doing so, it bases its claims at least in part on things subject to historical scrutiny. The texts which provide the experiential witness to and interpretation of these events are likewise historical products, written by real people in particular times, places, and circumstances. The language with which they speak, the examples and metaphors that they use, and the references they make to the world around them, all belong to time-bound, culturally shaped, historically circumscribed communication. The naive notion that the Scriptures can speak directly to a modern reader or interpreter simply by the soul's encounter with the words on the page must ignore the most basic fact that those words are a translation, achieved by the employment of secular human intellectual tools. The translator necessarily draws upon information outside of Scripture to even know what the individual words used in Scripture mean. There is no such thing, for example, as "biblical Greek," as a distinct and unique form of the Greek language known only from comparing biblical texts with each other.[37] The meaning of Scripture cannot be discerned without information drawn from non-scriptural, even non-Christian, Greek literature. That is not to say that such human intellectual tools provide the full and complete meaning of the text or that the meaning of Scripture can be reduced to lexical and denotative data. There is still the human encounter of the reader with the text that discovers significant connotations that inform faith. But that encounter cannot even begin without the mediation of human fields of knowledge. Even prior to translation, humanistic methods of analysis are required to determine the best attested wording of the biblical text—that is, to determine what should be regarded as the most reliable text, a necessary consideration given the many textual variants in biblical manuscripts. Individual readers cannot spiritually encounter that which they do not encounter at all, and the encounter with Scripture is mediated by processes of establishing the text and working out a translation that relies upon fields of study that

---

37. Adolf Deissmann, followed by many other leading lights of New Testament studies, demonstrated that the form of Greek used in the New Testament is not a distinct, self-contained dialect ("New Testament Greek") but simply the colloquial Hellenistic "koine" ("common") Greek found in the everyday nonliterary letters and documents of the period. *Light from the Ancient East: The New Testament Illustrated by Recently Discovered Texts of the Graeco-Roman World* (London: Hodder and Stoughton, 1927).

adhere to secular principles of evidence, validity, assessment, plausibility, and coherence.

The progress of historical research may uncover deeper and better understandings of the conditions assumed in the utterances of biblical authors. For example, Paul's advice for women to work at home (Titus 2:5) must be understood within an accurate understanding of economic production in the ancient world—in which, for example, most household goods were produced in private homes for sale in the marketplace, and women played a leading role in manufacturing. Paul, therefore, is not speaking of domestic "housework," but of women employed as manufacturers in an essential economic role in a location secure from various forms of exploitation, such as urban workshops. Understanding the likely motives of particular teachings through such historical critical investigation, therefore, allows the modern interpreter to stress the spirit of the teaching rather than its mere letter.

Through the study of the culture and society known to the New Testament authors, it has become clear that they learned not only the Greek language but also their compositional paradigms and rhetorical tropes from contemporaneous non-Christian cultural traditions. It adds to our hermeneutical toolkit to recognize when these are being employed and enables us to correctly discern the rhetorical effect intended in a particular passage.[38] That being the case, the particular turn of phrase biblical authors use or the mode of argument they employ may have connotations or implications that have nothing to do with the Christian kerygma. If we had, for instance, earlier expressions of the same kerygma preserved in its original Aramaic, it might have been expressed in fundamentally different terms, alternative imagery, and distinct rhetorical forms. Early Christian preachers were adapting the Christian

---

38. See Duane F. Watson and Alan. J. Hauser, *Rhetorical Criticism of the Bible: A Comprehensive Bibliography with Notes on History and Method* (Leiden: Brill, 1994); Vernon K. Robbins, *The Tapestry of Early Christian Discourse: Rhetoric, Society, and Ideology* (London: Routledge, 1996).

message to audiences in the latter's own terms and presuppositions, accommodating their traditions of discourse. This real-
ization carries over into forms of argument employed by both
Jesus and the biblical authors, which were based on certain logical assumptions held in their culture, but not necessarily valid
under modern standards of argument and proof. This historical
and cultural disconnect can cause modern readers to miscon-
strue or simply be baffled by the meaning of entire passages of
the Bible. For this reason, a conservative hermeneutic of Scripture would require someone to first convert to ancient Mediterranean cultural models in order to be rightly considered a
convert to Christianity, on the understanding that the faith is
once and for all fixed in the terms of that ancient culture.

The challenge faced by modern interpreters is that the
historically and culturally determined ways of communicating
the faith in the writings of the New Testament are not acci-
dents of communication but constitutive of the meaning, the
thinking itself of the biblical author. Insofar as modern readers
live in a society that no longer thinks in terms, for example,
of animal sacrifice as a religious act and way to relate to God,
the very logic of a core tenet of Christian faith may be at risk
of becoming meaningless and absurd. For the liberal Protestant, therefore, the essential task becomes one of identifying
a meaning that transcends culture, time-bound imagery, and
expression. This can take the form of popular creative rein-
vention that is not particularly informed by historical-critical
investigation, such as the often-repeated reinterpretation of
atonement as "at-one-ment," achieved by the same sort of
insight-by-pun that biblical authors themselves sometimes
employ, but which is not by any stretch of the imagination a
meaning for atonement that the biblical authors had in mind
(if for no other reason, because the pun only works in English).
It should also be recognized that a core, potentially translat-
able meaning can be arrived at by careful historical-critical
unpacking of the background and assumptions a biblical author
brought to a particular passage in their compositions, in this

way identifying something closer to the "author's intention" in the text.

Since the writings of the New Testament were authored by different individuals at different times and in different contexts, one should not read the ideas of one text into another. Each author has their own unique understanding of Jesus and the Christian faith. The theological work of synthesizing such sources into the principles of faith is ill-served by obscuring what each biblical author brings to the dialogue. Christian leaders who helped shape the canon boldly embraced four distinct Gospels, for instance, rather than synthesizing them into a single account of Christ. Differences can be seen between the Gospel authors, even on major points. For example, a divine, preexistent Christ appears only in the Gospel of John and is presented there in a manner that clearly indicates it to be an innovative insight that must be justified at great length. The other three Gospels are innocent of such an understanding of Christ; to read John's Christology into the title "Son of God" in the Synoptics fundamentally misconstrues what those other authors meant by what they wrote. Recognizing the separate and distinct authorship of the individual books of the Bible opens up the interpretive possibilities of intertextuality. Just as Luther detected the epistle of James responding to Paul, so can we elicit other examples of dialogue between the books of the New Testament and learn how the Christian voices within them were responding to each other. Following the scholarly consensus on the literary interdependence among the Gospels, for instance, we can observe how the Gospel authors make changes to their sources, and in this way come to a fuller understanding of how each sought to portray Jesus, which stories were thought valuable and which were passed over, and how each introduces recurrent themes that were not present in their sources.

This sort of intertextual dialogue does not cease at the boundary of the canon, of course. Most New Testament books exercise creative interpretation and reapplication of Old Testament texts, the significance of which would be lost if we insisted that the words could not be construed differently between the Old and New Testament contexts. To understand some New Testament texts more accurately, it may be necessary to detect their intertextuality with noncanonical literature, such as "intertestamental" Jewish literature of the kind recovered in the Dead Sea Scrolls (e.g., the epistle of Jude's citation of *1 Enoch*), or even non-Judeo-Christian literature with which biblical authors engage: Acts 17:28 (NRSV) quotes favorably the pagan poet Aratus on Zeus, "in [whom] we live and move and have our being . . . for we too are his offspring." Similarly, Titus 1:12–13 quotes the pagan poet Epimenides from another poem on Zeus. Recognizing such engagement with other spiritual traditions may have major implications for understanding salvation history.

For a number of reasons, therefore, attempts to interpret the writings of the New Testament will be inadequate and even misguided when the interpreter remains within the limits of the New Testament canon. Such interpretation cannot succeed because it fails to recognize that the canon was imposed later on a set of writings selected from a wide and diverse body of literature produced by early Christians at the same time. Artificially removed from this larger context and conversation, and read in isolation, the books of the New Testament might be seriously misconstrued. In sum, it is vital to recognize that each of the early Christian writings was shaped in its form, its ideas, its imagery, and even its linguistic expression by the larger religious and nonreligious culture of their time.

The recognition of these realities of the biblical text underpins the liberal Protestant hermeneutic, an approach to Scripture which seeks to adapt Christian theology, practice, and institutional structures to modernity in such a way that the faith remains vital and compelling to new generations of believers who do not share some of the experiences and understandings of the world assumed by their distant ancestors. This purpose orients liberal Protestants more toward the *meaning* than the *wording* of the biblical text to the degree that these can be teased carefully apart. For example, Rudolf Bultmann attempted the interpretive and theological project of *demythologization* as a result of his recognition that the conceptualization of the world found in the writings of the New Testament "is different from the conception of the world which has been formed and developed by science."[39] Since myth preserves and presents the particular world of a particular people at a particular time, it stands in the way of universalizing Jesus's message. Before Bultmann, Albert Schweitzer had already concluded that Jesus's apocalyptic eschatology, in its specific details and timeline, had proven to be untrue in the literal sense in which Jesus had apparently intended it. Schweitzer did not think it valid to fix this problem of the historical Jesus by reinterpreting his eschatology in some metaphorical or allegorical way. Rather, he saw the historical process of Christian development carrying forward the kernel of Jesus's ethical system wrapped in the chaff of the worldview of his time. In much the same way, Bultmann's *demythologization* project did not seek to find a way out of the fact that the writings of the New Testament earnestly adhere to the mythological world of their time. Instead, Bultmann proposed that the interpreter consider the ways in which the text speaks to contemporary readers who understood the world through science, just as Jesus and his disciples impacted ancient people in a world that was understood through myth.

Yet such a project presupposes that one is able to determine accurately the desired impact and core components of early Christian kerygma. Schweitzer was convinced that it was the ethical stance that Jesus modeled and commanded. The supernaturalism and myth in which it was expressed could be replaced by a modern equivalent. Bultmann, too, felt certain that he could identify an existential core to Jesus's message that could be successfully carried forward, stripped of the mythological mode in which it was communicated in the New Testament. But the question remains: how do we identify this authentically

---

39. Rudolf Bultmann, *Jesus Christ and Mythology* (New York: Scribner, 1958), 15.

Christian message apart from its mythic and socio-cultural context and discern what is central to the message of Jesus from what is related to its context? That is, how might we differentiate the "meaning" of Jesus's message from the "medium" in which it is communicated?[40]

One example with contemporary resonance involves the issue of homosexuality. Attitudes towards homosexual behavior expressed in the writings of the New Testament arguably have more to do with the prevailing socio-cultural environment of the time than with the Christian message. Many modern conservative Christians isolate and highlight Paul's identification of certain kinds of homosexual behavior in 1 Corinthians 6:9 and conclude that they warrant the exclusion of individuals from the church community and even the kingdom of God. Taking this position, however, entails extracting Paul's words from a much longer list of behaviors that Paul likewise thinks will exclude individuals from the kingdom (1 Cor. 6:10)—a list broad enough to capture most people in its dreadful net. Perhaps that was Paul's point, just as it seems to be in his only other reference to homosexual behavior in Romans 1:24–27. In the latter passage, Paul's brief reference to homosexual behavior leads to his declaration in the following chapters that every individual is a sinner. Needless to say, those who exhibit these other behaviors are not typically excluded from church communities, although they might be counseled in various ways.

When it comes to the interpretation of 1 Corinthians 6:9, therefore, we must be careful to address not only what was said, but also Paul's intention in making such lists. Does his instruction represent ideals to which the whole community should constantly be admonished to attain, however much they fall short? Do they address every possible such failing, or do they merely offer a cautionary selection? The careful consideration of the historical, social, and cultural contexts might shed further

---

40. See John Macquarrie, *The Scope of Demythologizing: Bultmann and His Critics* (New York: Harper, 1960).

light that brings nuance to Paul's meaning and complicate a straightforward application to contemporary issues. With regard to this specific subject, is Paul referring to homosexuality in the modern sense?[41] On this issue, too, a "canon within the canon" hermeneutic may offer a possible solution. As some interpreters often point out, Jesus never speaks of homosexual behavior as disbarring someone from the kingdom of God. Has Paul allowed his conditioning by cultural prejudices to lead him to presume the exclusion from the kingdom of those whom Jesus did not?

It is in the very nature of biblical scholarship to question, debate, and to disagree on matters relating to the interpretation of the New Testament. As advancements are made in various fields of study, several older interpretations become scrutinized and new proposals form, only to in turn face query. In its openness to the ongoing work of this discipline, therefore, liberal Protestantism does not await definitive answers and final positions. Instead, it employs new insights and discoveries to foster ever new explorations of faith. It seeks a progressive faith that returns again and again to its foundational texts in order to discover in them ways to keep pace with the different needs and demands of the unfolding future.

The New Testament Scriptures themselves are resources to be mined, voices with which to enter into dialogue—*inspiration* in the broadest sense of the term. Just as the Scriptures were used to shape and sustain the faith of the early Christians, they continue to be used today in different forms among individual Christians, without precluding community. The New Testament itself does not model a community where everyone thinks alike, acts alike, or is similarly influenced and impacted by Christian doctrine. Liberal Protestant hermeneutics, therefore, starts with the needs of the modern community and each distinct individual within it. It does not yield to a single

---

41. See W. L. Petersen, "Can *arsenokoitai* Be Translated by 'Homosexuals'? (1 Cor. 6.9; 1 Tim. 1.10)," *VC* 40 (1986): 187–91.

hermeneutical approach, but recognizes a variety of methods and tools that reflect the distinct concerns of different communities and individuals: Afrocentric, Asian, Hispanic, Indigenous, feminist, womanist, Mujerista, liberation, postcolonial, LGBTQ, and so forth.[42] Such interpretive approaches make explicit what is implicit in all hermeneutics: that the reader or interpreter is not a passive recipient of meaning and that one approaches the text in search of engagement on matters of personal interest and concern. The more approaches, the more potential discoveries and utilizations of Scripture emerge that nourish the community and the remarkably different people who find their home within it.

---

42. For a brief survey of such interpretive approaches, see John H. Hayes, *Methods of Biblical Interpretation* (Nashville: Abingdon, 2004), 297–384.

A ROMAN CATHOLIC PERSPECTIVE ON THE NEW TESTAMENT CANON

Ian Boxall

From a Roman Catholic perspective, the decisive date in the formation of the New Testament canon is arguably April 8, 1546, when the Fourth Session of the Council of Trent promulgated its "Decree Concerning the Canonical Scriptures." On that date the Council Fathers made definitive the canonical list earlier produced by the Council of Florence in its "Decree for the Jacobites" (February 4, 1442), a measure which sought to achieve union between the Catholic Church and the Copts. The list specified at Trent included forty-five books of the Old Testament (forty-six if Jeremiah and Lamentations are separated), and the standard twenty-seven of the New (albeit in a slightly different order from Florence, which had placed Acts just before Revelation). What made Trent's declaration so significant was its definitive statement, binding on Roman Catholics, about the parameters of the books considered canonical:

> If anyone does not accept as sacred and canonical *the aforesaid*
> *books in their entirety and with all their parts* [*libros ipsos integros cum*
> *omnibus suis partibus*], as they have been accustomed to be read in
> the Catholic Church and as they are contained in the old Latin
> Vulgate Edition, and knowingly and deliberately rejects the
> aforesaid traditions, let him be anathema.[1]

Trent is mainly remembered for what it says about the canon of
the Old Testament in response to the Reformers. However, its
definition regarding the New Testament is also of significance.
In part, it is a response to the reopening of early canonical
debates, including debates among Roman Catholics provoked
by humanism's return *ad fontes* ("to the sources"). Erasmus of
Rotterdam famously regarded Hebrews as non-Pauline, while
still viewing it as on a par with Paul. He also raised questions
about some of the Catholic Epistles (James, 2 Peter, 2 and 3 John,
and Jude in particular), and made ambiguous statements about
the Apocalypse. The Dominican Cajetan also raised questions
about the canonicity of Hebrews, James, 2 and 3 John, and
Jude, on the authority of Jerome, and confessed his inability
to interpret Revelation *juxta sensum literalem* ("according to the
literal sense"), though he was more favorable about 2 Peter.
Trent effectively left open the question of distinctions within
the canon, including the New Testament books, in opting for
its undifferentiated canonical list.[2]

Of course, Trent was not introducing anything new vis-à-vis
the New Testament canon, at least in terms of its contents. It
merely underscored the broad consensus reflected as early as
Athanasius' thirty-ninth Festal Letter of 367 CE, which listed
all twenty-seven New Testament books, a list reiterated by the

1. Henry Joseph Schroeder, *Canons and Decrees of the Council of Trent: Original Text with English Translation* (St. Louis: B. Herder, 1941), 18 (italics added).
2. Guy Bedouelle, "Biblical Interpretation in the Catholic Reformation," in *A History of Biblical Interpretation. Volume 2: The Medieval through the Reformation Periods*, eds. Alan J. Hauser and Duane F. Watson (Grand Rapids: Eerdmans, 2009), 428–49 (432–33); John W. O'Malley, *Trent: What Happened at the Council?* (Cambridge, MA: Harvard University Press, 2013), 89–102.

Third Synod of Carthage (397), Pope Innocent I (405), and the Council of Florence, and preserved in the Latin West in editions of the Vulgate. Where Trent made a novel contribution was in its authoritative statement about the canonicity of the listed books of both Testaments "in their entirety and with all their parts." We shall return to this phrase later, particularly as it pertains to the New Testament.

The remainder of this chapter will begin with a broad sketch of the factors leading to the New Testament canonical list widely recognized among Christians and defined at Trent. The theological question of the canon's authority and the basis for that authority from a Roman Catholic perspective will then be addressed. Finally, in a more practical sense, hermeneutical implications of this view of canonicity in general and the New Testament canon in particular will be explored. At this point, I raise two caveats. First, although I will seek to present a Roman Catholic position on these questions (a position broadly shared by the various Eastern Catholic Churches, even where their canonical history has been somewhat different), drawing on official ecclesial formulations, this will inevitably be a personal perspective, not least on the historical question. Second, though logically separable, these three strands—historical, theological, and hermeneutical—are inevitably interwoven, as will be evident in what follows.

The Formation of the New Testament Canon

The differing views of the complex historical process leading to the formation of the New Testament canon as we know it (twenty-seven books), views derived from the incomplete extant sources, have been well documented elsewhere, and many of the details will not be rehearsed here.[3] The surviving

---

3.   See, e.g., William R. Farmer and Denis M. Farkasfalvy, *The Formation of the New Testament Canon: An Ecumenical Approach* (New York: Paulist, 1983); Harry Y. Gamble, *The New Testament Canon: Its Making and Meaning* (Philadelphia: Fortress, 1985); Bruce M. Metzger, *The Canon of the New Testament: Its Origin,*

evidence, fragmentary though it is, would appear to support the following broad picture: that the main parameters for the core of the New Testament canon as *authoritative books* recognized as "inspired" were established by the second century, and that an expanded canon as *authoritative list* was widely accepted by the fourth, though allowing for some ongoing "fuzziness" around the edges. This description follows the now common terminological distinction between "Scripture" and "canon," understanding the latter as, in Gerald O'Collins' words, "a closed list of foundational, sacred books, acknowledged by the Church as divinely inspired, and enjoying a normative value for Christian belief, worship, and practice."[4] The New Testament canon as a definitive list is the result of a long and complex process of "canonization." This broad picture holds irrespective of whether one dates the influential Muratorian Canon to the late second to early third or the fourth century.[5] The complexity of the evidence also suggests the need to look for a variety of factors to explain the emergence of the New Testament canon.

While individual Roman Catholic scholars will reconstruct the historical evidence differently, Catholics root the beginnings of the New Testament process of canonization in the apostolic witness to Christ during the foundational period of the church's life. Vatican II's Dogmatic Constitution on Divine Revelation, *Dei Verbum* (1965), reiterating Trent and Vatican I though reshaping the discussion in a more patristic, and, therefore, a more ecumenical fashion, speaks of divine revelation being transmitted in a unique way in and through Christ, "in whom the full revelation of God the Most High is brought to completion," and through the commission to

  Development, and Significance (Oxford: Clarendon, 1987), 39–247; John Barton, *The Spirit and the Letter: Studies in the Biblical Canon* (London: SPCK, 1997), 1–62.

4.   Gerald O'Collins, *Inspiration: Towards a Christian Interpretation of Biblical Inspiration* (Oxford: Oxford University Press, 2018), 139.

5.   For a robust defense of the fragment as early and western, see Joseph Verheyden, "The Canon Muratori: A Matter of Dispute," in *The Biblical Canons*, eds. Jean-Marie Auwers and Henk Jan de Jonge, BETL 163 (Leuven: Leuven University Press, 2003), 487–556.

preach the gospel, fulfilled by the apostles "and others of the apostolic age who, under the inspiration of the same Holy Spirit, committed the message of salvation to writing" (*Dei Verbum* 7).[6] This somewhat blurs the distinction between Scripture and tradition (or "traditions," as the Council of Trent has it), viewing them not as two distinct sources of revelation but dynamically interconnected.

Ultimately, then, Christianity is understood not as a religion of the book, but as a religion of a person. The climax of revelation is found in the person of Jesus Christ, his teaching and his story, especially his passion, death, and resurrection, proclaimed by the first witnesses and preserved in authoritative writings from the first generations. In other words, just as there was "Scripture" before the "canon" (following Albert Sundberg's definition of "canon" as a closed collection), so too was there proclamation of the good news by the church before the composition of the New Testament Scriptures.

It is fairly uncontroversial to conclude, though there will be disagreement over the details, that the New Testament we possess is formed of collections of texts (the Gospels; Pauline letters; Catholic Epistles) that were originally preserved and circulated independently. There are indications within the New Testament itself that Paul's letters, despite their occasional character, were already considered as having wider application for first-century Christians. The invitation to the Colossians to have their letter read by the Christians in nearby Laodicea, and to read the letter "from Laodicea" (presumably a Pauline letter to that community), is one such piece of evidence (Col. 4:16). Another is the survival of such a brief letter as Philemon (and its wide attestation in canonical lists).

Certainly, by the time that 2 Peter was written, a collection of Paul's letters was known as "Scripture" (γραφή), along with a concern that these difficult epistles required careful interpretation

---

6.   English translation from Dean P. Béchard, ed. and trans., *The Scripture Documents* (Collegeville, MN: Liturgical, 2002), 21–22.

(2 Peter 3:16). The request in 2 Timothy to bring "the books, especially the parchment ones" (τὰ βιβλία, μάλιστα τὰς μεμβράνας, 2 Tim. 4:13) may be another indicator of an early Pauline collection. The growing authority of Paul as apostle is borne out by his importance for the Apostolic Fathers (Clement of Rome, Ignatius, Polycarp). The surviving manuscript evidence, together with divergent lists of letters (e.g., Marcion's ten letters, beginning with Galatians, contrasted with the early second century P[46], with nine extant letters, headed by Romans and Hebrews), supports the view that there were several collections of Pauline letters in circulation, as well as disagreement over the Pauline status of Hebrews.[7]

The origins of the four-Gospel canon are also obscure and complicated by the ongoing oral transmission of the Jesus tradition, particularly the sayings. This makes it difficult, for example, to state with any certainty whether the Apostolic Fathers are literarily dependent on the Gospel of Matthew. Moreover, it is plausible that in the earliest period specific communities possessed a single Gospel, dependent on geographical location. This seems to have been the conviction of some early Fathers, as in Irenaeus and Origen's view that Matthew was composed for Jewish converts and Jerome's belief that it was specifically addressed to believers in Judea (Irenaeus, *Adv. haer.* 3.1.1; Origen in Eusebius, *Hist. eccl.* 6.25.4; Jerome, *De Vir. Illustr.* 3). It may also be implicit in the prologue to the Gospel of Luke if one reads that as a critique of the insufficiency of earlier narratives (Luke 1:1–4). The Quartodeciman dispute over the date of Easter points to the authority of the Gospel of John in the churches of Asia Minor (though use by gnostic Christians such as Basilides, Ptolemy, and Heracleon also attests to its circulation in Egypt and Italy). Irenaeus' defence of the fourfold Gospel (*Adv. haer.* 3.11.8), however, may not be as pioneering as

---

7.   E.g., Harry Y. Gamble, "The Redaction of the Pauline Letters and the Formation of the Pauline Corpus," *JBL* 94 (1975): 403–18; Metzger, *The Canon of the New Testament*, 258–61.

is sometimes suggested.[8] Prior to Irenaeus, Tatian clearly knows and trusts the testimony to Jesus in the Gospels of Matthew, Mark, Luke, and John (irrespective of whether he also uses other sources), and uses John to provide his organizing chronological framework to his Gospel harmony. A similar use of the four Gospels is attributed by Jerome to Irenaeus' contemporary Theophilus of Antioch (Jerome, *Ep.* 121.6), while the longer ending of Mark (Mark 16:9–20), already known to Tatian and Irenaeus, attests to the use of all four Gospels in the mid-second century. In addition, Marcion's promotion of Paul, and his choice of Luke as a Pauline Gospel, would appear to presuppose not only the tradition of Luke as a companion of Paul but also Gospels associated with other rejected apostles. So, while the need to respond to Marcion, along with challenges provoked by gnostics and the Montanists, almost certainly contributed to the move towards the various fourth-century canonical lists, which are both more expansive than Marcion's and more restrictive than gnostic groups, the former's innovative role can be overstated.

Either way, there is a wide consensus in favor of the fourfold Gospel by the late second to early third century.[9] Though the manuscript evidence is contested, it is possible that there were codices containing all four Gospels earlier than P[45] (c. 250). It has been proposed, for example, that the early-third-century P[75], now containing only Luke and John, originally comprised all four Gospels. More controversial is the thesis that the second-century papyri P[4] (containing fragments of Luke), P[64], and P[67] (both containing fragments of Matthew) originally came from the same codex.[10] Certainly, support for the fourfold Gospel was not universal: Tatian's harmony, which came

---

8. See, e.g., Graham Stanton, *Jesus and Gospel* (Cambridge: Cambridge University Press, 2004), 65–68.

9. See, e.g., Clement of Alexandria in Eusebius, *Hist. eccl.* 6.14.5–7; Tertullian, *Adv. Marc.* 4.2; Origen, *Comm. John* 1.21–2; *Hom. Luc.* 1.2; also the Muratorian Canon on its earlier dating.

10. Edmon L. Gallagher and John D. Meade, *The Biblical Canon Lists from Early Christianity: Texts and Analysis* (Oxford: Oxford University Press, 2017), 33–34.

to be called the *Diatessaron*, was initially dominant in Syriac Christianity. Nor did it mean that other Gospels ceased to be read: both Clement of Alexandria and Origen know and can cite from other Gospels, while Eusebius attests to the use of the *Gospel of Peter* at Rhossos in Syria (Eusebius, *Hist. eccl.* 6.12). But these other Gospels seem to have failed to meet the canonical criterion of widespread use, and Origen became more discerning when he was exposed to the practice of Christian churches outside Alexandria. Indeed, in his *Commentary on Matthew* (written in Caesarea toward the end of his life), Origen famously wrote that the four Gospels "are the only indisputable ones in the Church of God under heaven" (quoted in Eusebius, *Hist. eccl.* 6.25.4).[11] Nor is there extant evidence for these other Gospels having been bound together with one of the four Gospels now regarded as canonical (unlike, e.g., the *Shepherd of Hermas* or the *Epistle of Barnabas*).

The case of the Catholic Epistles collection points to a longer process of formation, given the absence of certain letters in some lists, or evidence for ongoing debates about their status. First Peter and 1 John were accepted relatively early, and their prominence is still evident in the early fourth century, when Eusebius includes them, alongside the four Gospels, Acts, and the Pauline letters, among his "acknowledged books" (though Eusebius is aware of a collection of seven letters, he lists James, 2 Peter, 2 and 3 John, and Jude as "disputed": Eusebius, *Hist. eccl.* 2.23.25; 3.25.2–3). Something of the fluidity in the shape of the collection, if not its number, is still observable at the Council of Trent. Trent's canonical list places the two letters of Peter at the head of this section, perhaps reflecting a Roman emphasis on Petrine primacy, in contrast to the more usual order of James, 1 and 2 Peter, 1, 2, and 3 John, and Jude.

The number of seven letters may well be influenced, *post eventum* ("after the event"), by the symbolic significance of that number, already present in the messages to the seven churches

---

11.   Translation from Metzger, *The Canon of the New Testament*, 136.

of the Apocalypse (Rev. 2–3), and appealed to as justification for Paul having written to seven churches in the Muratorian Canon. The presentation of these seven letters suggests that they were to be regarded as applicable to the whole church and that the criterion of catholicity was starting to be recognized. This is not unrelated to content: readers will observe that they often lack some of the particularity of the Pauline letters to communities and individuals, and at least two are explicitly circular or "encyclical" letters (James 1:1; 1 Peter 1:1–2). Apostolicity, at least in its broadest sense, also contributes to the formation of this collection: all seven are attributed to prominent figures of the foundational generation, including at least two whose apostolic status was a matter of dispute (if James and Jude are identified as the brothers of the Lord). This may also explain the fact that, in the manuscripts, Acts is often bound with the Catholic Epistles, giving them a canonical priority over Paul as those "who were apostles before" him (Gal. 1:17; this order is also found in Athanasius' canonical list).

The Apocalypse of John deserves separate comment, given its rather unique early history. Though even here the evidence is fragmentary, it is not so much the case of a disputed text subsequently included in canonical lists, but rather a text which had relatively wide acceptance in the second and third centuries (Syriac Christianity seems to have been an exception, hence the absence of Revelation from the Peshitta), only subsequently to fall out of favor among Eastern Christians. In the West, the Apocalypse is regarded as authoritative by Justin, Irenaeus, Tertullian, Cyprian, Hippolytus, and Victorinus of Pettau, and in the East by Papias, Melito of Sardis, Theophilus of Antioch, Clement of Alexandria, and Origen. Though its use by the Montanists and those holding to overtly chiliastic interpretations raised some concerns in the early third century, it seems to have been the impact of Dionysius of Alexandria's challenge to apostolic authorship, *not* the book's authority (Eusebius, *Hist. eccl.* 7.25), that precipitated Eastern doubts. Despite support from important figures in the East such as Athanasius, the impact was strong and felt for centuries. This may be reflected in its absence from the lectionary, Eastern iconography, canonical lists (e.g., Cyril of Jerusalem, the Synod of Laodicea, Gregory of Nazianzus), and the lack of Greek commentaries before Oecumenius and Andrew of Caesarea (sixth to early seventh centuries).

In summary, the formation of the New Testament canon as a widely accepted, closed list of authoritative and normative early Christian writings was a long and complex process of community discernment. If there are early indications of the central importance of the four Gospels and Pauline letters, emerging as Scripture alongside Israel's Scriptures, there appears to have been more diversity around the edges. This is evident from the shorter twenty-two-book canon of the Peshitta, which agrees with the canon of the Chalcedonian churches on the Fourfold Gospel, Acts, and the Pauline corpus, as well as James, 1 Peter, and 1 John.

It is possible to detect various kinds of arguments at play in the process of canonization, some of which have been referred to already. However, as Morwenna Ludlow observes, what patristic discussions often seem to reveal is that "the Church is formulating *reasons* or *explanations* for why it has what it has, not *criteria* for choosing what it should have in the future."[12] In other words, there is a passive as well as an active dimension to the process of canon formation. We have noted a broad consensus concerning the core, understood by the second century as preserving the apostolic teaching, and therefore in conformity with the "rule of faith" (ὁ κανὼν τῆς πίστεως, *regula fidei*), as well as widespread use across the churches, especially in a liturgical context (the use of other texts in particular communities notwithstanding), paralleling the early Christian use of Israel's Scriptures.

---

12. Morwenna Ludlow, "'Criteria of Canonicity' and the Early Church," in *Die Einheit der Schrift und die Vielfalt des Kanons/The Unity of Scripture and the Diversity of the Canon*, eds. John Barton and Michael Wolter, BZNW 118 (Berlin: de Gruyter, 2003), 71.

Hence, the criterion of apostolicity may be more broadly conceived than a narrow focus on historical authorship by an apostle. On the one hand, the New Testament canon, even in its early core, reflects a maximalist view on the debate over whether or not the apostolate should be restricted to the original Twelve (e.g., Matt. 10:2; Acts 1:15–26; Rev. 21:14) or incorporate a wider group of early witnesses (e.g., Rom. 1:1; 16:7; 1 Cor. 9:1–6; 15:7, 9; Gal. 1:17, 19). On the other, not all works attributed to apostles came to be regarded as canonical. Discernment led to the rejection of texts clearly written at a later stage to fill in gaps (see, e.g., 1 Cor. 5:9; 2 Cor. 2:3; Col. 4:16). These include the *Epistle to the Laodiceans*, though it was transmitted in some manuscripts of the Vulgate, including the sixth-century Codex Fuldensis, and *Third Corinthians*, which was not widely accepted, despite its canonical status in the Armenian Church.

Catholicity, the conviction that these writings transcend the particularity of their production to speak to the whole church, is already evident in the formation of various collections, scribal editing of specific letters (e.g., Rom. 1:7, 15; possibly Eph. 1:1), and appeals to the symbolic significance of the number seven, employed in relation to the Pauline corpus, the Catholic Epistles, and Revelation. Other criteria only come to be used with the passage of time, as in the Muratorian Canon's appeal to antiquity in its rejection of the *Shepherd of Hermas* as canonical.

Certain of these arguments become more important in response to alternative views of authoritative books, although it was more likely the cumulative effect of Marcion, gnostic teaching, and Montanist enthusiasm, rather than any single factor, that precipitated the fourth-century canonical lists. The testimony of prominent churches, especially those regarded as having been founded by apostles, or communities to whom the texts were believed to have been originally addressed (e.g., Rome, Antioch, Ephesus), also played a role, as did the views of respected figures such as Origen, Jerome, and Athanasius. Irenaeus' appeal to bishops in the apostolic succession of teaching, and hence to their preservation of apostolic tradition, is an important plank in his refutation of gnostic appeals to the transmission of secret knowledge (*Adv. haer.* 3.1–25). Particularly appealing is William Farmer's suggestion, based on his study of Irenaeus and the *Letter of the Martyrs of Lyons and Vienne*, that persecution and martyrdom were important contributing factors. Hence the second-century core gives priority to the four Gospels, writings which speak of the martyrdom of Jesus and function as a hermeneutical lens for other Christian writings;[13] Acts, which testifies to the martyrdom of certain apostles and other figures such as Stephen; various epistles; and the Apocalypse, which almost certainly preserved the memory of Nero's persecution in Rome and came to be read as a book for Christian martyrs.

The Authority of New Testament Writings

Should the New Testament writings be regarded as more authoritative than other early Christian writings such as the *Shepherd of Hermas* or the *Gospel of Peter?* The Catholic Church's answer is a resounding yes, insofar as we are speaking of books which are normative for the church's self-understanding, worship, and life. That does not mean, as the ongoing use of texts like *Hermas* and *1 Clement* shows, that other books are not useful or beneficial for Catholic Christians, still less that they are unnecessary for a fuller historical understanding of early Christianity. Indeed, for Catholic Christians across the centuries, canonical Scripture has often been mediated indirectly through noncanonical devotional writings, preaching, visual art, and what Tobias Nicklas has called "landscapes of memory" (constructed from locations of biblical significance and rituals and texts associated with these locations).[14] These, however, remain on a different level than the defined twenty-seven books. In what follows, I shall reflect on the authority of

---

13. Farmer and Farkasfalvy, *Formation of the New Testament Canon,* 34–43.
14. Tobias Nicklas, "New Testament Canon and Early Christian 'Landscapes of Memory,'" *EC* 7 (2016): 5–23.

the New Testament books, discuss the significance of Trent's "with all their parts," and consider whether there is a "canon within the canon" for Catholic Christians.

The authority the Roman Catholic Church acknowledges in these twenty-seven books reflects the early recognition (albeit earlier for the central core than some of the marginal texts such as 2 Peter or 3 John) that these texts preserve in written form the foundational apostolic testimony to the fullness of revelation in Christ. That revelation—the period of Christ's earthly life and of the apostolic preaching—now belongs to the past. However, it is mediated to subsequent generations "in a special way in the inspired Books" (*Dei Verbum* 8). As noted above, this presupposes a broader concept of "apostolicity" than the narrower claim that these writings were composed by apostles, which in the case of much of the New Testament has been problematized by historical criticism. Apostolicity is understood rather as the preservation of the original apostolic response to the Christ event, first conveyed through the preached gospel, and preserved both orally in the ongoing transmission of the apostolic tradition, and in written form in the writings now recognized as canonical. The authority of the New Testament writings lies in their preservation of the authoritative testimony from "the closing period of foundational revelation."[15]

Therefore, the New Testament canon is not, as is often claimed, a straightforward consequence of ecclesiastical politics, even if political concerns and rivalries between prominent episcopal sees, as well as the views of influential bishops and theologians (like Athanasius, Jerome, and Augustine), undoubtedly played a role in the complex historical process. The fact that there was no universally binding ecclesial decree concerning the precise number of New Testament books prior to the Council of Trent counts against this. So does the fact that the canon enshrines theological diversity, which can undermine as well as confirm the politico-religious status quo.

---

15. O'Collins, *Inspiration*, 143.

To use the terminology of Hans Robert Jauss, the canonical writings are *weltbildend*, "world-shaping," and do not simply reflect the worldview and cultural assumptions of its readers (*weltanbildend*).[16] The anti-imperial Apocalypse of John, for one, would prove problematic for the Constantinian vision of a Christian Empire, a factor that may partly explain Eusebius' famous ambivalence about the book (*Hist. eccl.* 3.25.2, 4).

Catholics would describe the Church's role as one of discernment, not so much the giving of authority to these texts as the recognition of the authority they already possess. The First Vatican Council rejected the proposal that the Church conferred canonical status on books which had not previously possessed them:

> These [books] the Church holds to be sacred and canonical, not because, having been composed by simple human industry, they were later approved by her authority, nor merely because they contain revelation without error, but because, having been written by the inspiration of the Holy Spirit, they have God for their author and were delivered as such to the Church. (Vatican I, *Dei Filius* II.2)[17]

In other words, the inspired New Testament books are a gift to the Church (see also Lutheran-Roman Catholic Commission on Unity, *The Apostolicity of the Church* [2006], 4.5.1). The discernment of their authoritative status, reflecting a consensus of the churches in diverse geographical areas in the first four centuries, is viewed as a concrete example of the *sensus fidei* ("sense of faith"), the conviction that "the faithful have an instinct for the truth of the Gospel" (International Theological Commission, *Sensus Fidei in the Life of the Church* [2014], 2). There is a pneumatological conviction here that is not accessible

---

16. John Riches, *Galatians Through the Centuries*, Blackwell Bible Commentaries (Malden, MA: Blackwell, 2008), 6.

17. Béchard, *The Scripture Documents*, 17.

to the historian of the formation of the canon: that, in the messiness of the historical process, with its inevitable ecclesial and political rivalries, the discernment process was nonetheless guided by the Holy Spirit. We might call this a Johannine hermeneutic: the conviction, expressed by the Fourth Evangelist, that the Spirit-Paraclete "will guide you into all the truth" (John 16:13), a ministry manifested in the process of canonization, and not only in the writing of the scriptural books.

What of the Council of Trent's definition of the canonical status of the books "in their entirety and with all their parts"? Though the Council Fathers did not specify the parts, and the question is complicated by textual diversity in the Vulgate manuscript tradition, it is widely agreed that these include the longer ending of Mark (Mark 16:9–20, though not, apparently, the Shorter Ending or the Freer Logion), the *Pericope Adulterae* (John 7:53–8:11), disputed verses from Luke's passion narrative (Luke 22:19b–20, 43–44), and the Johannine Comma (1 John 5:7–8). The last had been omitted by Erasmus from the first edition of his *Novum Instrumentum omne* (1516), though it was restored under pressure in his third edition.[18]

Two comments are pertinent. First, Trent is making a statement about canonicity or normative status, not about authenticity nor about the inspired character of earlier forms of the canonical writings. These "parts" are declared to be without doctrinal error and suitable for reading and teaching in the churches. Like its definition of the list of books, Trent is essentially saying nothing new here, but recognizing a centuries-long history of widespread use of the longer form of certain books, especially though not exclusively in communities where the Vulgate was read authoritatively. Hence, Catholic scholars have as much liberty as their colleagues in exploring the textual-critical issues concerning these "parts" and their implications

---

18. Erika Rummel, "The Renaissance Humanists," in *A History of Biblical Interpretation. Volume 2: The Medieval through the Reformation Periods*, eds. Alan J. Hauser and Duane F. Watson (Grand Rapids: Eerdmans, 2009), 280–98 (291–92).

for exegesis. That the authenticity of the Johannine Comma remains an open question for Roman Catholics was affirmed in 1941 by the Pontifical Biblical Commission in its "Letter to the Archbishops and Bishops of Italy."

The implications of this perspective can be explored further by considering the longer ending of Mark, which had already become the *de facto* canonical ending long before Trent through its long history of preservation, circulation, and use. Trent's confirmation of this status does not undercut discussion of the original ending or of the latter's significance for the interpretation of the Gospel as a whole, as a survey of recent commentaries on Mark by Catholic scholars makes clear.[19] As an important stage in the inspired writing of the text, from the pen of the *apostolicus vir*, "apostolic man," Mark (*Dei Verbum* 18), the originally abrupt ending at Mark 16:8 retains its value, as do interpretations which presuppose such an ending (a similar openness to both endings is found centuries earlier in Eusebius and Jerome). It does, nonetheless, validate the public use of the longer ending, resulting in the irony that, at least in the modern Roman lectionary, the gospel for the Feast of St. Mark the Evangelist (Mark 16:15–20) comes from the one part of the Gospel almost certainly not composed by the evangelist himself. The longer ending is certainly canonical, though that does not thereby make it Markan. More positively, as Francis Moloney observes in his commentary, its widespread preservation is testimony to its successful resolution for many readers of Mark 16:8, as well as its development of motifs from earlier in the Gospel in a way which responded to the missionary dimension of the second-century community for whom it was first composed.[20]

---

19. E.g., Joachim Gnilka, *Das Evangelium nach Markus. 2. Teilband (Mk 8,27–16,20),* EKK II/2 (Zürich: Benziger/Neukirchen-Vluyn: Neukirchener Verlag, 1979), 337–58; John R. Donahue and Daniel J. Harrington, *The Gospel of Mark,* SP 2 (Collegeville, MN: Liturgical, 2002), 457–64; Francis J. Moloney, *The Gospel of Mark: A Commentary* (Peabody, MA: Hendrickson, 2002), 339–62; Adela Yarbro Collins, *Mark: A Commentary,* ed. Harold W. Attridge, Hermeneia (Minneapolis: Fortress, 2007), 779–818.
20. Moloney, *The Gospel of Mark,* 359–62.

Second, Trent does not claim that every part of those books, or every view espoused in them, bear the same weight.[21] Does this mean, therefore, that Roman Catholics operate with a "canon within the canon," whether formally or informally? Not in the sense that it grounds the canon "on a provisional, changeable theological standard"[22] that silences other canonical voices. Different time periods and different cultural contexts will have their own views on what is the norm, making this an appeal to shifting sands. The reception history of Revelation is instructive here, since although its canonical status has been, and in some contexts continues to be, disputed, the reasons for such dispute have varied significantly (e.g., its millenarianism, its perceived lack of apostolic status, its problematizing of the idea of a Christian empire, or the violence of its imagery). Whereas all Christian communities, the Roman Catholic Church included, have at times given more weight to parts of the New Testament—the importance of the Pastoral Epistles for a Catholic understanding of church order is an obvious example—the authority of alternative canonical voices has, at least in theory and at specific moments in practice, acted as a counterweight.

Nonetheless, the Catholic view of the New Testament canon does give hermeneutical priority to the four Gospels, since these are focused, not on the challenges of community formation (as are the epistles), but on the Christ event itself. *Dei Verbum* expresses this perspective as follows:

> It is common knowledge that among all the Scriptures, even those of the New Testament, the Gospels have a special preeminence [*Evangelia merito excellere*], for they are the principal

---

21. Nicolaas Appel, "The New Testament Canon: Historical Process and Spirit's Witness," *TS* 32 (1971): 624–46, esp. 641–42.

22. Jens Schröter, *From Jesus to the New Testament: Early Christian Theology and the Origin of the New Testament Canon*, trans. Wayne Coppins, BMSEC (Waco, TX: Baylor University Press, 2013), 253.

witness to the life and teaching of the incarnate Word, our Savior (*Dei Verbum* 18).[23]

This preeminence is reflected, not least, in liturgical practice, where the proclamation of the gospel is marked by particular solemnity: honored with a procession and incense, often sung, with the congregation standing. Here, the reasons for the early emergence of the fourfold Gospel are relevant. What distinguishes the four that would become canonical from many of the extracanonical gospels (the *Gospel of Peter* being a possible rare exception), is not only their earlier date but the central place they give to the life, teaching, death, and resurrection of Christ. This holds even for the Gospel of John, despite the claim of Ernst Käsemann that John's "naïve docetism" results in his passion narrative being "a mere postscript" to his Gospel.[24] Prioritizing the fourfold Gospel foregrounds Jesus's teaching as mediated by the evangelists for Christian praxis. The gospel pattern of Christ's life, death, and resurrection has the further effect of emphasizing those dimensions not only in the Pauline corpus (centered on the proclamation of Christ crucified) but also in Hebrews (Christ as sacrifice and high priest), 1 Peter (the example of the suffering Christ), and Revelation (the victorious Lamb). This does not come at the expense of a monochrome uniformity: the preeminent place of the four Gospels, in contrast to the *Diatessaron*, presupposes an authority in diversity. Benedict Viviano reminds fellow Catholics, for example, of "the dialectical mutual correction and balancing provided by different biblical books read in the same community of faith."[25]

---

23. Béchard, *The Scripture Documents*, 27.
24. Ernst Käsemann, *The Testament of Jesus*, trans. Gerhard Krodel (London: SCM, 1968), 7.
25. Benedict Thomas Viviano, "The Normativity of Scripture and Tradition in Recent Catholic Theology," in *Scripture's Doctrine and Theology's Bible: How the New Testament Shapes Christian Dogmatics*, eds. Markus Bockmuehl and Alan J. Torrance (Grand Rapids: Baker, 2008), 125–40 (132).

Hermeneutical Implications: The Case of Revelation

So what are the hermeneutical implications of this perspective on the New Testament canon, including Viviano's reminder of its dialectical character? A particular test case—the book of Revelation—has been chosen to focus the discussion. The hermeneutical question related to the Apocalypse of John can be addressed in at least four, albeit overlapping, ways: (1) the boundary between the canonical Apocalypse and what are now considered extracanonical apocalypses; (2) the christological implications of reading Revelation through the "rule of faith"; (3) the relationship of Revelation to other canonical texts; and (4) the question of canonical shape and order.[26]

First, for Catholic Christians, Revelation has an authoritative voice that places it in a separate category from the large number of other early Christian apocalypses, however influential they may have been. This holds even for the Greek *Apocalypse of Peter*, cited as Petrine by Clement of Alexandria (*Ecl.* 41) and accepted in the Muratorian Canon, albeit with the caveat that "some of us are not willing that the latter be read in church" (1.72).[27] Though the apostolic authorship of both apocalypses has at times been disputed (for Revelation, at least in the East, though hardly in the Latin West, at least until the sixteenth century), the criteria of catholicity and usage favor the Johannine Apocalypse. Its widespread acceptance in different parts of the church in the early period may well be due to its

---

26. Studies on reading Revelation as canonical Scripture include Robert W. Wall, "The Apocalypse of the New Testament in Canonical Context," in *The New Testament as Canon: A Reader in Canonical Criticism*, by Robert W. Wall and Eugene E. Lemcio, JSNTSup 76 (Sheffield: Sheffield Academic, 1992), 274–98; Tobias Nicklas, "The Apocalypse in the Framework of the Canon," in *Revelation and the Politics of Apocalyptic Interpretation*, eds. Richard B. Hays and Stefan Alkier (Waco, TX: Baylor University Press, 2012), 143–53; Külli Tõniste, *The Ending of the Canon: A Canonical and Intertextual Reading of Revelation 21–22*, LNTS 526 (London: Bloomsbury T&T Clark, 2016).

27. Translation from Metzger, *The Canon of the New Testament*, 307. For Eusebius, it belongs in his second category of disputed books, among those designated as "spurious."

explicit claims to convey prophetic revelation (Rev. 1:3, 11; 2:1; 22:7, 10, 18), underscored by its "integrity formula," recalling Deuteronomy (Rev. 22:18–19; cf. Deut. 4:2; 13:1; 29:19). This may have given it an edge over other writings that now form the New Testament, even some of those of the core.[28]

This canonical priority should have little practical impact on the work of Catholic New Testament exegetes, at least in terms of understanding Revelation in its original context. Extracanonical Christian apocalypses such as the *Apocalypse of Peter* or the *Ascension of Isaiah*, like their Jewish counterparts, rightly play a key comparative and illuminating role in a Christian interpretation of the Apocalypse. Without such comparison, the Revelation commentaries of R. H. Charles, David Aune, and Craig Koester would be substantially poorer. Where the difference does impact Christian, and specifically Catholic, exegetes is in Revelation's normative character, drawing upon the earliest Christian usage of κανών (*kanōn*) to refer, not to a closed list, but to a rule or measure (as in "the canon of truth" or "the rule of faith"). Here the earliest commentaries (e.g., by Victorinus of Pettau) provide some clues as to how the Apocalypse functioned normatively in the early period, prior to debates about its apostolic authorship and canonicity.

Theologians often speak of canonical texts as normative in three areas: doctrine, liturgy, and Christian praxis. At least in the second of these, Revelation has traditionally functioned as anything but normative. Its absence from the lectionary of Constantinople, and therefore even from the liturgy of Eastern Catholic Churches of Byzantine tradition, is well-known (though it retained its prominence in some Oriental Orthodox communities, especially the Coptic and Ethiopian Churches). But even in the Latin West, the public reading of Revelation, at least during the Eucharist, has been marginal. Moreover,

---

28. Though for arguments that other New Testament authors believed they were writing Scripture, see, e.g., D. Moody Smith, "When Did the Gospels Become Scripture?" *JBL* 119 (2000): 3–20; Francis J. Moloney, "The Gospel of John as Scripture," *CBQ* 67 (2005): 454–68.

this Roman Catholic liturgical minimalism is shared by other mainstream Christian churches with roots in Latin Christianity. As Harry Maier quips, "Such a close eye is kept on John, the miscreant nuisance from Patmos, that he has to behave himself or get kicked out of the church altogether."[29]

That is not the whole story, however. There is an important hermeneutic at work in the history of Roman Catholic public reading of Revelation. Early evidence, which would shape Western liturgical practice, attests to the reading of Revelation during Eastertide (e.g., Gaul, Spain, and Portugal) or specifically the Octave of Pentecost (e.g., Rome). This liturgical reading of the Apocalypse in the Easter season is preserved in the modern Roman lectionary (at least for Year C of the three-year Sunday cycle). Furthermore, in the Middle Ages, lectionary reading was bolstered by an "apocalyptic maximalism" in church art and architecture, as well as in drama and devotional literature. Medieval Catholics inhabited a symbolic universe shaped to a high degree by the language and imagery of the book of Revelation. If we take account of this more expansive "use," then the Apocalypse was much more formative in the Middle Ages than it is for Catholics today. This is a good example of how specific canonical texts can shift in their normative importance, even for the same ecclesial community.

Such an Easter hermeneutic presupposes a reading of Revelation shaped by the "rule of faith" and the canonical centrality of the four Gospels: the belief in God as creator who reveals himself in the history of Israel and acts decisively in and through the passion, death, and resurrection of Jesus. In some ways, Revelation provides a clearer doctrinal articulation of this rule than certain other parts of the New Testament canon. This is found, for example, in its presentation of "the one seated on the throne" as παντοκράτωρ (*pantokratōr*), who "created all things" (Rev. 4:11; cf. 1:8; 10:6) and whose judgment is

---

29. Harry O. Maier, *Apocalypse Recalled: The Book of Revelation after Christendom* (Minneapolis: Fortress, 2002), 6.

directed against "the destroyers of the earth" (Rev. 11:18), as well as its profound dependence on the Hebrew Bible, evident in almost every verse.

But this ancient Western practice of reading Revelation at Eastertime also directs a particular reading of the book's Christology. It reads the Apocalypse through the lens of the death and resurrection of Jesus, foregrounding its key vision of the slaughtered-yet-standing Lamb and critiquing alternative interpretations of the book, not least those which advocate violence against others or tame the radical nature of its prophetic message. This is not to deny that the Christ of Revelation could be understood in a more violent way, or that other, less salubrious passages could be given greater prominence (e.g., Rev. 8–9; 14:9–12). But a canonical reading through the lens of the four-fold Gospel constrains which interpretations are normative for church life. To take one example: the violent vision of Christ as Divine Warrior (Rev. 19:11–21) is read through this lens as another mythological description of Christ's sacrificial victory, the blood on his robe understood as the Lamb's own blood, and his white-clad cavalry an army of martyrs. Judith Kovacs and Christopher Rowland espouse a similar hermeneutic in the epilogue to their magnificent reception-historical Blackwell Bible Commentary on Revelation: "If one were to expound the Apocalypse in such a way that its images led to a practice at odds with the pattern of Jesus's life, death and resurrection as found in the Gospels, there would be an incompatibility with the gospel."[30]

Although the canonical centrality of the fourfold Gospel is at play here, it does not impose an alien framework on the Apocalypse; it simply prioritizes particular dimensions of the story it already tells.

This brings us to the third question: What does Revelation *do*, as part of the New Testament canon as a list, and particularly

---

30. Judith Kovacs and Christopher Rowland, *Revelation: The Apocalypse of Jesus Christ*, Blackwell Bible Commentaries (Malden, MA: Blackwell, 2004), 248.

as part of a text called the New Testament (whether in manuscript or printed form)? To state the question differently, if we allow that the New Testament canon's multiple voices sometimes sing in harmony, and at other times perform corrective roles, then how else might Revelation function as part of this canonical conversation? Tobias Nicklas encourages us to ask two questions about the Apocalypse: What does it contribute to the New Testament canon, and what does it lack (which is potentially corrected by its new position within a diverse collection of canonical voices)?[31] We have already noted Revelation's theocentric focus on God as creator and its saturation with allusions to and echoes of Israel's Scriptures, the latter serving as a robust critique of Christian crypto-Marcionism. Its radical critique of empire or of the corruption of political and religious power provides an important counterbalance to canonical perspectives which could too readily "baptize" the political or cultural status quo (compare, e.g., Rev. 13 with Rom. 13:1–7, or the Pastoral Epistles). While the Apocalypse is often an embarrassment to liberal Christians in the comfortable West, or alternatively read in a self-congratulatory manner by equally comfortable conservative Christians, for those experiencing political and economic exploitation or life-threatening persecution, it is a potent and destabilizing proclamation of the gospel. It has long been so for martyrs and other marginal groups across the Christian centuries.

On the other hand, Revelation needs alternative canonical voices to constrain some of its more problematic aspects. Among these, Nicklas notes the anti-Jewish potential of John's references to the "synagogue of Satan" (Rev. 2:9; 3:9), in a text which is otherwise strongly Jewish-Christian, and its minimal interest in the love of God and neighbor.[32] To these we might add, paradoxically, the need for a canonical counterweight

---

31. Tobias Nicklas, "Revelation and the New Testament Canon," in *The Oxford Handbook of the Book of Revelation*, ed. Craig R. Koester (Oxford: Oxford University Press, 2020), 361–75.

32. Nicklas, "The Apocalypse in the Framework of the Canon," 151–53.

to the overconcentration on Revelation's radical critique of empire, important as it is. Although the church is undoubtedly called to a countercultural witness, there are other canonical voices (e.g., the Pastorals, the Parable of the Leaven) that invite a more nuanced engagement with society. Indeed, without this balance, the Christian use of the Apocalypse risks obscuring the particular circumstances of this book's composition. It is not necessarily the case that empires and other political structures are evil and corrupt; rather, it is the corruption of a particular empire (Rome as Babylon) at a specific historical moment, which requires the kind of resistance John of Patmos describes. Viviano's reminder of the canon's dialectical character is at work here, albeit in a more complex fashion. There is indeed an important corrective dialectic between different canonical voices. But there is also a dialectic between the historical particularity of Revelation and its canonical reconfiguration as a text with universal meaning for Christians, in which the latter does not silence the former. In light of this, historical criticism of Revelation is crucial to a responsible canonical reading.

Finally, how does the canonical order and shape of the New Testament affect the interpretation of Revelation? One must first acknowledge that the shape of the New Testament has not remained consistent, and certain conclusions can only be drawn once all New Testament books are combined, or linked with the Old Testament, in a single volume or set of volumes, whether a codex or a printed Bible. The shifting position of Acts and the Catholic Epistles (the latter placed in between Acts and the Pauline corpus in Athanasius' letter and in Codex Vaticanus, giving them a more central place than Paul) illustrates the point well. Still, fairly stable patterns eventually emerge which shape, consciously or unconsciously, Christian interpretation and use. The presence of the fourfold Gospel at the beginning of the New Testament does not merely reflect the chronological priority of Jesus to the apostolic church; it also provides the bridge between the Old and New Testaments (especially Matthew with its focus on continuity, appearing first in almost all manuscripts) while arguably supporting the priority of the Gospels as the key hermeneutical lens of the canon.

The canonical location of Revelation at the end of the New Testament, and therefore of the whole Christian Bible, is also fairly consistent in the manuscript tradition (leaving aside Greek manuscripts in which it is bound with extracanonical texts or appears as part of the Apocalypse commentary of Andreas of Caesarea). This is explicable in terms of its subject matter, ending as it does with visions of final judgment and ultimate salvation (especially Rev. 17–22), and thereby completing the overarching New Testament story (incarnation; death and resurrection; gift of the Spirit and emergence of the church). Whether this canonical arrangement overemphasizes the extent of future eschatology in Revelation at the expense of its visionary presentation of what Christ has already achieved, or its prophetic concern for the welfare of the churches, is a moot point.

Still, Revelation's current location as the climax to the canon certainly shapes expectations concerning the whole. It now functions, along with Genesis, as one of two "bookends" of the Christian Bible, which together function as textual Alpha and Omega revealing the divine Alpha and Omega (see Rev. 1:8; 21:6; 22:13). This gives prominence to the intertextual echoes of Genesis (e.g., Rev. 1:7; 2:7; 9:14; 10:6; 11:11; 12:9, 17; 14:10; 18:5; 22:1–2), sometimes obscured by focus on Revelation's reworking of Israel's prophetic tradition (especially Ezekiel, Daniel, and Zechariah). This hermeneutical significance is already acknowledged in the patristic and medieval periods. According to the *Monarchian Prologue to John*, a text that widely circulated throughout the Middle Ages, Revelation's supposed authorship by John the "virgin" is used to explain its fitting location at the climax to the biblical canon. Just as Genesis provides an *incorruptibile principium* ("incorruptible beginning") to Scripture, so the virgin apostle's Apocalypse supplies the Bible with its *incorruptibilis finis* ("incorruptible end"). Genesis begins humanity's story in a garden; Revelation brings it to completion in a garden-city. Christians may debate the precise contours of the story in between, while concurring that the Apocalypse presents its resolution in a fashion that returns to, if also moving beyond, its beginning.

Conclusion

Those in search of a neat process for the emergence of a New Testament canon are likely to be disappointed. On the one hand, the history of the canon's formation, fragmentary though the evidence is, seems to point to an early, if not unanimous, consensus across diverse geographical areas that certain core texts (notably the four Gospels and collections of Pauline letters, probably the book of Revelation) are normative for Christians. On the other hand, the emergence of the canon as we know it, as a closed list of twenty-seven writings, appears to be the result of a much longer process in which various criteria, some essentially passive, others more active (particularly when it came to questions of exclusion), were at play.

That being said, the Catholic conviction is that the writings listed by Athanasius and explicitly defined by Trent, even those which at times have been disputed (such as 2 Peter or Jude), can be trusted as authoritative witnesses to the apostolic faith, with the four Gospels having a preeminent place given their focus on Christ's life, teaching, death, and resurrection. The New Testament canon reflects the early church's Spirit-led discernment of this authority, reflected in widespread use and conviction that these texts had universal and not merely local relevance (catholicity). The formal definition of Trent, though simply reiterating the consensus of the fourth century in terms of the number of New Testament books, particularly emphasized the criterion of use in its assertion of the authority of the books "with all their parts." By the time of Trent, their normative status had been underscored by centuries of usage within the churches.

For Catholic Christians, this canonical unity does not result in the muting of canonical diversity. In practice, certain canonical texts have been more important at particular times

than others. But as part of a canonical whole, they cannot ultimately be isolated from a wider canonical conversation. It may
be appropriate to recall Irenaeus' discussion of the tetramorphic
Gospel, in which he famously likens the Gospels to the four
living creatures in the visions of Ezekiel and Revelation. These
creatures are both frightening and ultimately untamable, as a
parallel vision in the *Apocalypse of Abraham* makes clear (*Apoc.
Abr.* 18). The canon sets parameters, while also providing a
dialectic of mutual correction and balance. Having an established and closed canon of normative texts is just the beginning
of the process, not its end.

AN ORTHODOX PERSPECTIVE ON THE NEW TESTAMENT CANON

George L. Parsenios

The Orthodox Church adheres to the same twenty-seven-book New Testament shared by Roman Catholics and Protestants. But to tell the story of how the Orthodox Church selected its Bible is to tell a story with an unexpected ending. In one way of looking at things, the story has no ending. No single decision or historical event serves as the defining moment when this official canonical list of Scripture was established. Although there is absolute uniformity across the Orthodox world on the limits of the New Testament, this uniformity is not the product of an ecumenical decision in a church council. The twenty-seven-book New Testament has been codified, rather, by the practice of the church. This is not to suggest that the question remains open, or that the Orthodox Church is unclear about the limits of the New Testament. The practice of the church, guided by the Holy Spirit, is definitive on this point. In order to explain how this can be the case, the following chapter will unfold in three parts. The first part will explore the historical factors that led to the establishment and recognition of the canonical Scripture in the Orthodox Church. The second part will explain how the writings of the New Testament relate to other early Christian writings. Finally, the third part will discuss the hermeneutical approaches and presuppositions that underly the Orthodox understanding of the canonical New Testament.

Factors Precipitating the Establishment and Recognition of a Canonical Scripture

We may begin with the historical factors that determined the delineation of the canonical Scriptures. The most thorough treatment of the place of the Bible in the Orthodox Church is the work of Theodore Stylianopoulos, who discusses the development of the New Testament at some length.[1] Following Harry Gamble, Stylianopoulos sees four factors that served as criteria in the recognition of biblical writings: apostolicity, catholicity, orthodoxy, and traditional use.[2] The first two are significant, but require little comment, while the third and fourth criteria will need to be addressed in greater detail. The issue of orthodoxy is especially significant, because it raises a series of related concerns. As Stylianopoulos sees it, the criterion of "orthodoxy" refers only to the doctrine expressed in a given book. That is to say, a disputed book might satisfy other criteria, such as having an apostolic lineage (apostolicity), or it may have been known generally to the whole church (catholicity). If it contains false teaching, however, it must be rejected.[3] But the issue of orthodoxy, as it relates to the canonical Scripture, can be extended considerably, as is done by John Behr in his book *The Way to Nicaea*. The first line of this book repeats the question asked by Jesus to his disciples in the region of

---

1.   Theodore Stylianopoulos, *The New Testament: An Orthodox Perspective* (Brookline, MA: Holy Cross Orthodox Press, 1997), 9–10, 27–28, 48–50, 56–59. See also Stylianopoulos, *The Making of the New Testament: Church, Gospel, and Canon* (Brookline, MA: Holy Cross Orthodox Press, 2014).
2.   Harry Y. Gamble, "Canon: The New Testament," *ABD* (1992) 1:837–61 (857–59).
3.   Stylianopoulos, *The New Testament*, 59.

Caesarea Philippi, "Who do you say that I am?" (Matt. 16:15).
Behr then adds, "This question, posed by Jesus Christ, is the
one that Christian theology seeks to answer."[4] Behr begins his
survey of the theology of the early church by tracing the development of a canonical Scripture, focusing on subjects such as
the early stages of this process in the second century and the
writings of prominent theologians of the church such as Clement, Tertullian, and Irenaeus, who battled Marcion, Valentinus,
and others.[5]

In the early chapters of his volume, Behr focuses upon
Irenaeus' consideration of the books that are to be read as
Scripture and what hermeneutical presuppositions should
govern their reading.[6] For Irenaeus, both sides of this equa-
tion are necessary for the preservation of the apostolic teaching
about Jesus. One must recognize the correct books and read
them with the proper theological convictions. Irenaeus does
not, however, invent these concerns in a vacuum. He develops
them, rather, in combat with his opponents, who were likewise engaged in the exercise of determining which books have
authority and how they should be read. Marcion, for example,
famously refuses to accept as authoritative any Christian writings except an edited version of the Gospel of Luke and some of
the letters of Paul, because he is unable to find any compatibility
between the god of the Old Testament and the god of the New.
Because of his conviction that law and gospel are incompatible,
he refused to read the Old Testament allegorically or to recognize the ways in which the New Testament complements and
fulfills the Old. His treatment of the Scriptures, then, was both
theological and exegetical in nature.[7] As John Barton writes,

---

4.   John Behr, *The Way to Nicaea*, Formation of Christian Theology 1 (Crestwood,
NY: St. Vladimir's Seminary Press, 2001), 1.

5.   Behr, *The Way to Nicaea*, 17–48.

6.   Behr, *The Way to Nicaea*, 30–48.

7.   Behr, *The Way to Nicaea*, 18. For further discussion, see John Barton, *Holy
Writings, Sacred Text: The Canon in Early Christianity* (Louisville: Westminster John
Knox, 1997), 53–62. The precise role that Marcion played in the production of a
collection of canonical writings is not entirely clear. Did he reduce a canonical list

> The harmony an allegorical reading produced (or assured) between the Old Testament and Christian faith proved unacceptable to Marcion because he was already convinced that the God of the Jews, the creator-god, was irreconcilable with the God in whom Christians believed. . . . Marcion's prior conviction that the Old Testament was not "Scripture" for a Christian led him to read it in the ways that non-scriptural texts were read, that is, non-allegorically.[8]

Marcion, again, produced a list of acceptable scriptural texts, as well as a method of reading that cohered with his theological presuppositions. Hermeneutical methods, theological convictions, and one's perspective regarding the extent of the canon are clearly interrelated subjects regardless of one's perspective on these subjects.

The same occurs with gnostic writers. Unlike Marcion, who rejected the majority of Christian literature, however, the theological presuppositions of the gnostics did not lead them to recognize only a small body of writings. To the contrary, they produced several additional writings which describe and explain the gnostic myth of salvation. According to the classic version of the gnostic story of salvation, as expressed in works such as the *Secret Book according to John*, the material world was created by mistake, and the God who created it was not the ultimate God, but a confused and misshapen being. The story of salvation, then, is a story of return to the harmony and repose that

---

that was longer or did he inspire the creation of a larger list by publishing his own limited collection? Following Adolf Harnack, many have concluded that Marcion was the first to assemble a canonical list of biblical books, and that Irenaeus was merely responding to him. It is just as possible, however, that Marcion did not develop a new list, but that he simply cut apart the one already in use. Barton quotes Harnack as saying that "the catholic New Testament beat the Marcionite Bible; but this New Testament is an anti-Marcionite creation on a Marcionite basis." See John Barton, "Marcion Revisited," in *The Canon Debate*, eds. Lee Martin McDonald and James A. Sanders (Peabody, MA; Hendrickson, 2002), 341–54 (342). For further discussion, see Charles E. Hill, *Who Chose the Gospels?* (Oxford: Oxford University Press, 2012).

8.   Barton, *Holy Writings*, 54.

comes with true knowledge about the true purpose of existence from a counterfeit existence on earth that is under the sway of a counterfeit deity.[9] Not content to promote their teaching from these books alone, the gnostic authors found ways to use orthodox books like the canonical Gospels and the letters of Paul to expand and explore their teaching.

Finally, the second-century gnostic Valentinus raises the same hermeneutical problems as Marcion and other gnostics, but in noticeably different ways and with very different results. He relies on neither a fixed list of Scriptures nor a fixed set of theological presuppositions. Indeed, he excerpts passages from the New Testament in the way that the New Testament excerpts passages from the Old Testament in order to produce what might be described as a new myth of salvation. For Valentinus, the truths revealed in the New Testament are not exclusive and simply point us to things that can be learned from a variety of sources. According to his perspective, all writings, canonical or otherwise, are best understood as secondary expressions of the truth that emanates from the inner life of the true believer. Valentinus says precisely this when he refers to the works of pagan antiquity as "publicly available books" and the Christian New Testament as "the writings of God's church." As he explains, "Many of the things written in publicly available books are found in the writings of God's church. For this shared matter is the utterances that come from the heart, the law that is written on the heart."[10]

---

9. Although we often use the label "gnosticism" as an umbrella term for broad religious tendencies in the ancient world, the teachings and texts that are included in this category show a great deal of diversity. For recent discussion on the complexity of the category and the variety of belief and behavior associated with it, see David Brakke, *The Gnostics: Myth, Ritual and Diversity in Early Christianity* (Cambridge, MA: Harvard University Press, 2012). For variations on the story of salvation especially, see pages 52–70.

10. From Clement of Alexandria, *Stromata* 6.52.3–4; trans. as Fragment G, in Bentley Layton, *The Gnostic Scriptures: Ancient Wisdom for the New Age* (New York: Doubleday, 1987), 243.

Valentinus does not need a canonical set of writings, therefore, since the truth that he teaches is a personal truth. As
Behr writes, "Having such direct access to wisdom, Valentinus no longer recognized any distinction between Scripture
and commentary, between source and interpretation. Rather,
he reconfigured the language and images of Scripture in the
light of his experience, and the results are themselves new
compositions."[11] In very different ways, therefore, Marcion,
Valentinus, and the other gnostics created a problem that
Irenaeus addressed by appealing to apostolic tradition, both in
written and oral form. Where Marcion restricts Scripture very
narrowly and Valentinus expands it infinitely, Irenaeus offers a
defense in his *Against Heresies* (*Adv. haer.*) of the apostolic tradition that had been passed down in its various forms.

Irenaeus first insists that heterodox teaching does not
cohere with that which has been passed down openly in all the
churches by the apostles. These heresies do not agree, in the
language of 1 John 1:1, with what was passed down "from the
beginning." Irenaeus insists, indeed, that he himself was able
to sit as a young man at the feet of Polycarp, who had learned
from the very apostles (*Adv. haer.* 3.3.4). None of these figures
taught what the heretics teach. He adds that, even if there had
been no sacred writings, the tradition that the apostles passed
down in the churches is enough to know the truth about
God's work in Christ. As he writes, "For how should it be
if the Apostles themselves had not left us writings? Would it
not be necessary in that case to follow the course of the tradition which they handed down to those to whom they did
commit the Churches?" (*Adv. haer.* 3.4.1).[12] But there is, in
fact, a written record of the apostles' teaching that is contained
in the four Gospels. As Irenaeus explains: "We have learned
from no others the plan of our salvation from those through
whom the Gospel has come down to us, which they did at one

---

11.   Behr, *The Way to Nicaea*, 21.
12.   Translation from Behr, *The Way to Nicaea*, 43.

time proclaim in public, and at a later period, by the will of God, handed down to us in the Scriptures, to be the ground and pillar of our faith" (*Adv. haer.* 3.1.1).[13] These writings are defended, most importantly, because they accord with what was passed down "from the beginning." The message that was passed down orally by the apostles in their churches coheres with the message passed down in writing in the four Gospels. The problem arises, however, when even the heretics recognize these particular books but read them in a fashion that supports their aberrant doctrine.

This leads to an important question: If influential Christian writings are interpreted differently, how can one know if a given reading of Scripture is correct? In order to distinguish true from false teaching, and a true reading from false readings of Scripture, Irenaeus calls his readers to adhere to what had been publicly taught by the apostles and their disciples. The tradition that originated with the apostles becomes for Irenaeus and others the "criterion of truth," something that is itself beyond dispute but allows one to determine or verify the veracity of a teaching.[14] Hellenistic philosophical schools had long debated the criteria of truth, and the Christian discussion is an extension of their work. A "criterion" in philosophy was a final arbiter in determining truth, some factor that did not need to be defended or supported by itself but that could support what is true or convict what is false in other matters (see Lucretius, *On the Nature of Things* 4.469–521).

These criteria are not in and of themselves open to debate, as they were understood to be self-evident. Epicurus, the primary innovator in this pursuit, made use of a key epistemological term, *kanōn* (κανών). A *kanōn* was a tool for making a straight line or for measuring, much like our modern ruler, and its close synonym in the thought of Epicurus is the term

---

13. Translation from Behr, *The Way to Nicaea*, 39.
14. This discussion depends heavily on Behr, *The Way to Nicaea*, 30–48. It is important to add that for Clement of Alexandria the chief first principle of all Christian life, beyond dispute, is faith (*Stromata* 7.16.95.4–6). See Behr, *The Way to Nicaea*, 33.

"criterion" (cf. *Letter to Herodotus* in Diogenes Laertius 10.37–38). The three criteria posited by Epicurus include sensation (*aisthēsis*), preconception (*prolēpsis*), and feeling (*pathos*). If our sensations lead us to make an improper judgment, then the fault does not lie with the sensations, which are accurate, but with the judgment that was founded on them. The Stoics developed this program with a slightly different orientation, locating the criterion of truth not in sense impressions themselves but in the cognitive impressions made by the senses. Both the Epicureans and the Stoics sought to develop criteria of truth in their struggle with the Skeptics, that is, members of a philosophical school of thought who suspended all judgment about truth (see Plutarch, *Col.* 1122A–F). Their purpose was to destroy any foundation that other philosophers established in order to force their opponents into an ever-expanding infinite regression of argument. As a result, they rejected completely the existence of a criterion of truth. In the theological debates of the second century, the concern among Hellenistic philosophers for finding a "criterion of truth" became a central concern of early Christian theologians. Irenaeus argues that his opponents would develop a new line of argument in every debate (*Adv. haer.* 1.18.1; 1.21.5), leading to the same infinite regress that the Stoics and Epicureans tried to avoid in their encounters with the Skeptics. For this reason, Irenaeus looked to the "rule of faith" as the "criterion of truth." With regard to false readings of Scripture, Irenaeus declares,

> Anyone who keeps unswervingly in himself the canon of truth (τὸν κανόνα τῆς ἀληθείας) received through baptism will recognize the names and sayings and parables from the Scriptures, but this blasphemous hypothesis of theirs he will not recognize. For if he recognizes the jewels, he will not accept the fox for the image of the king. He will restore each one of the passages to its proper order and, having fit into the body of the truth, he will lay bare their fabrication and show that it is without support. (*Adv. haer.* 1.9)[15]

---

15.   Translation from Behr, *The Way to Nicaea*, 34–5.

Irenaeus describes the canon of truth as "the faith in one God the Father Almighty, Creator of heaven and earth . . . and in one Lord Jesus Christ, the Son of God, who was enfleshed for our salvation; and in the Holy Spirit" (*Adv. haer.* 1.10.1).[16] He then goes on to speak about the virgin birth, the passion of Christ, his resurrection, and his second coming. The one who holds this canon of truth, he suggests, will be able to ascertain which books are to be recognized as Scripture and which should not, and will be equipped to rightly discern the true message of the Scriptures. It should be noted, however, that the apprehension of the truth is not merely an intellectual exercise involving dialectic and proof. The true first principle of Christian theology is faith, as Clement of Alexandria says. This faith is indemonstrable, and, as a gift from God, empowered by the Holy Spirit.[17] From the perspective of Orthodox writers, Marcion and gnostic writers such as Valentinus read the Scriptures with no regard for the rule of faith, an omission that inevitably led to erroneous readings of the apostolic books as well as the recognition of additional books of their own creation.

This anti-heretical impetus is not confined to the second century. Gamble, for instance, understands that it was also important during the fourth century. As he observes, "While impulses toward the limitation of the scope of scripture were never absent, they did not take full effect until the fourth century, when definitive canon lists became the order of the day."[18] This is the century in which we see for the first time the

---

16. Translation from Behr, *The Way to Nicaea*, 35.
17. With regard to Clement's emphasis on the criterion of truth, Eric Osborne writes, "Faith is a grace which goes beyond the indemonstrable principle to what is entirely simple, and in no way material. The point of Clement's argument is that it shows how faith and God are correlative. For Paul, faith depends on the God who justifies the ungodly (Rom. 4:5), raises the dead and creates out of nothing (Rom. 4:17). Such a God is the ultimate first principle and not accessible except by faith." See Eric Osborne, "Arguments for Faith in Clement of Alexandria," *VC* 48 (1994): 1–24 (14).
18. Harry Y. Gamble, "The New Testament Canon: Recent Research and the Status Quaestionis," in *The Canon Debate*, eds. Lee Martin McDonald and James A. Sanders (Peabody, MA: Hendrickson, 2002), 267–94 (294).

lists that are now normative in the Orthodox Church, written down in several places. This includes the famous thirty-ninth *Festal Letter* (*Ep. fest.* 39) of Athanasius of Alexandria in 367 CE as well as the Synod of Hippo Regius in 393 CE and the third Synod of Carthage in 397 CE.[19] Gamble cites several factors that may have led to the formation of the official lists that were produced during this century, but theological concerns are prominent.[20] The struggles against Arianism, in which Athanasius played a definitive role, would have been significant, since the Arian debates were often fought over exegetical questions, and a debate over the proper meaning of Scripture would necessitate a clear delineation on which books were to be regarded as authoritative Scripture.[21] Likewise, Cyril of Jerusalem writes in his *Catechetical Lectures* (4.36), "Then of the New Testament there are four Gospels only, for the rest have false titles and are harmful. The Manichaeans also wrote a Gospel according to Thomas, which being smeared with the fragrance of the name Gospel destroys the souls of those who are rather simple-minded."[22] Thus, from the Orthodox perspective, one of the critical factors in the development of a recognized

---

19. The specific decisions promulgated by the Synod of Hippo have not survived, though it is thought that Canon 24 of the Synod of Carthage affirmed the same list of writings that were recognized at Hippo.

20. Chief among them is the orderliness that Constantine sought to bring to ecclesiastical life, in keeping with his broader efforts to standardize practices throughout the entire Empire. Technological advances in book production also played a role, in concert with imperial interest in the church. Eusebius tells us that Constantine commissioned the production of fifty Bibles, which demonstrates that book production had reached a sufficient level of efficiency to be able to create multiple copies of books for distribution. If the Scripture is to be published in large numbers, a decision about what counts as Scripture is important, and so Gamble even sees publishing technology as playing a role. Gamble's final, and greatest, insight is that several factors play into the development of these authoritative lists, and all must be accounted for: theological, ecclesiastical, political, social, and exegetical. But he does see imperial influence as especially important in the fourth century. See Gamble, "Recent Research," 221.

21. See T. E. Pollard, *Johannine Christology and the Early Church* (Cambridge: Cambridge University Press, 1972), 184–245, for the place of Scripture, especially the Gospel of John, in the Arian controversy.

22. Translation from Bruce Metzger, *The Canon of the New Testament: Its Origin, Development and Significance* (Oxford: Clarendon, 1987), 311; cf. discussion, 209–10.

collection of canonical Scripture can be summarized with the term "orthodoxy," as long as the term refers to the effort to preserve the apostolic faith in its fullness. In sum, certain books were set aside as Scripture because they preserve the apostolic deposit of faith. Similarly, one can only discern which books should be recognized, and how to read them properly, if one shares this apostolic faith.

Having discussed the criterion of orthodoxy at some length, we can deal more briefly with the next criterion elevated by Stylianopoulos, "traditional use." This criterion is far more significant, it appears, than each of the other categories. Barton may make the point too strongly but nevertheless offers a helpful explanation of the influence of this criterion when he states,

> In the case of the New Testament, Marcion was already too late in trying to reduce the Gospels from four to one. Though Irenaeus might produce reasons to justify a four-Gospel "canon," their very speciousness points to the truth that by then people simply "knew" that Matthew, Mark, Luke and John were holy books, and it was much too late to do anything about that. . . . No other reason for accepting books as canonical or scriptural even approaches in importance the argument that they have always been so accepted.[23]

While this historical claim has been embraced by scholars such as Gamble and Charles Hill, others have suggested that Marcion played a more instrumental role in the development of the canonical process. It is not necessary for us to decide the matter here as a historical problem, because Orthodox writers have always affirmed what Barton says.[24] Irenaeus himself says that he is not inventing anything but simply transmitting what had already been passed down to him (*Adv. haer.* 3.1.1–2; 3.2.2). Similarly, Orthodox theologians would say that the

---

23. Barton, *Holy Writing*, 59.
24. See Gamble, "Canon," 858–59; Stylianopoulos, *The New Testament*, 59–60.

church has simply received and transmitted the teaching of the apostles in a chain extending to Paul, who says, "For I delivered to you as of first importance what I also received: that Christ died for our sins in accordance with the Scriptures, that he was buried, that he was raised on the third day in accordance with the Scriptures, and that he appeared to Cephas, then to the twelve" (1 Cor. 15:3–5).

The books that would eventually be accepted as authoritative Scripture were not delineated until the fourth century, but even at this time there was not a universal consensus, as may be demonstrated by alternative lists. In his *Catechetical Lectures* (4.6) in 350 CE, for example, Cyril summarizes the Christian faith for catechumens preparing to enter the church and in the process instructs them on which books to read and which to avoid. Noticeably absent is the book of Revelation. The same is true of a poetical list of the New Testament drawn up by Gregory of Nazianzus, which excludes the book of Revelation (*Carmen* 1.1.12). Figures from the church of Antioch seem to have an even more abbreviated canonical list. John Chrysostom, for example, does not appear to cite from 2 Peter, 2–3 John, Jude, or Revelation, omissions which conform to the state of the Peshitta text in use in Antioch at this time.[25] In 363 CE, a local synod met in Laodicea and cited a list of scriptures which also appears to have excluded Revelation. It should be noted, however, that the authenticity of Canon 60, the record which refers to Revelation, is disputed.[26]

This situation continues much later than the fourth century. Bruce Metzger and B. F. Westcott both express consternation at what Westcott refers to as "the picture of confusion which was allowed to remain" in the Byzantine world well after the fourth century.[27] As evidence for this

---

25. Metzger, *The Canon of the New Testament*, 214–15.
26. For discussion, see Metzger, *The Canon of the New Testament*, 312.
27. Brooke Foss Westcott, *The Bible in the Church: A Popular Account of the Collection and Reception of the Holy Scriptures in the Christian Churches* (New York: Macmillan, 1905), 227; Metzger, *The Canon of the New Testament*, 216.

state of confusion, we may briefly note some of the developments that took place into the sixth and seventh centuries. Of particular interest is the Council in Trullo, which convened in 692 CE in response to the concern of the Emperor Justinian that the work of the fifth and sixth ecumenical councils, held in 553 CE and 681 CE respectively, was incomplete.[28] The previous councils addressed doctrinal matters, but they delivered no disciplinary canons regarding church order. Metzger's concern is with Canons 1 and 2 of this council because in his eyes it created an anomalous and unworkable situation. Canons 1 and 2 listed all of the previous authorities and synods that it viewed as authoritative, including the local synods of Laodicea and Carthage, as well as the *Apostolic Constitutions*. It also listed several individual hierarchs who were regarded as authoritative. The problem is that these various authoritative synods and individuals published lists of Scripture do not agree with one another. Seeing this confusion, Metzger writes, "The Council thereby sanctioned implicitly, so far as the list of biblical books is concerned, quite incongruous and contradictory opinions."[29]

Even after the Council in Trullo, the matter is not completely settled. As late as the tenth century, Westcott cites as many as six different lists of canonical Scriptures circulating in Byzantium.[30] Indeed, no ecumenical council ever delineates a final canonical list of Scripture. Why is this so? To understand this question, we must be aware of the character of Orthodox

---

28. Because the council in 692 CE continued the work of these previous councils, it is sometimes called the *Quinisext*, based on the words for "fifth" and "sixth" in Latin, or the *Penthekti*, which is based on the same numbers in Greek. It is also called the council "in Trullo," after the hall in which it met in the imperial palace.

29. Metzger, *The Canon of the New Testament*, 216. See also the landmark volume Richard Price, *Canons of the Quinisext Council (691/2)*, Translated Texts for Historians (Liverpool: Liverpool University Press, 2020). Price covers several aspects of the Council in Trullo and includes detailed notes on each canon. For an accessible discussion of the Council in Trullo, see also Leo Donald Davis, *The First Seven Ecumenical Councils (325–787): Their History and Theology* (Collegeville, MN: Liturgical, 1983), 285–88.

30. Westcott, *Bible in the Church*, 227.

canon law. As Lewis Patsavos explains, "Unlike the canon law of the Roman Catholic Church, the canon law of the Orthodox Church has not been codified. Neither is it prescriptive in character, anticipating a situation before it actually takes place; instead, it is corrective in nature, responding to a situation once it has occurred."[31] Orthodox canon law is not prescriptive. Rather, it responds to problems. The Orthodox Church, for example, had venerated icons for centuries before the seventh Ecumenical Council was convened for the purpose of defending the practice in 787 CE. Because of its prior use, there was no need to explain the role of icons until they began to endanger the Church's Christology.[32] The Orthodox Church had, likewise, called Mary *Theotokos* long before the title was enshrined in the Council of Ephesus in 431 CE.[33] The use of this title required canonization by an ecumenical council because it raised critical issues regarding the two natures of Christ. Each of these situations led to debates that involved the entire Orthodox world and that ran to the heart of what it meant to believe in Christ. Whatever variation existed in the New Testament regarding the canonical status of books such as Revelation never rose to this level of urgency. Variation was thus permitted and may be observed over an extended period of church history.

We may conclude that the evolution of the canonical Scripture did not end completely until 1672 CE when the Council of Jerusalem presented the Orthodox Bible, both Old and New Testaments, as it is now construed. The New Testament

---

31. Lewis J. Patsavos, *Spiritual Dimensions of the Holy Canons* (Brookline, MA: Holy Cross Orthodox Press, 2007), 6.

32. For the Christological concerns in the iconoclastic controversy, with particular attention to the writings of John of Damascus, see Andrew Louth, *St. John Damascene: Tradition and Originality in Byzantine Theology* (Oxford: Oxford University Press, 2004), 193–219.

33. The title *Theotokos*, according to the Byzantine historian Socrates (*Hist. eccl.* 7.32.14), goes back at least to Origen. The term was certainly so common in Constantinople prior to the Council of Ephesus in 431 CE that when Nestorius opposed the term, he seemed like an innovator who offended the piety of the majority of the city's population. For discussion, see Nicholas P. Constas, *Proclus of Constantinople and the Cult of the Virgin in Late Antiquity* (Leiden: Brill, 2003), 53.

writings listed in *Question* 3 in the *Acta* of the council of 1672 are the same twenty-seven books referred to in Athanasius' *Festal Letter* 39, while the Old Testament includes the so-called Deutero-canonical books of the Old Testament as Scripture. The Old Testament is outside our purview, but this is a document in the modern period that confirms the list of Scriptures as we have them now in the Orthodox Church.[34] The Synod of Jerusalem, however, may give some indication of one factor that led the transition from a more fluid to a more established state of the canon. This synod, like the earlier Synod of Jassy in 1642 CE, was convened to counter the teachings of Cyril Loukaris, a Patriarch of Constantinople influenced by Calvinism.[35] Loukaris had rejected the so-called deutero-canonical books of the Old Testament under the influence of his Calvinist leanings. The Council of Trent, after all, had in 1545–1563 CE defined the limits of Scripture for the Roman Catholic Church in response to the Protestant Reformation. It is possible, therefore, that a late factor leading to a more definitive recognition of the extent of the canonical Scripture was the need to define the Orthodox Scripture in relation to Protestants and Catholics. Even the Synod of Jerusalem in 1672 CE, however, was merely a local synod that was not binding on the ecumenical church. Nevertheless, it is indicative of the practice of the church at this time.

Furthermore, it is highly unlikely that the conveners of the Synod of Jerusalem were engaged in anything more than simply recognizing what the church had long affirmed. The latter years of the Byzantine Empire were a period of homogenization on a variety of ecclesiastical levels, such as the liturgy. As the Empire continued to decline in the face of various invasions, the great diversity that had characterized all forms of ecclesiastical life

---

34. For the text of *Question 3* in the Confession of Dositheus, which was ratified at the synod, see J. Leith, *Creeds of the Churches: A Reader in Christian Doctrine from the Bible to the Present* (Philadelphia: Westminster Press, 1982), 507–8.

35. For the career of Loukaris, see Paschalis Kitromilides, "Orthodoxy and the West: Reformation to Enlightenment," in *The Cambridge History of Christianity: Eastern Christianity*, ed. Michael Angold (Cambridge: Cambridge University Press, 2006), 187–209, esp. 193–202.

began to form into a single, consistent system. This process has been called "Byzantinization," though what it really means is simply that the practices of Constantinople became consistently used throughout the Greek East. We see this process, for example, in the way that the church of Jerusalem slowly lost its distinctive liturgical practices in favor of those associated with Constantinople, a lengthy process that culminated in the thirteenth century.[36]

Thus, the practice of the church over time is determinative, and it is necessary at this point to stress that, from the Orthodox perspective, the traditional practice of the church is not a subjective phenomenon, or something that could casually change to something else. The practice of the church is an essential factor in determining and defining the church's faith in many essentials. When Basil the Great sought to defend the divinity of the Holy Spirit in the fourth century, for example, he relied on many forms of evidence, several of which are drawn from the "unwritten" teachings of the church, including the baptismal formula by which Christians are baptized, a formula which places equal emphasis on the Father, Son, and Holy Spirit. When discussing the relationship between Scripture and the church's practice, Basil writes,

> Have any saints left for us in writing the words to be used in the invocation over the Eucharistic bread and the cup of blessing? As everyone knows, we are not content in the Liturgy simply to recite the words recorded by St. Paul or the Gospels, but we add other words both before and after, words of great importance for this mystery. We have received these words from unwritten teaching. We bless baptismal water and the oil of chrismation as well as the candidate approaching the font. By what written authority do we do this, if not from secret and mystical

---

36. Daniel Galadza, *Liturgy and Byzantinization in Jerusalem* (Oxford: Oxford University Press, 2018). For a more accessible treatment, see Robert Taft, *The Byzantine Rite: A Short History* (Collegeville, MN: Liturgical, 1992), 78–84.

teaching? Even beyond blessing the oil, what written command do we have to anoint with it? What about baptizing with three immersions, or other baptismal rites . . . ? Are not all these things found in unpublished and unwritten teachings, which our fathers guarded in silence? (*On the Holy Spirit* 27)[37]

The practice of the church that has passed down over the centuries is not merely a series of functional procedures that could have developed otherwise or that could have been easily discarded or changed. These practices are expressions of the church's faith and are guided by the Holy Spirit and the sources of theological reflection about the nature of Christian faith and belief. Even more importantly, they express the presence of the Holy Spirit as it guides the church. Vladimir Lossky defines these unwritten practices of the church as follows: "The pure notion of Tradition can then be defined by saying that it is the life of the Holy Spirit in the Church, communicating to each member of the Body of Christ the faculty of hearing, of receiving, of knowing the Truth in the Light which belongs to it, and not according to the natural life of human reason."[38] The practice of the church sometimes takes time to become solidified. It is not simply the case that every little thing the church has ever done is considered "tradition." In many instances, the practice of the church takes time to find its proper expression. Before the Council of Nicaea, for example, the term *homoousios* was the opposite of "traditional," and yet it was seen to express the tradition in the reflection of the church fathers. The same is true of the gradual development of the canonical Scripture.[39] Tradition, as Irenaeus said earlier, is the life of the Holy Spirit in the church, guiding it in the truth.

---

37. Translation from St. Basil the Great, *On the Holy Spirit*, trans. David Anderson (Crestwood, NY: St. Vladimir's Seminary Press, 1980), 99.
38. Vladimir Lossky, *In the Image and Likeness of God* (Crestwood, NY: St. Vladimir's Seminary Press, 1974), 141–68 (152).
39. Lossky, *Image and Likeness*, 159.

The Relationship Between the New Testament and Other Early Christian Writings

This emphasis on the role of tradition in the church—both in its unwritten and written form—requires us to address a theological question that is related to the historical subjects we have previously surveyed. If the written and unwritten tradition of the Orthodox Church has such a high standing, how does the honor given to tradition relate to the reverence given to Scripture? What defines the authority of Scripture, especially in relation to all the written and unwritten elements of holy tradition? Or, more to the point, how do the New Testament writings relate to other early Christian writings?

The most straightforward category of noncanonical writings we might discuss are those which are deemed heretical such as the *Gospel of Thomas*. Though valuable as historical artifacts, they do not point to the Christ of Scripture, nor are they consistent with tradition. As a consequence, they have no positive theological standing. Rather than directing the reader to a fuller understanding of Christ, they lead to incorrect answers regarding the question of Christ, "Who do you say that I am?" Other noncanonical texts from early Christianity, such as the *Didache* in the late first century, the various writings of the Apostolic Fathers composed during the second century, and other patristic literature from later periods, present a more complicated case. Collectively, these texts fall under the umbrella of holy tradition, but how do they relate to the New Testament writings?

The first and most important thing that must be said at the outset is that Scripture and tradition cannot be separated, as though tradition is something that is added but unnecessary, or as though Scripture stands entirely on its own without tradition. As we have just seen, for the Orthodox, the limits of the Scripture are established and solidified precisely by the church's tradition, that is, the church's practice. Scripture does not stand alone. We might ask, however, if Scripture and tradition are distinct. The definition of their relationship posited by Georges Florovsky may be overly simplistic, but it is a useful place to begin. As Florovsky writes, "The easiest answer to this question is the least satisfactory: one may suggest at once that the Scriptures are the only authentic record of the revelation, and everything else is no more than a commentary thereupon. And commentary can never have the same authority as the original record."[40] The temporary value of this formula lies in the fact that it labels Scripture as the record of revelation. The necessity to delimit the boundaries of the sacred Scripture is a theological necessity. The Scriptures, taken in total, are a historical record of what God has done to guide his creation, a work which culminated in the incarnation of the Son of God. Ultimately, the Scripture is closed because the revelation of God has reached its completeness in Jesus Christ. As Dumitru Staniloae writes, "Supernatural revelation came to its close in Christ. For in him . . . the plan to save and to deify creation has reached its fulfillment. This plan cannot lead any higher. God draws no closer to man than he has in Christ. The union between God and man cannot advance any farther nor can we grow to any higher fulfillment than the one available to us in Christ."[41] Simply put, the Bible is closed because the Word of God has become flesh. The Bible has God as its content, and it narrates the history of how God has revealed himself to his creation, revelation that came to its fulfillment in the revelation of Jesus Christ. Both the Old and New Testaments are a history of this revelation, and they have Christ as their center. He is promised in the Old Testament and finally revealed in the New. Thus, as the written record of this revelation, the Bible is distinct from all other written and unwritten tradition in the Church. As Florovsky

40.   Georges Florovsky, "Revelation and Interpretation," in *Biblical Authority for Today*, eds. Alan Richardson and W. Schweitzer (Philadelphia: Westminster, 1953), 163–80; repr. in Florovsky, *Bible, Church, Tradition* (Vaduz: Buechervertriebsanstalt, 1987), 29–30.

41.   Dumitru Staniloae, *The Experience of God: Revelation of the Triune God*, Orthodox Dogmatic Theology 1, trans. Ioan Ioanita and Robert Barringer (Brookline, MA: Holy Cross Orthodox Press, 1998), 37.

describes it, the tradition of the Church serves as commentary on that revelation.

But, as we saw with the formulas of Basil described above, the practices of the church defined as holy tradition—its sacraments, hymnography, ascetical life—are not *just* commentary on the Christ described in Scripture; they are the lived experience of Christ in the present. This is where Florovsky's previously cited definition needs to be set aside for what he states elsewhere:

> The Bible is complete. But the sacred history is not yet completed. . . . The Church stands by its testimony and witness. But this witness is not just a reference to the past, not merely a reminiscence, but rather a continuous rediscovery of the message once delivered to the saints and ever since kept by faith. Moreover, this message is ever re-enacted in the life of the Church. Christ himself is ever present in the Church, as the Redeemer and head of his Body.[42]

It is, of course, this very lived experience that brings people again and again to the Scriptures, to ensure that the church is seeking the right Christ, the true Christ. And each believer is drawn ever more into union with God through reading the Scriptures. With regard to this "living dialogue with Christ" that occurs in scriptural reading, Staniloae writes that "sacred Scripture is one of the forms in which revelation keeps on being effective as God's continuous appeal. . . . Through the word of Scripture, Christ continues to speak to us and to provoke us to make a response in our deeds, and thus to be actively at work in us too."[43] One final category of written text requires attention. There are also texts, such as the *Protevangelium of James*, which some may assume to be among the gospels rejected by the church such as the *Gospel of Thomas*. The *Protevangelium* is

---

42. Florovsky, "Revelation and Interpretation," 26, 35.
43. Staniloae, *The Experience of God*, 40.

certainly not included in the New Testament, nor is it read in the church. But it is also not rejected completely. Indeed, its contents lie behind iconographic traditions, such as the scenes in the Church of the Chora in Constantinople, where Mary experiences the Annunciation while visiting a well, as she does in the *Protevangelium*. As Lossky observes regarding this phenomenon,

> Thus one uses apocryphal sources, with judgment and moderation, to the extent to which they may represent corrupted apostolic traditions. Recreated by the Tradition, these elements, purified and made legitimate, return to the Church as its own property. This judgment will be necessary each time that the Church has to deal with writings claiming to belong to the apostolic tradition. She will reject them, or she will receive them, without necessarily posing the question of their authenticity on the historical plane, but considering above all their content in the light of Tradition.[44]

Hermeneutical Issues Pertaining to the New Testament Canon

Hermeneutical questions have already been raised in a few different ways throughout this chapter, especially in the discussion of Irenaeus and the "canon of faith." Several additional issues may now be raised. I will focus on two issues in particular. With respect to the canon of Scripture, I would suggest that (1) there is an essential unity in the message of all the Scriptures, just as God is one, and (2) the Scriptures are an expression of God's condescension to human understanding. These concerns will be shown to be intimately connected to the questions raised earlier in this chapter regarding the limits of the canonical Scripture. As we have previously observed, Behr introduced his work with the pivotal question of Jesus, "Who do you say that I am?" (Matt. 16:15). The rule of faith and the

---

44. Lossky, *Image and Likeness*, 158.

Scriptures to which it accords were composed and preserved in order that God's people might answer the question correctly and encounter the true face of Christ.

The affirmation that Scripture has a single message or purpose that spans both the Old and New Testaments might seem simplistic and restrictive, but the opposite is in fact true.[45] To make the point, Maximus the Confessor compared the Scriptures to water. In the same way that water behaves and interacts differently with different species of plants and animals, so too is the Bible amenable to a variety of interpretations which are conditioned upon the state of the soul in which it flows. As Maximus emphatically stated, "the divine word could never be circumscribed by a single interpretation, nor does it suffer confinement in single meaning."[46]

Maximus, of course, does not intend what he says here in a postmodern sense.[47] The openness of the Scripture to unlimited significance does not imply that Scripture has no essential meaning or that its meaning can forever be deferred. Maximus always stresses, by contrast, that readings of Scripture should not be "unworthy of the Spirit."[48] As Maximos Constas explains, "Biblical interpretation unfolds within a framework of ethical, doctrinal and ecclesial commitments, which are constraints on any potential infinity of interpretations. One must therefore understand this as a potential infinity of *viable* interpretations."[49] We have already discussed the doctrinal and ecclesial commitments that Constas mentions. In addition to these important commitments, it should also be recognized that the ethical commitments of the reader are also of hermeneutical significance. While it is not possible

---

45. Maximos Constas, trans. and introduction, *Maximus the Confessor: On Difficulties in Sacred Scripture, The Responses to Thalassius* (Washington, DC: Catholic University of America Press, 2018), 38.

46. *Responses*, Introduction, 1.2.8. As Constas notes, Maximus himself will regularly develop up to ten interpretations of a given passage, 39.

47. Constas, *Responses*, 39.

48. *Question* 55.1 (cf. 54.130). Translation from Constas, *Responses*, 355.

49. Constas, *Responses*, 39.

here to describe the various stages of spiritual development in different Orthodox authors, we may observe that the ability to recognize the unity of the Scripture's message plays an important role in the larger process of ascetical ascent toward God. To the extent that a person has cleared one's mind and soul of earthly cares, one will see more clearly and deeply into the Scriptures. As Constas observes,

> The disordered movements of the passions, to the extent that they impel the mind to attach itself to the material surface of the world, create the conditions for a profound hermeneutical crisis. . . . The passions are interested in pleasure, not truth, and a mind dominated by the passions perceives neither the metaphysical ground of creation nor the spiritual meaning of Scripture . . . a failure that inevitably leads to the abuse of both nature and Scripture.[50]

This insight leads to an additional element that underlies Orthodox hermeneutics, the idea that the Scriptures are an expression of divine condescension. As explained by Staniloae, Scripture allows human beings to have a "living dialogue with Christ" in one's ascetical life.[51] In the same way that Christ emptied himself and became flesh so that he might achieve union with humanity, so too does God continue to communicate with his people through the Scriptures. God expresses himself in forms that human beings can understand in order to elevate them to a more spiritual manner of living. As Maximus the Confessor states, "Scripture fashions God speaking in terms relative to the underlying disposition of the souls under his providence" (*Question* 44.2).[52] Elsewhere, when discussing the fourfold Gospel, Maximus makes the following argument:

---

50. Constas, *Maximus*, 23.
51. Staniloae, *The Experience of God*, 86.
52. Translation from Constas, *Responses*, 249.

> I would even venture to affirm that every thought capable of
> forming an impression in the intellect is nothing other than an
> elementary outline, pointing to realities that are beyond it. This
> is why the Gospels are four in number, so that they might be
> intelligible to those who are still under the sway of sense percep-
> tion and corruption, for this world consists of the same number
> of elements [i.e., four elements]. (*Ambiguum* 21.5)[53]

The Bible is a product of the material world, he argues, and it
participates in its realities in order that it might speak to those
who belong to it. Since there are four elements underlining all
matter and four virtues governing human morality, there are
four Gospels, each of which corresponds to a particular virtue
and to a particular material element.[54]

In addition to this emphasis on the distinct character of
each of the evangelists and their work, Maximus also affirms
the unity of their message, a unity that applies not only to
Matthew, Mark, Luke, and John, but to all of sacred Scripture.
"If the meaning of the whole of Sacred Scripture is properly
and piously smoothed out," he contends in *Ambiguum* 21.14,
"the disagreements perceived on the literal level of the text will
be seen to contain nothing contradictory or inconsistent."[55]
In order to further explore this process of smoothing out the
inconsistencies on the literal level of Scripture, we should pause
for a moment to recognize that it is now clear that the unity of
Scripture is connected to its character as an act of divine condescension. Indeed, the hermeneutical principle of divine condescension assumes that the same God speaks throughout Scripture. God is the same, but his message takes many forms because

---

53. Translations of the *Ambigua* are taken from Maximos Constas, *On Difficulties in
the Church Fathers: The Ambigua, Volume 1*, Dumbarton Oaks Medieval Library
28 (Cambridge, MA: Harvard University Press, 2014). The translation of the
passage cited here is from Constas, *Ambigua*, 425.

54. In *Ambiguum* 21.6, Maximus says that Matthew represents earth and justice;
Mark represents water and temperance; Luke represents air and courage; John
represents fiery ether and understanding.

55. Translation from Constas, *Ambigua*, 441.

it is spoken into widely divergent types of circumstances. This principle spans the patristic interpretation of Scripture.

When he defends the veneration of icons, for example, John of Damascus sees precisely this kind of divine condescension in God's work. While the Damascene recognizes that the Decalogue forbids images in Exodus 20:4 and Deuteronomy 5:8, he also recognizes that this is not God's only comment in the Old Testament relating to sacred art. God elsewhere tells Israel to place cherubim on the cover that protects the ark of the covenant (Exod. 25:19–20). God has, thus, said two different things about images. The Damascene explains the contradiction as follows:

> Answer me this question: "Is there one God?" You will answer, "Yes, I assume there is only one Lawgiver." What? Does he then command contrary things? The Cherubim are not outside creation. How can he allow Cherubim, carved by the hands of men, to overshadow the mercy-seat? He allows the image of Cherubim . . . to be made and shown as prostrate in adoration before the divine throne, overshadowing the mercy-seat, for it was fitting that the image of the heavenly servants would overshadow the image of the divine mysteries. (*On the Divine Images* 1.15)[56]

In this case, then, images were to be carved on the encasement of the ark of the covenant in order to do what was appropriate in regard to the Law, that is, to treat it with the honor and the respect that it deserves. Things that relate to God deserve special honor. In the case of the ban on images in the Decalogue, however, the people of Israel were in a different situation and were thus in need of alternative instruction. As John writes, "These commandments were given . . . because

---

56. Translations of John of Damascus are taken from David Anderson, trans., *St. John of Damascus: On the Divine Images* (Crestwood, NY: St. Vladimir's Seminary Press, 1980).

of their proneness to idolatry" (*On the Divine Images* 1.8). Two different teachings are given for two different circumstances, but both teachings have the same goal of giving proper honor and glory to God.

The incarnation has created yet another circumstance related to the acceptability of images (*On the Divine Images* 1.16). To justify this stance toward Scripture, the Damascene refers to Ecclesiastes 3:1, which teaches that there is a time for everything under heaven, as well as Hebrews 1:1, which states that God previously spoke in "many and various ways." The same God speaks, but he speaks to a humanity that consistently faces changing circumstances. Of the ban on images in the Decalogue and the importance of images for Christians, he explains that while they are different, they share the same goal. Images were banned in the Decalogue in order to ensure that Israel did not worship anything but the one true God (*On the Divine Images* 1.6), while Christians must venerate images in order to be reminded of the fact that they are no longer under custodians and have come to fuller knowledge of God (*On the Divine Images* 1.8). In both cases, the intention of God's command is to teach his people to worship him properly. With a change of circumstances, often comes a change in the proper manner of worshipping God.

The approach to Scripture that recognizes God as an adaptable Good Shepherd begins very early in the church fathers, with figures like Tertullian and Clement of Alexandria.[57] The initial source of this type of thinking in Christianity goes to the very origin of written Christian literature, to the apostle Paul, who says in 1 Corinthians 9:22, "I have become all things to all people, that by all means I might save some." As the passage reveals, it was Paul's practice to adapt his message to changing circumstances. This principle of "adaptability" has been

---

57. See Margaret M. Mitchell, "Pauline Accommodation and Condescesion (συγκατάβασις)," in *Paul beyond the Judaism-Hellenism Divide*, ed. Troels Engberg-Pedersen (Louisville: Westminster John Knox, 2001), 197–214 (201–5).

studied extensively in Paul's ministry, as it permeates every aspect of his pastoral work.[58] It is not unique to Paul, of course. Ancient philosophers also extolled the virtues of adaptability and applied it in their work, often comparing the care of the soul to the medical treatments that healed the body.[59]

Such pastoral adaptability is a principle of all life in the Orthodox Church. It is a key tool in pastoral care, as expressed in the *Apophthegmata Patrum*, where three monks went to Abba Achilles and asked him for assistance in making fishing nets. He refused the first two, because he was busy, but the third had a very bad reputation among the monks. With him Achilles agreed to work. When the others whom he had refused asked for an explanation, Achilles responded, "If I had not made one for him, he would have said, 'the old man has heard about my sin, and that is why he does not want to make me anything.'" This would have disheartened the brother and separated him from Achilles. "But now," Achilles adds, "I have aroused his soul."[60] The monks are treated differently because their circumstances are different. The monks are called to the same life and the same retreat from sin into purity, but they are brought there through different paths.

Thus, the exegetical principle of adaptability is not confined to exegesis and is common in the life of the church. David Rylaarsdam also has shown how Chrysostom understands the work of God in the Old Testament, as well as of Jesus and St. Paul in the New Testament—and even of the Christian priesthood—according to the principle of adaptability.[61] Based on God's dealings with his people, we may observe

---

58. The seminal study in regard to Paul is Clarence Glad, *Paul and Philodemus: Adaptability in Epicurean and Early Christian Psychagogy* (Leiden: Brill, 1995).

59. See Glad, *Paul and Philodemus*, 133–4, 152–5.

60. Achilles 1 (*PG* 65:124BC). Translation from Douglas Burton-Christie, *The Word in the Desert: Scripture and the Quest for Holiness in Early Christian Monasticism* (Oxford: Oxford University Press, 1992), 284.

61. David Rylaarsdam, *John Chrysostom on Divine Pedagogy* (Oxford: Oxford University Press, 2014). See also Margaret M. Mitchell, "'A Variable and Many-Sorted Man': John Chrysostom's Treatment of Pauline Inconsistency," *JECS*

that adaptability is a method that God uses to lead humanity toward deeper intimacy with him and greater virtue. God is a father and physician, but also a teacher who deftly adapts his instruction to the level of understanding of his students. In light of this, we may conclude that God uses Scripture to elevate humans in their weak state and to provide them with a greater knowledge of him.

How the principle of adaptability works is demonstrated in Chrysostom's commentary on Jesus's encounter with the Samaritan woman, commentary that appears in his homilies on the Gospel of John. As Chrysostom observes, Jesus's interaction with the Samaritan woman takes place in a manner markedly different than his previous correspondence with Nicodemus. As the conversation continues, her understanding of Jesus noticeably increases. Jesus, according to Chrysostom, recognizes that the Samaritan woman presents a different case: "The woman, therefore, believed immediately and appeared much more discerning than Nicodemus. Not only more discerning, but also more courageous. For, although he heard countless such things, he urged no other person onward, nor did he himself act boldly, while she displayed the works of an apostle, evangelizing everyone" (*Hom. Jo.* 32.1).[62] Even so, Jesus accommodates the woman's weakness and meets her in her current state:

> He still continues to use language appropriate to the senses, for she was not yet able to comprehend the spiritual matters with precision. Indeed, if he had said, "If you believe in me you will never thirst," she would not have understood what he said, since she didn't know at all who the one talking was, or about what sort of thirst he was speaking. Why, though, did he

---

6 (1998): 93–111; Robert Charles Hill, *St. John Chrysostom, Commentary on the Psalms, vol. 1* (Brookline, MA: Holy Cross Orthodox Press, 1998), 21–41; Fabio Fabbi, "La Condiscendenza divina nell'inspirazione biblica secondo S. Giovanni Crisostomo," *BIB* 14 (1933): 330–47.

62. Translations of Chrysostom's Homilies on John are my own.

> not do this also among the Jews? Because they had seen many signs, while she had seen none, but heard these words first of all. (*Hom. Jo.* 32.1)

Jesus does not leave her in the lowly state, however, but slowly brings her to the state of higher insight. Chrysostom writes,

> Do you perceive how he led her upward, little by little, to the loftiest of his teachings? At first, she thought that he was a transgressor of the Law. . . . Next, after he had responded to this accusation, when she heard of "living water," she thought water perceptible to the senses was meant. But later, having learned that he was speaking of spiritual things, she believed. (*Hom. Jo.* 32.1)

Christ meets the Samaritan woman in a manner appropriate to her earthly realities but leads her upward gradually to the point of seeing him as the savior of the World.

What Chrysostom sees happening with the Samaritan woman is what occurs to anyone who reads Scripture properly: it elevates one's consciousness, step by step. The dominant image in adaptability, then, is that God is a teacher or a physician who first diagnoses the circumstances of his people, and then offers them the cure for their spiritual diseases or the instruction that will fill the lack in their knowledge. There is one destination, and one message, but that message is expressed differently depending on the capacity and the circumstances of the hearer. By seeing that God adopts to different circumstances, one sees the same God working throughout Scripture. To the extent that the interpreter lives a life that gradually elevates him from earthly to heavenly concerns, the deeper unity of Scripture will become clearer, and the exercise of reading Scripture will result in an ascent toward God.

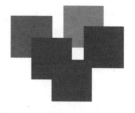

RESPONSE OF
DARIAN R. LOCKETT

Whether told from a conservative or progressive evangelical perspective, a liberal Protestant, Roman Catholic, or Orthodox perspective, the story of how the New Testament canon came to its final form is a complex yet important one. Both the fragmentary nature of the evidence and the fact that the formation of the New Testament canon cuts across historical, theological, and hermeneutical concerns answer for the story's complexity. Yet, as challenging as the task might be, appreciating the significance of the New Testament canon is crucial not only to give an historical description of how the canon came to be (its origin), but also for the way in which the canon functions as Scripture for the church (its authority).

As this volume demonstrates, one's academic and ecclesial location affects one's understanding of how the issues of the canon's history, theology, and hermeneutical function are related. While acknowledging the distinctive contribution of each of the views articulated in this volume, these perspectives are not mutually exclusive in all aspects. I very much appreciate having opportunity to make my own contribution alongside the colleagues included in this volume. In what follows I attempt to trace some lines of agreement and disagreement among these views as I see them.

Response to David Nienhuis

I agree with Nienhuis' concern with prioritizing historical reconstruction of the canon over its theological character (or ontology). To treat the New Testament as if it were a historical artifact—defining its ontology as merely human or creaturely—misses the canon's theological nature and function. Furthermore, Nienhuis is right when he laments that many historical accounts of canonization specifically lack careful theological articulation of the relation between human and divine agency. This is helpfully illustrated by calling out the disastrous consequences of separating biblical studies and theology. With Nienhuis, I think it is crucial to articulate an ontology of the canon as the product of divine-human word-making, yet in my perspective this gives warrant for speaking of the inspiration of Scripture at its composition. One cannot understand what canon *does* until one understands what canon *is*. Furthermore, I agree that one should understand the historical process of canonization under the larger category of God's providential ordering of history.

Nienhuis of course is not an advocate of a naïve and uncritical reception of the New Testament, but I fear that he poses too sharp a conflict between a scholar's historical reading and a layman's theological appropriation of the canon. I too recognize the importance of describing the canon's theological ontology; however, I do not think this necessitates pitting history against theology, or emphasizing the *use* of Scripture in the sanctification of the church at the expense of Scripture's historical composition. I will expand on both these points of disagreement in turn.

First, I fear that Nienhuis overstates the contrast between the "'informed' scholarly reader" and the "'uninformed' lay reader." Though he is careful to say he has no quarrel with historical analysis *per se*, throughout the essay he seems dismissive regarding the necessity of such analysis in understanding the authority and interpretation of the New Testament canon. This is demonstrated by the fact that he only allows for two sharply opposing positions: a naive historical positivism that articulates the meaning of the New Testament canon relying only on scholarly reconstruction of original author, audience, and social-historical situation over against a faithful theological Trinitarianism that receives the sanctifying work of the Spirit by means of Holy Scripture. One need not approach the text exclusively as a natural artifact when interpreting the New Testament canon with reference to its historical origins. I agree that historical reconstruction on its own is not sufficient either to give a full account of what the New Testament canon *is* or to interpret the text *as Scripture*. However, in acknowledging its insufficiency, Nienhuis implies that historical analysis is unnecessary for understanding and interpreting Scripture. Despite his attempt to address the overreach of a kind of historical positivism in historical-critical methodology, I find that his bifurcation between history and theology ultimately fractures the necessary connection between history and theology.

As an example of this kind of bifurcation between history and theology, consider Nienhuis' claim that the "reception of these books into a larger canonical whole provided them with a *new* authoritative setting, one that displaced the social world of author and first readers in favor of the literary setting of the biblical canon." It is true that the boundaries of the New Testament canon constitute an authoritative recontextualization of these texts; however, it does not follow that the historical context of composition is therefore *displaced*. Though often fragmentary, the context of composition (author, audience, context of origin) plays a necessary (though not exclusive) role in determining meaning. Canonical recontextualization *relativizes* the compositional context without *displacing* (or dispensing with) it.

Second, whereas it is crucial to understand the theological ontology of Scripture, it should not be determined by the ways in which the church made *use* of it. Nienhuis argues that if a New Testament text was anonymous, pseudepigraphical, or even historically sub-apostolic it would be of no consequence because the Spirit God is able to use any such text for God's purposes. Furthermore, emphasizing the role of historical author or the context of composition in general risks misplacing "the authoritative center in a creaturely reality and not in the Persons and work of the Triune God." Rather, Nienhuis stresses the significance of how the texts are *used* by the church as Scripture. It is this *use*, in the end, that determines the texts' authority and significance as canon.

I disagree with the implicit claim that God inspires creaturely compositions only in their *use* and not their *origin*. If God can take up creaturely texts after their composition, why could he not be active in the very writing of those texts? It seems to me that the writers of the New Testament and the Fathers of the church understood that God was not only active in the *use* of the New Testament texts, but in their *composition* as well— the concern in the early church to establish apostolic authorship of these texts bears witness to this fact. Furthermore, whereas I share his concern over misplacing the authoritative emphasis on "creaturely reality," I fear Nienhuis might unwittingly place authoritative emphasis on a different kind of "creaturely reality," namely, the church's profitable *use* of the text as a sanctifying instrument. Ecclesial *use* of the text surely is as "creaturely" as apostolic *authorship* of the text.

Finally, though Nienhuis appeals to John Webster in his argument for the church's use of Scripture, I do not think Webster actually endorses Nienhuis' position. It is possible that Nienhuis did not intend to imply that Webster endorses his view of "canon as use"; however, his essay is easily read this way. Webster argues that the church's use of canon is distinctively *passive* in character: "canonicity is not a function of use but use a function of canonicity (which is itself a function of divine approbation and use). Affirmation of the canon is thus a commitment to allow all the activities of the church (most of all, its acts of worship, proclamation and ruling) to be as it were enclosed by the canon."[1]

---

1.   John Webster, *Holy Scripture: A Dogmatic Sketch* (Cambridge: Cambridge University Press, 2003), 65.

Webster makes the following four theological assertions regarding the church's action regarding the process of New Testament canonization. First, the church's *reception* of the New Testament canon is an act of confession. This confession, according to Webster, "has noetic but not ontological force, acknowledging what Scripture is but not making it so."[2] Second, the church's *confession* of the canon is an "act of submission before it is an act of authority."[3] Any claim the church has for its own authority is grounded in its acknowledgment of the canon as the norm it stands under—the church is authoritative only as it submits to God's self-disclosure in the canon. Third, in confessing and submitting to canon, the church makes, as it were, a *backward reference*. In other words, the church receives and affirms that its life and testimony moving forward are grounded on the prior reception of the apostolic testimony. When the church receives and acknowledges the canon, it does so as it points beyond (and behind) itself to the testimony that precedes it. Finally, in the church's act of confession, submission, and backward reference it *binds itself* to this normative canon in all its actions.[4]

Whereas I very much appreciate Nienhuis' contribution to this volume, and his important work that addresses the canonical interpretation of the New Testament more broadly, his emphasis upon the moment of canonization at the expense of the moment of composition and his emphasis upon the church's *use* of the text both give me pause.

Response to Jason BeDuhn

BeDuhn's openness to reevaluation of the canonical process and early church development in light of the historical evidence is commendable. Both the academy's and the church's engagement of the New Testament should be open to the questions

---

2.   Webster, *Holy Scripture*, 63.
3.   Webster, *Holy Scripture*, 63.
4.   These points are all from Webster, *Holy Scripture*, 62–65.

and evidence of history. However, arguing that the results of historical-critical study of the Bible demand the fundamental reformation of the Christian church overstates the scope of his methodology. This is to give the historical-critical method a kind of role it cannot bear. Arguing that historical-critical study should be used to assess (and transform) the foundations of Christianity itself seems to indicate a commitment to a methodological naturalism that predetermines what kind of evidence is relevant in such a reassessment. Furthermore, his commitment to historical criticism lacks a satisfactory description of divine and human agency in the development of the New Testament canon. It is this methodological naturalism and some particular claims that concern me most regarding BeDuhn's contribution.

Again, whereas historical criticism *per se* is a helpful tool, the way BeDuhn takes up this approach leads to a somewhat dismissive attitude toward the church's reception of the New Testament canon. For example, in his discussion of Irenaeus' argument for the limitation of the canonical Gospels to four on the grounds of the four cardinal directions and the four winds emanating from those directions, one might expect a more precise and (historically) contextualized critique of Irenaeus' logic. BeDuhn seems to dismiss Irenaeus' logic based implicitly upon what one believes should count as evidence in a modern framework. In addition, he claims Irenaeus' argument regarding the fourfold Gospel "comes like a bolt out of the blue." However, one could argue that Irenaeus' defense of the fourfold Gospel (*Adv. haer.* 3.11.8) is not as "out of the blue" as BeDuhn claims. Theophilus of Antioch, a contemporary of Irenaeus, argues that the four canonical Gospels were inspired by the Spirit of God just like the Old Testament (*Autol.* 3.12), whereupon he then cites Matthew and Luke as examples and later clearly interacts with John's Gospel. Though Theophilus is silent about Mark, it is telling that he ended up producing a fourfold Gospel harmony very much like Tatian's *Diatesseron* (see Jerome's comment in *Ep.* 121.6, noted in Boxall's essay). This might suggest that in his endorsement of the fourfold Gospel Irenaeus was not as pioneering as BeDuhn claims. I am not suggesting that Irenaeus' logic and evidence are beyond historical assessment, rather that they should not be dismissed out of hand because of one's (modern) methodological commitments.

Furthermore, BeDuhn makes the sweeping claim that during the second century Christians continued producing texts that "would become serious contenders for canonical status." He offers no further argument for this claim, nor does he provide any evidence. Though other gospels were produced in the second and third centuries, they did not meet the canonical criterion of widespread use. It should be noted that there are no surviving early codices in which a noncanonical gospel was bound together with the four canonical Gospels. Of course, we can point to the *use* of noncanonical gospels within the early church (Clement of Alexandria's use of the *Gospel of the Egyptians* or the *Gospel of the Hebrews*, or the Christians at Rhossus reading the *Gospel of Peter*), but one must ask what *kind* of use was made of such texts and what that use might indicate. For example, there seems to be no clear sign that the Christians at Rhossus were reading the *Gospel of Peter* in worship *as Scripture*. Furthermore, it is doubtful that Bishop Serapion would have allowed such a practice especially for a gospel with which he had so little knowledge.

BeDuhn argues that the New Testament texts are merely human compositions, records of their spiritual experiences. Therefore, rather than divine words, the New Testament texts are but merely human words. Interestingly his prime example of the human character of the texts is Paul's personal greetings. These ephemeral comments are taken as proof that Paul writes without any consciousness of producing timeless Scripture. Therefore, because they are merely human words, the authority of the New Testament lies in the events or experiences recounted rather than in the particular words themselves, and as such these words must be recognized as products of fallible human beings (who, themselves, were fallible).

These conclusions influence BeDuhn's hermeneutical approach to the text. Because the texts are fallible, we must interpret them "as time-bound relics," products of their original context. The culturally relativized texts of the New Testament thus hold only relative authority for its readers, but the historical-critical study of the New Testament can help interpret the spirit of the teaching rather than the mere letter. In light of these judgments, BeDuhn argues that limiting interpretation of the early Christian texts to that of the New Testament collection alone is inadequate and misguided. He insists that such interpretation "cannot succeed because it fails to recognize that the canon was imposed later on a set of writings selected from a wide and diverse body of literature."

I fundamentally disagree with these claims. BeDuhn's assertions here beg the question: Which collection and which set of associations should we attend to when interpreting the New Testament? One does not escape the hermeneutical logic of selection and arrangement when arguing for historical-critical dismantling of the New Testament canon. That is, one's interpretation of these texts will be influenced by selection and arrangement, whether these are guided by the logic of the Christian canon or by the logic of historical-critical reconstruction. Because interpretation is always guided by notions of collection and association, the interpreter must become aware of the underlying logic of such decisions. I am arguing that whereas historical associations are important and useful, the canonical collection of the New Testament and the associations it generates should take precedence. I do not think such a collection and association have been imposed upon these texts, but rather that they represent the right understanding of their content.

Whether or not BeDuhn is committed to metaphysical naturalism, his dependence upon historical criticism suggests a kind of methodological naturalism which limits the ability of his position to assess *both* the historical and *theological* elements of the New Testament canon.

Response to Ian Boxall

I find Boxall's sketch of the canonical development of the New Testament quite helpful. Though acknowledging the complexity of the historical process of canonization, I think Boxall is correct in his conclusion that the available evidence points to an early consensus regarding at least the core texts of the New Testament, including their normative status for Christians. I especially appreciate Boxall's argument for the development of the New Testament canon as a collection of collections (Gospels, Pauline Corpus, Catholic Epistles) and that these collections circulated and were received as Scripture early on. Moreover, his conclusion that Marcion's innovative role in the development of the New Testament canon can be (and I would add, often is!) overstated is certainly correct.

Finally, I appreciate Boxall's nuanced discussion of the authority of the New Testament canon. He flags both apostolicity and catholicity as necessary criteria, yet he does not understand apostolicity narrowly as historical authorship by an apostle, but rather the preservation of the original apostolic teaching. The New Testament's authority, therefore, rests in the preservation of this testimony. My only objections are with Boxall's argument for the definitive closure of the New Testament at the Council of Trent and his commitment to interpreting the text via the lens of the Gospels.

Boxall understands the definitive moment of closure for the New Testament canon as an official decision of the church represented in the conclusions of Trent. Though I appreciate the acknowledgment of the church's reception of the canon as the community addressed in and formed by Scripture, I do not think there is one "conscious, retrospective, official" moment of canonical closure, nor do I think the canon should be defined strictly as a closed corpus. Doing so causes problems in understanding the relationship between canon and Scripture and is liable to foreclose talk of a New Testament canon until later in the process (fourth or fifth century). Furthermore, these texts are not granted their authority (and thereby their canonicity) by the church's official decree or practical use. Though Boxall qualifies his appreciation for Trent by noting that its conclusions "merely underscored the broad consensus reflected as early as Athanasius' thirty-ninth Festal Letter of 367 CE," emphasizing Trent's authority implicitly stresses the church's role in canon formation.

Later in his essay, Boxall notes both a passive and an active dimension to the church's role in canon formation. I am in full support of his approving citation of Morwenna Ludlow's comments: "the Church is formulating *reasons* or *explanations* for why it has what it has, not *criteria* for choosing what it should have in the future."[5] Boxall goes on to state clearly that "Catholics would describe the Church's role as one of discernment, not so much the giving of authority to these texts as the recognition of the authority they already possess." This is quite helpful and, at least in my estimation, distinguishes Boxall's understanding of the church's use of these texts from Nienhuis' position. However, I am still not completely clear regarding Boxall's understanding of the church's *active* role in canon formation.

Recognizing the consensus of the early church over the acceptance of the core texts of the New Testament, Boxall argues that the four Gospels have pride of place in interpretation. He notes that the "Catholic view of the New Testament canon does give hermeneutical priority to the four Gospels" because they are focused on "the Christ event itself." The Gospels function as a kind of lens that is able to bring the entire New Testament into focus. He argues that the placement of the Gospels at the beginning of the New Testament marks the chronological priority of Jesus, provides a bridge between Old and New Testaments, and establishes the "Gospels as the key hermeneutical lens of the canon."

I very much appreciate Boxall's reflection on the collection and order of the New Testament as it influences interpretation;

---

5.   Morwenna Ludlow, "'Criteria of Canonicity' and the Early Church," in *Die Einheit der Schrift und die Vielfalt des Kanons/The Unity of Scripture and the Diversity of the Canon*, eds. John Barton and Michael Wolter, BZNW 118 (Berlin: de Gruyter, 2003), 71.

however, I would like to hear more detail regarding how the Gospels function as a hermeneutical lens. Can the Gospels be prioritized hermeneutically without displacing other New Testament texts? Attending to the shape of the New Testament like this in interpretation is warmly welcome, yet more explicit detail regarding the kind of hermeneutical priority the Gospels should be given would be helpful.

Response to George Parsenios

The central thrust of Parsenios' essay, as I understand it, is that the Orthodox consensus regarding the New Testament canon is a result of the Holy Spirit's guidance of the church's practice. I appreciate his stress on the criteria of apostolicity, catholicity, orthodoxy, and traditional use. However, this last criterion, as Parsenios presents it, raises a central concern. He argues that Scripture and tradition cannot be separated. The Orthodox position insists that Scripture cannot stand on its own without tradition. Thus, "the limits of the Scripture are established and solidified precisely by the church's tradition, that is, the church's practice." Because there is little difference between text and tradition for Parsenios, the development of second-century Christian orthodoxy is indistinguishable from canonical development. Whereas I agree that issues of the rule of faith are directly related to the development of canon, in Parsenios' telling they are the same story.

Furthermore, Parsenios argues that in the canonization of the New Testament "the practice of the church over time is determinative." In his presentation, the church's practice determines the boundaries of the canon. As noted above, I would argue that the church's role in canon formation is a passive one of reception and recognition.

Conclusion

I am grateful that this volume calls attention to the importance of the New Testament canon. Stephen B. Chapman is correct when he notes, "The church's concept of a canon lay precisely at the fault line between history and theology."[6] Each of the perspectives in this volume understands that the historical and theological characteristics of canon constitute a crucial way forward in various ways. Though I have found reason to question or disagree with the other contributors, this in no way is an indication of my lack of appreciation or respect for their position or their work. It is an honor to be included in this dialogue and I certainly have learned much from this interaction.

Perhaps in closing I can attempt to summarize my own contribution to the conversation. In my essay I attempt to demonstrate how the early origin of the New Testament canon, especially understood as the development of very early subcollections, is in keeping with the theological persuasion that the canon is the authoritative and inspired word of God. One unique contribution of my essay is its argument for the close relationship between the concepts of Scripture and canon and its definition of canon in broader terms (both a list and a rule). Furthermore, in my essay and in my responses above, I argue that a canonical approach to the New Testament must be careful to avoid pitting canonization against composition or defining canon by appealing to the church's *use* or performance of the text. Rather, the church stands under the text of Scripture as canon, joyfully receiving and confessing its authority and rule.

---

6.   Stephen B. Chapman, "Reclaiming Inspiration for the Bible," in *Canon and Biblical Interpretation*, eds. Craig Bartholomew et al. (Grand Rapids: Zondervan, 2006), 167–206 (167).

RESPONSE OF
DAVID R. NIENHUIS

I want to begin by expressing my honest appreciation for my co-contributors and the editors who invited them to submit their perspectives. The essays in this volume demonstrate well the wide range of orientations and approaches to the New Testament canon held by Christians of different ecclesial traditions. Though I disagree with some of what each of my colleagues presents in their essays (sometimes quite strenuously!), I can say without hesitation that I learned something from all of them, and for that I am truly grateful.

The fact is, I find myself in the somewhat ironic position of discovering my perspective has far more in common with that of my Roman Catholic and Eastern Orthodox colleagues than that of my two fellow Protestants. Perhaps it simply makes good sense that disagreement would be sharper among brethren who dwell in closer ecclesial proximity? Regardless, as will be plain to those who read my essay, I am deeply sympathetic to the unabashedly ecclesial and pneumatological approach to canonization presented by those who have written from their respective locations in the ancient Eastern and Western Christian traditions. By contrast, I find more reasons for concern in the perspectives presented by those representing the "conservative" and "liberal" wings of Protestantism. I'll begin by responding to those with whom I largely agree and move on to those with whom I perceive greater difference of opinion.

Response to Ian Boxall

Boxall and I appear to be making many of the same claims, albeit in language that occasionally differs. I certainly agree with Boxall's desire to utilize a wider-angle lens when viewing the canonization process, which unavoidably results in a blurring of "the distinction between Scripture and tradition . . . viewing them not as two distinct sources of revelation but dynamically interconnected." Such a view enables one to unapologetically appreciate the fact that the formation of the New Testament canon was a long and complex process of communal discernment. Indeed, Boxall and I are obviously quite comfortable affirming the vital role the church played in the discernment process that resulted in the eventual recognition of canonical Scripture. In this regard I especially enjoyed his brief reminder of the relationship between canonical texts and the many noncanonical writings, preaching, and visual arts that grew up alongside them as part of the larger ecclesial "landscapes of memory" (so Nicklas)[1] that mediated canonical texts to the faithful.

Given the Spirit's involvement, there is no reason to be overly concerned about the "inevitable ecclesial and political rivalries" unearthed in the historian's examination of the canonization process. We have no need to nervously defend against possible evidence of human mechanisms or machinations; we simply presume God's superintending involvement throughout the process. Hence it is not only historically dishonest to pretend that "tradition" played little to no role in the divine delivery of these texts to the church, it is also completely unnecessary. To this end, I found his definition of "apostolicity" quite helpful: rather than offering a narrow claim about a text's *authorship* (which historical inquiry has made difficult to

---

1. Tobias Nicklas, "New Testament Canon and Early Christian 'Landscapes of Memory,'" *EC* 7 (2016): 5–23, cited in Boxall.

maintain) or about a text's *content* (so Luther), apostolicity is better conceived as referring to "the *preservation* of the original apostolic response to the Christ event, first conveyed through the preached gospel, and preserved both orally in the ongoing transmission of the apostolic tradition, and in written form in the writings now recognized as canonical (emphasis mine)." Apostolicity as *preservation* thus enables the extension of canonization as a Spirit-guided process unfolding through time. It helps Protestants like me to thicken our conceptualization of God's providence by linking the origin and content of these texts together with the history of the church's experience of recognizing, gathering, and tending those texts.

Response to George Parsenios

Of course, the Protestant in me would have liked to have heard a bit more detail from Boxall about the precise relationship between the oral and written preservation of apostolic tradition. The essay by Parsenios fills in this gap with a very helpful presentation of the apostolic rule of faith as it is enshrined and embodied in the living practices of the Orthodox Church. Like Boxall, Parsenios insists that what we call "canonization" must be understood as part of a much larger apostolic *paradosis,* the transmission of "what has already been passed down . . . recognizing what the Church had long affirmed." Yet unlike its Western counterparts, the Orthodox Church never delineated a final list of Scripture. Theirs is a deeply pneumatological understanding that aims to dwell in the richness of Christian heritage while resisting the encroachment of institutional or doctrinal controls: what the Orthodox call "tradition" is simply "the life of the Holy Spirit in the Church."

Perhaps knowing that his essay would be set alongside three Protestant perspectives, Parsenios offers a detailed definition and defense of "unwritten teaching" (particularly in regard to liturgical practice) and its relation to the canon, asking specifically, "how does the honor given to tradition relate to the reverence given to Scripture"? This is precisely the Protestant question! He quotes Florovsky approvingly: "the Scriptures are the only authentic record of the revelation, and everything else is no more than a commentary thereupon. And commentary can never have the same authority as the original record." Amen to that. But then he goes on to formalize the distinction between written and unwritten tradition by focusing on Scripture's *content*: Scripture is "the record of revelation. . . . Both the Old and New Testaments are a history of this revelation." The practices of the church, by contrast, "are not *just* commentary on the Christ described in Scripture; they are the lived experience of Christ in the present" (emphasis original). Scripture is intended to function as a check on these holy practices, as the church's immediate experience of the living Lord "brings people again and again to the Scriptures, to ensure that the church is seeking the right Christ, the true Christ."

To be sure, Parsenios does not intend to suggest that Scripture is merely an inert source that refers believers to a set of past events, for like the church, Scripture is also a site of divine encounter. As Staniloae states, "Through the word of Scripture, Christ continues to speak to us and to provoke us to make a response in our deeds, and thus to be actively at work in us too." Thus the relationship between written and unwritten tradition finds its symbiotic power in the presence of the living Lord: the church's witness in the world is the "continuous rediscovery of the message" of Scripture that "is ever re-enacted in the life of the Church."

I confess to being caught in a bit of a conundrum at this point. I wish I could so easily proclaim the uncomplicated, living unity of Scripture and tradition, but that is not my inheritance as a Protestant Christian. So in my essay I was obliged to express deep admiration for the church's living "rule of faith" that guides and directs our reading of Scripture, "provided that the rule does not become so grand and overly articulated that it ends up simplifying our reception of the message and thus displaces God's guiding and convicting presence." In the end, "the canon of Scripture in all its wild messiness must always assume a position of priority over any of the clean and precise tools that are brought in to help us read it." Thus I am immediately led to worry (for instance) about Parsenios' approval of Maximus' insistence that the meaning of Scripture must be "properly and piously smoothed out." That "pious smoothing" has a long history that has not always served God's people well.

Let me be perfectly clear on this point: unlike many Protestants, I am not driven to subordinate unwritten to written tradition out of any anti-ecclesial sentiment. It is simply because, unlike Parsenios, I am a recipient of apostolic tradition as it has been refracted through the lens of a divided church. Sadly, Protestantism has spent much of its history treating schism as a virtue, and those of us who live and work among mostly Protestant Christians simply do not have the luxury to appeal to a shared, "thick" ecclesial rule or set of liturgical practices beyond the canon of Scripture itself. I have come to believe that this state of affairs is a tragedy that God continues to redeem in countless ways. For all its many failures, Protestantism helped to set the canon of Scripture loose in the world. Yes, Scripture without a shared interpretive guide has resulted in a cacophony of voices, but it has also demonstrated the rich breadth of the Spirit's capacity to extend the Word through unexpected voices and in unauthorized places.

No doubt this is part of what Parsenios was after when he closed his essay by focusing on God's identity as an adaptable Good Shepherd who seeks us wherever we may be found and draws us from those disparate places into deeper communion. As Parsenios puts it, "What Chrysostom sees happening" in Jesus's encounter with the Samaritan woman at the well "is what occurs to anyone who reads Scripture properly; it elevates one's consciousness, step by step." But given the inseparable symbiosis of Scripture and ecclesial practice Parsenios outlines, can Protestants ever be said to read Scripture "properly"?

Response to Darian Lockett

In the end, my disagreements with Boxall and Parsenios are quite minor, given the fact that our shared ecclesial and pneumatological convictions keep us speaking mostly the same language. I wish I could say the same about the perspectives shared by my Protestant brethren. I began my own essay by making the case that an understanding of the Bible as the church's Scripture requires a careful, theological articulation of the relation between human and divine agency in history; one must be able to deal honestly with the historical evidence "from below" while making a case for God's superintending activity "from above." I noted that more conservative perspectives on the matter "tend to lapse into apologetics in an attempt to defend the authority of Scripture against presentations of its canonical history that emphasize intricate human involvement in a manner they perceive as threatening to its divinely rooted authority." By contrast, more liberal perspectives insist on a sharp separation of theological and historical evidence "under the presumption that theological commitments only get in the way of ascertaining the 'real' truth of the matter, which is of course the truth as it is reconstructed by the professional historian who is (supposedly) able to operate unencumbered by the imposition of a religious filter." While both Lockett's and BeDuhn's essays had much of value to share, it seemed to me that each of them offered a relatively accurate performance of my characterization of typical conservative and liberal Protestant approaches.

Lockett and I have known each other for years, and over that time we have mapped out a good deal of agreement and disagreement in our respective positions on the New Testament canon. As with the others, I find much to appreciate in his essay. We agree, for instance, that it is a mistake to conceive of the canonization process with a fixed end in mind, as though everything hangs on precise determinations of when the final form can be said to have arrived. To this end, I valued his recounting of the so-called "canon debate" that raged among Protestants over the course of the twentieth century.

Of course, one must ask *why* such an extended reflection is thought to be required in the first place. Lockett does not leave his readers wondering about his intention: throughout, he makes it plain that he seeks to defend the authority of Scripture independent of any ecclesial authority. This is unsurprising, given his "conservative Protestant" location. Right at the outset he names his conviction that the Scripture was "recognized (rather than created) by the church." To get there, he labors to show that the canon began developing at an early period in Christian history, and that it did not come about as a result of later ecclesial decisions: "the recognized authority and inspiration of the texts that were eventually collected into the New Testament was not something that was granted by the church, but was, rather, an intrinsic property of those texts that was recognized by the church." I find it somewhat ironic that both our Roman Catholic and Eastern Orthodox contributors appear to completely agree with Lockett on this point! But where the others (and I) would speak of this recognition as a Spirit-guided process of communal discernment, Lockett's focus throughout is weighted toward the protection of divine agency. As a fellow Protestant I respect this, but his presentation of Scripture's self-authenticating nature consistently demonstrates the sort of anti-institutional commitments common to conservative Calvinists that lead to rather forced assertions that are open to critique.

Lockett insists, "The church's inheritance of the New Testament canon indicates that from the very beginning, *from the composition* of the apostolic writings, it had authority in the churches where they were known" (emphasis mine). How could such a claim ever possibly be demonstrated? These proto-New Testament writings were "spontaneously" and "automatically . . . received as Scripture without any formal or institutional judgment needed." It is obvious that these texts were received as authoritative by *someone* or they would not have been preserved; in this regard, no *formal* or *institutional* judgment was needed. But insisting these writings were spontaneously and automatically received as Scripture requires us to imagine that there was no judgment or discernment to be made at all—no prayerful human participation, no testing of the spirits to see which are from God, no parading and performing of texts in different configurations over decades to determine which sequence best communicated the apostolic message. It leaves us with the sense that God found it necessary to override human agency in the desire to give humans the Bible.

In another place, Lockett quotes Childs' recognition that "the formation of the canon was not a late extrinsic validation of a corpus of writings, but involved a series of decisions deeply affecting the shape of the books." But Lockett extends this insight to insist that "the pressures that led to the formation of the Old and New Testaments . . . were not manipulative of the texts themselves." What does he mean by this? Does he mean to say that no scribal shaping took place as the canon developed? How on this basis does one account for the ending of Mark's Gospel or the *Pericope Adulterae* (John 7:53–8:11)? Lockett appears to want to speak about the development of the canon without acknowledging any meaningful role for the community wherein that development took place. Throughout, one hears a nervous concern to protect a pristine text unaffected by human processes.

Response to Jason BeDuhn

While I have raised concerns with Lockett's more antiinstitutional perspective, at least I can share with him a scholarly commitment to approaching the Bible according to its primary identity as Christian Scripture. I do not think I can say the same for BeDuhn. Indeed, where Lockett seems to want to secure biblical authority against human agency, BeDuhn seems equally committed to protecting human agency against the authority of the Bible.

It is only right that I begin by listing off points of appreciation. In various places BeDuhn persuasively demonstrates the value of historical inquiry and reconstruction. I respect his detailed opening overview of canon formation "from below," as it presents a good deal of evidence against simplistic assertions of intrinsic scriptural authority that attempt to sidestep human processes. I also truly value his honest narration of how the rise of historical criticism "pressed forward with the Reformation," especially its recognition that the latter "stopped short of bringing to the New Testament canon the same critique it made of the Old Testament canon and other church traditions," for it is on this basis that the authority of the New Testament is routinely qualified by liberal Protestants.

I found it illuminating how BeDuhn twice points out that his approach is really no different from that which emerges from those who are not affiliated with any religious tradition. This is not particularly surprising; modern biblical scholarship has long insisted that the only way to read the Bible rightly is to read it a-theistically—to pretend that it is *not* Christian Scripture, but little more than a collection of "humanly composed records of spiritual experiences and insights" written by fallible human beings. The presumption of an inherently fallible Bible is what then opens the door for modern critics to reject "various aspects of their texts that, in the judgment of Christian communities, somehow fall short of Christian ideals." But how are such "Christian ideals" developed when one is working with such a fallible source text? That is the job of the enlightened critical historian, who must strive "to understand not just the literal meaning of the words of the Bible but the inner logic and intended effect by which these words functioned in their original context. By doing so, we may then consider the possible meaning that transcends time and place."

Perhaps I simply misunderstood, but I confess to being rather dumbfounded by what struck me as a stunningly uncritical modernist epistemology operative throughout BeDuhn's essay. Is he unaware of the devastating critiques that have been leveled against this Western dream of a value-free, neutral scholarly observer who can so easily separate the wheat of timeless truth from the chaff of those "time-bound relics of the original context"? The presumption of an a-cultural, disembodied, "timeless" knowing is one of the more dangerous elements of the European heritage. Reading the Bible in this fashion has a long history of turning the book into little more than a magic mirror we peer into only to discover that it perfectly reflects our own "Christian ideals" right back to us.

It is arguable that this turn to the priority of "human religious experience" as an interpretive rule of faith is precisely what shattered the Protestant movement into a thousand pieces. Most Protestants I know seem to be quite content with this state of affairs, but this "progressive evangelical" is not. Our shared history has made it plain that neither the biblical text nor our own hearts are self-interpreting or self-authenticating. The apostolic tradition, written and unwritten in its many varied forms, is ultimately an auxiliary of the One Spirit who proceeds from God to spread the healing Word throughout our troubled creation. I do not know precisely how God will perform that healing, but I am convinced Christian scholars of the Bible will only play a role if the Spirit finds us on our knees, working prayerfully together across denominational lines. This *Five Views on the New Testament Canon* project is one such collaborative endeavor. As my Orthodox friends like to say, "May it be blessed."

RESPONSE OF JASON DAVID BEDUHN

Christianity is not some sort of transcendental philosophy; it is a religion at whose core stands the belief in a God who is involved in the world and in the earthly lives of human beings. That earthly life stretches across a history, and indeed, the Christian account of salvation is a salvation *history*. The Christian God does not inhabit some otiose realm quietly awaiting mystics to discover it but reaches into the world and reaches out to human beings above all through a flesh-and-blood historical figure whose connection to God Christians regard as unique and decisive, and who changed the world at one stroke some two thousand years ago. This historical characteristic of the Christian religion renders it vulnerable in a way a transcendent philosophy is not. In staking a claim on history, Christianity submits itself to the publicly accessible, secular standards by which such claims are assessed. This is not some novel notion I am asserting; it is little more than a paraphrase of the words recorded by Paul in 1 Corinthians 15:14.

Although there have been times in the last two thousand years when history did not seem to matter much to many Christians, that cannot be said of the age in which we are living now. Modern Christianity seems especially entangled with questions of historicity, as if there has arisen a discomfort in faith communities about relying on their own naked authority. There exists in modern Christianity the trait of having something to prove. And the proof in question must be made by the modern coin of the secular realm, whether that be science or history. While not everything discussed by the contributors to this volume falls under the standards of such "objective" fields, much of it does, as their own words and mode of presentation attest. This approach reflects the wish to speak the language of the age in order to persuade modern people; but it also results in the vulnerability I have mentioned.

After all, a religious community is perfectly entitled to tell any story of origins it wishes. It may relate its preferred narrative of how its scriptures came to be written and teach its adherents a gratifying tale of how the same set of texts it now values so greatly has always served as the touchstone of the faith. It may treat the process of canon formation as inevitable, indeed, foreordained. Yet most of the contributions in this volume have offered as part of such accounts that secular coin: *historical evidence*. They endeavor to prove that their account of the formation of the New Testament is not only gratifying and edifying, but objectively, historically true. In this regard, liberal Christians have the advantage of being already committed to giving all due deference to the findings of objectively conducted historical study, even as those findings change in light of ongoing discoveries. Taking account of such historical conclusions does not entail for them the dilemma of either defending or compromising some prior account on which they staked absolute and final certainty. The strain of that dilemma is evident in some of the contributions within this volume representing other forms of Christianity.

The current liberal Protestant understanding of the historical process of canon formation is closest to those offered in this volume by Boxall and Parsenios, representing respectively the Catholic and Orthodox positions. This proximity of viewpoint results from the recognition within the Catholic and Orthodox communities of historical development of the faith. Both churches acknowledge a process of what these authors term "discernment," by which Christians over time arrived at new understandings of the faith, even while retaining continuity with core commitments of the apostolic age. Both Catholic and Orthodox Christians embrace the historical evidence that Christianity in the apostolic age operated primarily in the oral medium, passing on traditions about Jesus and how to live a Christian life in face-to-face personal encounters. In Boxall's words, there was "proclamation of the good news by the church before the composition of the New Testament Scriptures." Written texts came later, as distillations from this vibrant oral tradition, even while the latter continued alongside the gradually spreading authority of the new texts, which took several centuries to arrive at even an unofficial consensus. In fact, the interdependence and complementarity of these two sources of authority was such that—as Boxall and Parsenios both note—binding declarations of a New Testament canon only appeared in these communities very late (Catholic Council of Trent 1546, Orthodox Council of Jerusalem 1672), primarily as a response to the Protestant emphasis on Scripture at the expense of tradition. By excluding an essential role for tradition, both before and alongside of Scripture, Protestantism (including its evangelical forms) pressures itself to create a myth of Christian origin that places Scripture at that origin point, as the source and font of everything Christian. Lockett well represents this attitude. While acknowledging with the other contributors the historical evidence that the full New Testament canon appears only in the fourth century, he seeks for evidence of the earlier existence of subsets of that later canonical material, and even maintains that the individual books had scriptural authority from the time they were composed. Let us take each of these claims in turn.

For there to be evidence of proto-canonical sets of writings, the writings need to be cited *as sets*. That is, an author needs to show use of all four Gospels, rather than isolated allusions to a Gospel here or a Gospel there. One needs to cite multiple

Pauline letters, not just one or two. Yet all the evidence from before the mid-second century is of the latter type. The first direct evidence of knowledge of all four of the Gospels that will later be canonical derives from Tatian, from circa 170 CE, closely followed by Irenaeus. Paul is in slightly better shape, because Marcion knows a set of Paul's epistles (albeit a smaller one than later becomes canonical) by the 140s CE. Any conjecture that such later evidence of sets "probably presupposes" earlier and widespread circulation[1] is just that: conjecture without evidential corroboration. Sifting early Christian sources for corroboration of later canonical views operates in a one-sided, circular manner, finding and interpreting evidence in a selective manner. Mere allusion to another text does not confer on it "scriptural" or "canonical" standing, nor do early Christian sources confine themselves to alluding only to texts that would later be included in the canon. Even more, allusion to noncanonical texts is quite likely in these sources, but we are unable to recognize allusions to texts that have since been lost. The whole endeavor, therefore, is a highly tendentious reading of later views of Scripture and canon into earlier materials that are innocent of them, and unlikely to yield historically valid results.

Lockett's assertion that the books that went into the New Testament had authority from the time of their composition can be accepted, but only if it is carefully qualified. Paul's letters, for instance, clearly did have authority from the time of their composition: the personal authority of Paul over the churches he founded. This authority operated between Paul and these individual churches, whose distinctive and peculiar issues in that time he directly addressed; and certainly Paul sought to create a network that united those churches into a wing of the Christian movement. But this was a very small

---

1.   Larry W. Hurtado, "The New Testament in the Second Century: Text, Collections and Canon," in *Transmission and Reception: New Testament Textual-Critical and Exegetical Studies*, eds. Jeff Childers and David Parker, Text and Studies: Contributions to Biblical and Patristic Literature 4 (Piscataway, NJ: Gorgias, 2006), 3–27 (21).

circle within the larger movement, and Paul (or someone speaking for Paul) even complains about losing his authority over some of his communities (2 Tim. 1:15). Given that Paul's personal authority was hotly contested in his own lifetime, as he himself tells us, the missing part of the story is how the personal authority Paul invested in his letters came to have wider recognition—ironically, perhaps precisely through the letters, which circulated further than Paul personally ever did. In other words, Lockett is largely correct that the process of developing Christian Scripture and canon does not involve texts that had no authority having it later bestowed upon them; rather, it involves texts that did have authority from the start, albeit limited, local, interpersonal authority based on the relationship of the author to the community for which he or she wrote, with that authority gradually widening and spreading as they circulated among early Christian audiences. As Nienhuis puts it, speaking for progressive evangelicals, "texts that were initially considered valuable artifacts of the Christian past came increasingly to function also as authoritative Scripture for life in the Christian present."

This picture is a far cry from the characterization Lockett quotes from Stephen Chapman, that the Christian church can be "said to have *inherited* a scriptural canon."[2] This is simply incoherent as a statement about history. The New Testament did not constitute itself, after all, and talking as if it did is not a normal manner of speaking of occurrences in history, but a special theological language that presupposes forces outside of history. It is mythic speech, rather than historical speech. There is nothing wrong with mythic speech, unless it tries to pass itself off as historical speech, for then it moves into a different realm of assessment. By some theological standard, the church may well be considered "not competent" to confer authority on Scripture, but nonetheless it historically did so; and if it did not, there would

---

2.   Stephen B. Chapman, "The Old Testament Canon and Its Authority for the Christian Church," *ExAud* 19 (2003): 125–48 (140).

be no Christian Scripture. For the church to "inherit" a scriptural canon, there must have been a prior constituter of it to pass it on.

So the overarching problem for those who argue for what we might term "original authority" in the texts from the time of their composition, or the early formation of recognized sets of Scripture, is the lack of an authority structure that could have instituted such decisions within the Christian movement in its first two centuries. The only way around this historical fact is to argue for some sort of spontaneous or organic collective recognition of certain books as Scripture. This is a scenario posited by most of the other contributors to this volume, and I have no objection to the idea that leaders often had to yield to pressures "from below," so to speak, in such matters. Yet a key question is when, exactly, the new Christian compositions came to be known and used in church meetings. There is plenty of room for debate about what sort of circulation and use the authors had in mind; but actual evidence for reading such works in church meetings only emerges in the mid-second century. In the words of Parsenios, "the practice of the church over time is determinative," but "the practice of the church takes time to find its proper expression." Once the practice of reading Christian compositions in church started, the kind of spontaneous and organic recognition of Scripture described by the other contributors occurred with frequency. The wrinkle is that it involved both books later included in the canon and books left out; it involved both smaller sets and larger sets of Scriptures than ultimately would gain official standing as canon. So there is nothing wrong with saying that church leaders were not necessarily the instigators of a work's scriptural status, and that they did not necessarily force Scriptures on their communities. On the other hand, it was such leaders who sanctioned the ultimate canonical lists, accepting some and rejecting others of the community's scriptural wish list.

A religious community is perfectly entitled to determine the contents and extent of its sacred Scriptures. It may determine any criteria of selection and sanctification it wishes and need not submit these to any external examination or approval. It may regard the decisive element making a work "scripture" as some-thing "intrinsic" to the work, innocent of any institutional or political project. It may place the name of any of its traditional heroes upon them as it sees fit to lend them persuasive authority and need not submit to historical measures of authenticity. The community is under no compulsion to take into account any new discoveries or insights into the origin or meaning of its Scriptures coming from outside the community, up to and including the unmasking of forgery. To take this most extreme case, a forged Scripture is nevertheless Scripture if the community says it is.

Most of the other contributors to this volume recognize the obstacles to verifying—that is proving with historical evidence—the identity of the authors of the New Testament books. Speaking for progressive evangelicals, Nienhuis states,

> As it is, we know very little about who wrote these texts and where they came from; many of the New Testament texts are anonymous, and much of what we claim to know about their authors simply combines the scant historical evidence available to us with trust in the titles and corresponding narratives of origin that have been passed down as part of the *traditum* ("tradition").

This situation poses no great crisis, however, Nienhuis contin-ues, "because the authority of the text is not rooted solely in the context of its historical provenance." Rather, "the ultimate determinant of canonical authority is the Spirit's profitable use of a text in the churches and not strict determinations of authorship *per se*." Therefore, "ultimately the 'apostolicity' of a text had less to do with the actual author and more to do with a text's spiritual utility." Similarly, for the Catholic position, Boxall states that the authority of a biblical passage as part of the canon does not necessarily entail its historical authenticity as the work of the author to which it is traditionally ascribed. He speaks instead of a broader, looser sense of apostolic credential, namely, "preservation of the original apostolic response to the Christ event." The "discernment" involved in the canonization process, therefore, did not depend on the personal authority of a historical author, as illustrated by the church's rejection of a large number of texts circulating under apostolic names. Liberal Protestants would largely agree with such characterizations of the basis of a text's canonicity, without necessarily embracing the strong hand of divine providence that both these authors envision in the canonization process.

Quite different is the conservative evangelical view represented by Lockett, by which the authors composed their writings *as Scripture*, with a "canonical consciousness" from the start.[3] I frankly admit that I have no idea what feature of the texts this phrase is supposed to reference. It is difficult to imagine writings with less "canonical consciousness" than the letters of Paul. By sending personal greetings, providing travel updates, and addressing ephemeral interpersonal issues within the communities, Paul shows that he had no notion that his letters would have lasting application. Naturally he made some effort to formulate careful arguments and reasons, as well as to assert his authority as a guide to the proper understanding and practice of Christian faith. These characteristics of his immediately relevant labors could later form the basis for treating the letters as having lasting, "scriptural" authority, and allowed the later church to exert creative reapplication of passages to matters unrelated to those Paul understood himself to be addressing. In short, their "spiritual utility" was "discerned" through their wider circulation and use over time, culminating in their eventual treatment as "scripture." This picture of gradual scripturalization, with which liberal Protestantism is comfortable, appears to be shared by progressive evangelicalism, as Nienhuis articulates it in contrast to Lockett, when he states that "the proto-New Testament texts were not *written* as Scripture *per se*

---

3.   Lockett cites this concept of writings being composed with "canonical consciousness" from Brevard S. Childs, *The New Testament as Canon: An Introduction* (London: SCM, 1984), 21.

but *became* Scripture as they were gathered together into fruitful relationships with other texts."

To greater or lesser degrees, however, all of the other contributors appeal to something operating outside of normal historical processes or human agency in making these particular texts special, and hence scriptural and canonical. In doing so, all the other positions represented in this volume downplay or deny the political dimension of authority in Christian history. Instead, everything is "spontaneous," "organic," "the will of the people," "Spirit-led," "providentially guided." Thank goodness that the long history of the Christian church was never marred by assertions of power, hierarchies of authority, conflict between clergy and laity, theological or moral mistakes, or even any difference of opinion! Except that it was, and we all know that it was; we continue to observe it directly in the operation of churches and denominations today. This is something that liberal Protestantism not only acknowledges as historically undeniable but takes seriously as an issue that must form part of the ongoing work of the Christian church. In the eyes of liberal Christians, denying the political dimension of Christian history precludes the possibility of emending the abuses that leaders or even whole communities have made in the past when human failing prevailed over Christian spirit. Liberal Protestants recognize that figures in authority acted in Christian history to exclude certain texts from use in the churches, and in that way curtailed any momentum toward accepting them as Scripture. The same authorities made final delimitations of the canon, exerting control over the mix of voices and the preponderance of certain emphases within the final collection. While liberal Protestants find "spiritual utility" in every New Testament book, they remain alert to the possibility that selection or modification of texts occurred in order to promote certain agendas that were not wholly in accord with core Christian values. For example, by adding books or interpolated passages that had a more socially conservative view of women within them, male leaders of the church may have acted outside the bounds of the Christian spirit, seeking to counteract the fundamentally egalitarian views of gender found within that core of New Testament books that, as my fellow contributors rightly note, did enjoy early and widespread recognition as authoritative.

This brings us to an implicit "canon within the canon." The Pastorals, for instance, are more socially conservative than Paul's principal letters; Paul is more socially conservative than the Gospels. By "more socially conservative," I mean that they are more supportive of the status quo of the society around Christianity, which at that time was hierarchical, patriarchal, ageist, sexist, and classist. Jesus verbally attacks and rejects this state of the world as Satanic, and clearly instructs his followers (for example, in the Sermon on the Mount) to form communities that break with these characteristics, as a way of anticipating the coming kingdom of God. Liberal Protestants affirm Jesus as he is found in the Gospels as the highest authority within the canon, from the vantage point of which one may find other scriptural passages deficient in their full grasp of the gospel ethos. On behalf of the Catholic tradition, Boxall adopts a similar "canon within the canon" centered on the Gospels, since they provide accounts of the life and teachings of Christ, which have preeminence in shaping Christian belief and practice.

A religious community is perfectly entitled, furthermore, to interpret its own sacred Scripture in any fashion it chooses to legitimate. It is under no obligation to treat the text literally or to allow linguistic or historical insights into its meaning to shape the text's interpretation. It can assume that its Scriptures speak with one voice, despite any surface differences, and that the teachings they contain stand in perfect harmony with one another, despite passages that initially seem contradictory. The community can assert that what it teaches is identical to what these Scriptures say and can employ any erudite and clever technique to discover those teachings within them.

That said, religious communities survive and thrive by being persuasive to people whose lives extend beyond the walls of the church, and who engage with language and meaning in other settings where ordinary, secular understandings of grammar and syntax are expected. Debates over the proper interpretation to be applied to the books of the New Testament, therefore, center around how much "scripture" operates with its own unique rules of meaning, distinct from those of ordinary speech. Both Nienhuis speaking for progressive evangelicals and Parsenios speaking for Orthodox Christians advocate for the idea that Scripture must be interpreted primarily from itself, under the assumption that it speaks with one voice. Any apparent contradiction must be dissolved into harmony; any ambiguity of meaning in one book must be resolved by the interpretation that matches the meaning of the other books. As Nienhuis puts it,

> The ultimate reception of these books into a larger canonical whole provided them with a *new* authoritative setting, one that displaced the social world of author and first readers in favor of the literary setting of the biblical canon. Thus, a more theological understanding of canonization will address the historical significance and hermeneutical implications of a text's ultimate placement within the New Testament canon rather than focusing solely on its historical point of origin.

There are both opportunities and dangers in this view.

On the opportunities side, Nienhuis' position affirms the idea of a "canon within the canon" by which any isolated deficiencies in specific passages may be rectified. The canonical complementarity of the books of the New Testament means, as Nienhuis explains, that "the pressure is off for any text to be immaculate"; "texts may include material that is questionable . . . or offensive . . . or unjust . . . or uncouth," but they are counterweighted by neighboring texts in the Bible. Nienhuis attributes this coordination of meaning among the Scriptures to the Spirit, which acts as a kind of conductor that brings together human compositions in an orchestration that is the proper locus of scriptural authority and meaning. Liberal Protestants would generally agree with Nienhuis, while perhaps tending to speak in more "naturalized" terms of the community finding "spiritual utility" in the complementarity of imperfect human works, whose blended voices capture the spirit of the movement better than any individual voice can. This is something discerned and acted upon by the community, and that is where the "spirit" operates.

On the dangers side, Nienhuis' devaluing of what he considers "a myopic focus on a text's point of composition and a reconstruction of the meaning derived from its first readers" runs the risk of decontextualized interpretations and proof-texting. After all, the actual words of the New Testament are not transmitted by the Spirit; they are written originally in Greek, transmitted in manuscripts, and translated into the languages through which modern Christians access their meaning. None of the contributors in this volume represent communities that approve of an interpretive free-for-all. The actual words of the text must be the starting point for the meaning of the Bible. It is perfectly correct to say that comparison of what one book of the New Testament says to what is said in another offers possible clarification, since both texts stem from the same language, time, and community of discourse. But why stop there? If comparison to other contemporaneous literature within the New Testament aids interpretation, why not comparison to an even broader set of literature from the same language and time—both within the canon and without, both from within the Christian movement and from outside of it? The New Testament authors did not invent a new language; they spoke the language of the surrounding culture and chose their expression to be understood and persuasive. As modern readers, we must be prepared for the possibility that we are misunderstanding a biblical text, and have perhaps misunderstood it for centuries, because we have been missing part of the context in which it was originally composed. If we truly value the "apostolic" character of the books of the New Testament, we should welcome new insights from the study of ancient language and culture that help us to understand their message in the way those authors intended.

All the contributors to this volume would certainly agree with Parsenios that it is important to find the common spirit, values, and worldview shared among the writings of the New Testament and among the books of the Bible as a whole. That is precisely the "spiritual utility" of having a Scripture in the first place, an anthology of foundational texts whose complementary voices collectively display the common spirit of the Christian religion. But it is asking too much to expect modern readers (who, after all, can *read*) to reduce all the distinct voices and perspectives within the Bible to an amorphous mass of sameness. The richness of the Bible rests in these differences. Modern people cannot be expected to accept the kind of contortions by which earlier theologians tried to explain away the differences between individual books of the Bible in even basic statements of fact. Most importantly, the Bible does not ask for this help. It does not insist on its own sameness or request that we avert our gaze from its tensions. The spirit behind the writings of Scripture, however we think of it, has trusted itself to the minds of the individual authors and the conditions that shaped their experience and expression. The church, in gathering these writings together, has likewise trusted in the strength of dialogue rather than monologue. *Four* Gospels, not one; the authority of Paul *and* the authority of James. If modern Christians are not to silence the spirit, then they must discern it between and among the many voices collected into the one Scripture.

RESPONSE OF
IAN BOXALL

I am grateful to my four colleagues, not only for the thought-fulness and insight provided by their respective contributions, but also for their ecumenical sensitivity in avoiding traditional polemical language which might risk obscuring the profound degree of agreement between different traditions. In terms of broad consensus, two issues in particular stand out, which I note here before turning to the individual contributions.

First, there is a broad agreement that the historical task of describing the process whereby the New Testament canon emerged is complex. Despite a shared recognition of the limited and fragmentary nature of the evidence, however, there is also a consensus that at least a partial reconstruction of that process is possible. Inevitably, there is some disagreement in the details, the significance of particular moments in the "canonization" process, and the authority to be accorded the New Testament canon in the contemporary church.

A second common motif is a recognition, already acknowl-edged in the secondary literature, that differing terminologi-cal definitions shape the terms of the debate. Is "canon" to be used in its original sense of a rule or measuring rod? Or does it describe a normative or authoritative list of books, or even the books themselves? Appreciating how an author is using the term is an important first step in understanding what they are seeking to affirm or deny and can help avoid misunderstanding or misrepresentation.

My own contribution, therefore, meshes in significant ways with aspects of perspectives offered in the other chapters. My particular emphases include the following: a concept of the canon which identifies specific books as normative for the church's life and worship, the end result of a lengthy process viewed as a Spirit-guided communal discernment; an explication of what the Council of Trent's decree means for Catholics, including its key phrase "with all their parts"; an appreciation of the dialogical character of the canon, which does not obscure the different canonical voices, nor the light shed by historical criticism on the interpretation of specific texts; an appreciation, nonetheless, of the canonical priority given to the fourfold Gospel and how its pattern of Christ's life, death, and resurrection functions as a hermeneutical lens through which to read other canonical texts. With that in mind, I now turn to my responses to the other four chapters.

Response to Darian Lockett

Lockett's contribution is nicely nuanced in its appreciation of how the definition of "canon" and "canonization" shapes the terms of the debate and in its recognition of the challenges involved in describing the history of the canon's formation. In doing so, Lockett helpfully summarizes the three main positions regarding the origins of the New Testament canon in the modern scholarly debate (Zahn, Harnack, Sundberg) and demonstrates that these essentially disagree, not over the surviving evidence, but the interpretation of that evidence and appropriate terminology for doing so. He also clearly articulates what are in his view the three distinctive elements of a conservative evangelical perspective: (1) an early dating of the New Testament canon; (2) the church's role as recognizing textual authority rather than creating it; and (3) the importance, both historical and hermeneutical, of authorial intention. I will address each of these in turn.

The first two elements could be points of convergence between a conservative evangelical and a Roman Catholic perspective, though these both invite further elaboration for clarity. To address the first: the historical evidence, fragmentary though it is, would seem to support the conclusion that the identification of specific books as normative, and suitable for public liturgical reading alongside Israel's Scriptures, begins early. But "begins" is the operative word, suggesting that the simple claim of an early dating for "the New Testament canon" requires some qualification. In fact, Lockett's own historical treatment of the canonization process is more nuanced. He highlights the production of what he calls mini-collections or "subcollections" emerging at different points in the long drawn-out process of canonization that culminates in widespread acceptance of twenty-seven New Testament texts. The relatively early emergence of a four-Gospel canon and the Pauline corpus are obvious examples, even if there remains legitimate disagreement on historical grounds as to precisely how early they emerged. Whether these "subcollections" should also be appropriately described as "sub-closures," however, is arguably undermined by evidence for different versions of an early *Corpus Paulinum*. "Sub-closure" may be more appropriate to later stages in the process. That being said, Lockett's encouragement to focus on the various stages in the process leading to a (relatively) universally accepted New Testament canon, rather than its final and official closure, opens up a fruitful conversation.

Lockett's second distinctive element, the question of the church's role in the canonical process, again invites further discussion and clarification. The fundamental claim that the church did not so much confer authority on the texts we call scriptural as recognize the authority they possess has considerable merit. The First Vatican Council virtually stated the same for Roman Catholics (*Dei Filius* II.2). The Scriptures are, in a profound sense, a divine gift to the church. Yet some qualification is needed. The church's act of discernment was surely not a negligible thing, nor, given the lengthy process of canonization, something achieved all at once. Morwenna Ludlow's historical study of the criteria employed in the formation of the New Testament canon proposes both *passive*—explaining why the church has what it already has—and more *active* criteria—making judgments especially about more disputed texts, such as some of the Catholic Epistles.[1] Allowing for the contribution of internal and even external human factors, at particular moments in the process or in response to specific movements, is not incompatible with a conviction of the canon as a divine gift. Nor need one posit a formal decree by bishops meeting in council, à la Nicaea or Trent, to acknowledge the role played by the people of God in discerning which texts were considered normative for church belief and praxis.

Lockett himself acknowledges the importance of considering the divine-human relationship, not only in the original composition of the books which now comprise the New Testament canon, but also in the canonization process itself. Indeed, I appreciate his opening of an important conversation, well worth pursuing, as to whether the emergence of the canon should be viewed as part of divine inspiration or categorized differently under the doctrine of providence. Where it may be complicated is in determining when the process of Scripture's "composition" ends. In the case of Mark's Gospel, for example, the so-called Longer Ending which includes the entire text of Mark 16:9–20 has become the de facto canonical ending even though it was likely composed during the second century when the canonization process was already underway.

I would like to have seen further elaboration of Lockett's third distinctive feature: the historical and hermeneutical importance of authorial intention. I took this to mean the intention of the human rather than the divine author. Yet this question does not appear to feature prominently in his chapter.

---

1.   Morwenna Ludlow, "'Criteria of Canonicity' and the Early Church," in *Die Einheit der Schrift und die Vielfalt des Kanons/The Unity of Scripture and the Diversity of the Canon*, eds. John Barton and Michael Wolter, BZNW 118 (Berlin: de Gruyter, 2003), 71.

Rather, his insightful discussion centers on the hermeneutical significance of the canonical arrangement of New Testament texts, as part of that "two-testament reality" which is the Christian Bible. The canonical priority of Matthew, or the separation of Luke from Acts, are two specific examples where the canon overrides conclusions concerning authorial intention. In other words, Lockett's discussion has the effect of relativizing authorial intention, with the canon providing a "recontextualization" of the individual texts, and original meanings, for a new ecclesial context. This was surprising, given the emphasis on its importance for a conservative evangelical perspective.

Response to David Nienhuis

Perhaps the most significant feature of Nienhuis' chapter is his perceptive observation concerning the ordering of the three questions proposed for this volume (the historical, the theological, and the hermeneutical). Such a sequence of questions, Nienhuis argues, essentially presupposes the orthodoxy of modern biblical criticism, especially historical criticism, which privileges historiography, the quest for origins. In other words, the order in which we address questions, no less than the questions themselves, inevitably shapes the answers we give. This is an important consideration. Nor is such a methodology any respecter of ecclesial boundaries: my own contribution to this volume, from a Roman Catholic perspective, is as indebted to this prioritization of the historical as are others. Therefore, Nienhuis' contribution left me wondering how, with hindsight, I would have written my own chapter differently.

Nienhuis' argument for a different starting-point, or at least one which avoids the alternatives—whether a blurring of *Historie* and *Geschichte*, a historical reductionism which regards theological commitments as a hurdle to the truth, or the formation of a new "scholar's canon"—does not reject the significance of history. What it advocates is a model for describing canon formation which keeps in some kind of balance the human, historical dimension "from below" with a coherent theological understanding of God's involvement "from above." In other words, what is needed is a "theology of canonization," and Nienhuis proposes an essentially Trinitarian model, which he argues has the potential to undercut some of the typical dualisms found in discussions of the New Testament canon (creator vs. creature, natural vs. supernatural), as well as attempts to prioritize either author, text, or reader.

In doing so, Nienhuis makes a compelling case for taking seriously the thoroughly theological nature and function of the New Testament from origins to canon closure. He underscores the importance of understanding the New Testament authors as theologians, as well as appreciating the theological concerns of the editors at every stage, down to the addition of titles to individual books, the emerging sequence of texts, and the subcollections within the canon. This means that the New Testament should be viewed less as a resource or a set of building blocks for theological construction, but rather as "an artifact, designed of God's providence, using human hands, for the purpose of transforming readers into holy hearers made fit for divine actions." This raises a similar question to that provoked by Lockett: whether the emergence of the canon is an aspect of divine inspiration or evidence for God's providential activity. Though Nienhuis uses the language of providence, one wonders whether his model better supports viewing the canon itself as integral to the inspiration of Scripture.

The theological appreciation of the original authors means that historical origins are not ignored. Yet it is true to say that Nienhuis seeks to shift the focus for understanding individual books to their historical placement within the canon and the hermeneutical implications of such a placement. This extends to relationships with other canonical subcollections. For example, the canonical Paul can only be read correctly in light of the Acts of the Apostles which precedes, framing him as a Jewish collaborator with the original apostles, and the "corrective" role of the Catholic Epistles which follow (e.g., James and Paul placed in a canonical conversation over faith and works). One might qualify this by noting that the canonical placement of certain texts has occasionally shifted, which is itself hermeneutically significant. Acts, for example, has not always served as the bridge between the Gospels and Epistles in canonical lists or actual collections (in Codex Sinaiticus, it comes after the *Corpus Paulinum*). Similarly, in the so-called "Eastern order" preserved in Athanasius and Codex Alexandrinus, the Catholic Epistles are placed before Paul, potentially giving these a more central role for New Testament theology.

Nienhuis articulates this canonical focus in terms of texts not being written as Scripture but becoming Scripture in their new relationship with other texts. This might require some qualification. In its favor, it gives space to the gradual discernment of the Christian community that certain texts are authoritative, literary instantiations of the (originally oral) apostolic testimony to God's self-revelation in Christ. It helps explain the presence within the canon of pastorally motivated correspondence to specific congregations, together with brief texts which might have been intended as covering letters (e.g., Philemon or 2 John). Presumably, phrasing this as a process of *becoming* Scripture is articulated "from below," without passing judgment on divine intention "from above." Yet even as an account of the human processes, the evidence is mixed. The Apocalypse of John presents itself as a work of prophecy and emulates Deuteronomy by its "integrity formula" (e.g., Rev. 1:3; 22:7, 18–19), whilst some recent scholars have argued that other New Testament authors were self-consciously writing Scripture.[2]

Despite these qualifications, I found Nienhuis' contribution particularly refreshing, thought-provoking, and challenging. One remaining question is how much theological or hermeneutical significance the historical point of origin should

---

2.   D. Moody Smith, "When Did the Gospels Become Scripture?" *JBL* 119 (2000): 3–20; Francis J. Moloney, "The Gospel of John as Scripture," *CBQ* 67 (2005): 454–68.

be accorded. In particular, is there any value in the (inevitably provisional) "scholar's canon," not as a replacement for the church's canon, but as a valuable dialogue partner? I think, for example, of the work of Luke Timothy Johnson, utterly committed to the hermeneutical importance of the canon, yet whose close literary and theological reading of Luke and Acts together illuminates the distinctive voice of Luke within the fourfold Gospel.[3]

Response to Jason BeDuhn

The essay by BeDuhn helpfully lays out the liberal Protestant view of the Bible with implications for the New Testament canon: an openness to the findings of historical criticism and a serious consideration of its implications for the contemporary church. The second part means that historical study of the New Testament texts is not directed toward narrowly historicist concerns. Rather, it aims at understanding the "inner logic" of the faith experience of the earliest Christians, to provoke an analogous experience for contemporary believers, whose social conditions and worldview will be very different from, for example, the first audiences of Paul or John. The underlying presumption is that the scriptural writings are "humanly composed records of the spiritual experiences and insights of key figures and communities within early Christianity." In other words, the locus of inspiration has shifted from the texts themselves to the communities and individuals which produced them.

BeDuhn's historical reconstruction of the emergence of the New Testament contributes helpfully to the debate, reminding us of the human processes involved in original composition and in canonization. In many ways, his account closely parallels the narrative sketchily recounted by me and our other colleagues: the emergence, some of them in parallel, of subgroups or what

---

3.   Luke Timothy Johnson, *The Gospel of Luke*, SP 3 (Collegeville, MN: Liturgical, 1991); Johnson, *The Acts of the Apostles*, SP 5 (Collegeville, MN: Liturgical, 1992).

BeDuhn suggestively calls "tentative proto-canons," with early prominence being accorded to some form of Gospel or Gospel collections and groups of Pauline letters. I would argue that he overemphasizes the influence of Constantine in the move toward a closed Christian canon, as well as the novelty of Irenaeus' appeal to a fourfold Gospel. But he acknowledges the ecclesial role in determining the content and shape of the New Testament. His suggestion that the Reformation gave new weight to the biblical canon as ultimate authority, after centuries of indeterminacy, is an intriguing one.

BeDuhn also draws attention to the importance of *use* as a major criterion in the process of canonization, rather than explicit appeal to inspiration (though the two are not necessarily mutually exclusive). This is surely right, historically speaking, as is his observation that widespread, universal use of these texts required an editorial process of depersonalization. But I would nuance his statement that in canonical discussions, early Christians were concerned with determining which texts should be read publicly. Much of the discussion seems rather to have focused on which texts were *already* being used. In other words, use and catholicity (or recognition of universal relevance) were closely related.

Two particular issues stand out to me from BeDuhn's chapter. First, there seems to be a tension, somewhat unresolved, between the view that historical-critical methods are essentially objective methods (particularly expressed in the earlier part of the chapter) and an appreciation of the subjective, perspectival character of all interpretation, historical criticism included (especially in the reference to advocacy readings in the final paragraph). In much of the discussion, the former point of view seems to dominate, at least implicitly. But doesn't this set up something of an artificial dichotomy between "objective" historical reconstruction and the "subjective," theology-driven canonical process?

The second issue is related: what are the criteria for assessing the "normativity" of texts, and authoritative voices for

the church, from a liberal Protestant perspective? BeDuhn
helpfully offers a survey of different approaches found among
liberal Protestants, including the quest for a "canon within
the canon." But in establishing a canonical "core" or hermeneutical principle, what should be the determinative criterion, and why? If the authority of specific passages is to be
judged according to "Christian ideals," how are those ideals
to be determined? Doesn't this approach essentially require a
modern version of the "rule of faith"? Or if priority is to be
given to Christ, why specifically to Jesus's teachings, or more
specifically those teachings deemed as authentic according to
the criteria of authenticity (which will yield widely divergent
results, as a comparison of the Jesus Seminar with the works
of scholars such as John Meier reveals)? Why not the pattern
of Christ's life, death, and resurrection as presented in the
canonical Gospels, rather than a focus on sayings? Or if there
is an inner-Pauline core, should historical questions of authorship be the determining factor, which seems to be narrower
than the appeal to "apostolicity" by the early church? Doesn't
grounding scriptural authority on historical judgments of
contemporary interpreters necessitate the remaking of the
canon for every generation?

One final observation: I appreciate BeDuhn's dialogical
approach to the New Testament canon and agree that this is an
integral part of how the canon functions. In his final paragraph,
he describes the New Testament Scriptures as "resources to be
mined, voices with which to enter into dialogue." However,
I wonder whether "voices" and "resources" are synonymous.
Resources are to be utilized or left on the shelf as the case may
be, but they lack personal identity. Voices, by contrast, initiate
conversations, as well as responding to, provoking, and challenging other voices. In that dialogical engagement and judg-
ment-making, which is the church's engagement with the various voices comprising the New Testament canon, how much
space should be given to those voices interrogating, provoking,
and challenging us?

Response to George Parsenios

Parsenios' chapter, from an Orthodox perspective, is an invaluable contribution to the discussion, framing the conversation through an eastern theological lens which helps articulate the issues differently than the western theological tradition (which, for all their differences, the Roman Catholic and various Protestant perspectives have in common). His resulting discussion therefore has several surprises and illuminating perspectives, even where he shares common ground with his western colleagues. I will briefly describe those which I found most insightful, before raising a couple of issues for further clarification.

Perhaps most surprising for westerners is Parsenios' observation that there is no discernable "moment" which marks the "end" of the canonical process for Orthodox Christians. Not even the 1672 Synod of Jerusalem, which clearly articulated the limits of both Old and New Testaments, has the status that the Council of Trent has for Catholics, given its local nature. This does not mean that there is significant debate about the parameters of the New Testament canon for Orthodox Christians. Agreement on this, however, was not the result of a specific formal decree of bishops meeting in council. Instead, Parsenios sees the formation of the New Testament canon as emerging from the practice of the church, a concept which he elaborates at considerable length. It is important for western Christians not to reduce this eastern claim to an appeal to specific practices or customs. Rather, it is an expression of the guiding presence of the Spirit within the church, a more pneumatological articulation akin to what Roman Catholics might call the *sensus fidei* or "sense of the faith," an instinctive sense of what is in accord with the faith of the church. The biblical books may be "given," but that "givenness" only emerges over time through ecclesial discernment, which is itself a gift of the Spirit (cf. John 16:13).

Hence the fact that some fuzziness around the edges of the canon persisted for several centuries is not problematic for Orthodox Christians. Parsenios' narrative of the historical process of canonization is unfazed by the lack of a universal consensus in the fourth century (notably the disagreements over the book of Revelation or the briefer Peshitta canon) or by the observation that there were no less than six different canonical lists still circulating in Byzantium as late as the tenth century. Intriguingly, he proposes an explanation for this in terms of the contrast between western and eastern canon law, the latter being reactive and corrective rather than prescriptive. Hence, unlike the veneration of icons or the use of the title *Theotokos* for Mary, the precise parameters of the New Testament canon did not, from an Orthodox perspective, rise to a level of urgency. This fact is intriguing, and it suggests that there is a longer story about the function of the canon within Orthodoxy waiting to be told.

Beyond this question regarding the lack of urgency in Orthodoxy to determine the shape of the New Testament canon, two further issues raised by Parsenios invite further clarification. The first concerns the relationship between the New Testament and other early Christian writings. In thinking about the special authority of the New Testament writings, Parsenios proposes three categories of noncanonical writings: those deemed heretical such as the *Gospel of Thomas*; those like the *Didache* and Apostolic Fathers, which fall under the umbrella of "holy tradition"; and those, like the *Protevangelium of James*, used judiciously because, in Vladimir Lossky's terms, "they may represent corrupted apostolic traditions."[4] I understand the first category, which is related to the canonical criterion of orthodoxy or the "rule of faith." But is the distinction between the second and third categories so clear-cut, given the more positive use of the *Protevangelium*, not only in iconography but also in popular devotion?

The second, more hermeneutical question concerns the unity of the biblical canon. That there is an underlying unity to the Scriptures is an axiom for Orthodoxy, as is the conviction

---

4.   Vladimir Lossky, *In the Image and Likeness of God* (Crestwood, NY: St. Vladimir's Seminary Press, 1974), 158.

that understanding that unity is the fruit of Christian asceticism. The diversity among the four Gospels and other scriptural texts, as well as the variety of interpretations of specific texts, is an indication of divine condescension, an accommodation to the circumstances of human recipients. Still, one would have hoped for a more explicit articulation of the nature of that unity and of the Orthodox view of the shape of New Testament canon in relation to it.

Concluding Thoughts

What is striking in the thoughtful contributions of my colleagues is the substantial amount of common ground concerning the New Testament canon, the complex process of its formation, and the significance of canonical order and shape. In my response, I have described insights gained from the other chapters, as well as raising questions for an ongoing conversation. In several key areas, therefore, my own contribution meshes well with aspects of others.

One obvious area of divergence concerns the hermeneutical significance of canonical shape, and especially how this relates to the interpretation of specific New Testament texts provided by historical criticism. Does the former override the latter or should the latter be allowed to critique the former? Or does the growing acknowledgment of the perspectival character of all interpretation, historical criticism included, complicate the issue? This provides plenty of raw material for an ongoing, respectful, but critical conversation.

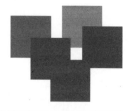

RESPONSE OF GEORGE L. PARSENIOS

William Wrede insisted that the canon of Scripture played no role in the interpretation of the books of the New Testament. He stated his position starkly and I will quote him here in order to introduce my response to the foregoing essays in this volume. Wrede wrote:

> No New Testament writing was born with the predicate "canonical" attached. The statement that a writing is canonical signifies in the first place only that it was pronounced canonical afterwards by the authorities of the second- to fourth-century church. . . . So anyone who accepts without question the idea of the canon places himself under the authority of the bishops and theologians of those centuries. Anyone who does not recognize their authority in other matters—and no Protestant theologian does—is being consistent if he questions it here, too.[1]

These comments articulate in a few lines how closely related are the historical, theological, and hermeneutical issues that each

---

1. William Wrede, "The Task and Methods of 'New Testament Theology,'" in *The Nature of New Testament Theology: The Contribution of William Wrede and Adolf Schlatter*, trans. and ed. Robert Morgan (London: SCM, 1973), 70–71.

essay in this volume has addressed. By accepting the twenty-seven-book New Testament, one inherently accepts the authority of the people who developed it and the image of Jesus they professed. Although Wrede expresses this position in a negative sense, the Orthodox Church holds the same position, expressed in a positive fashion. This inherent connection between the canon and the church presents a problem for anyone who affirms the authority of a canonical Scripture but denies the authority of ancient bishops. The essays in this volume present an array of perspectives on the dilemma that Wrede presents.

The liberal Protestant view expressed by BeDuhn, for example, follows Wrede in rejecting both the historical authority of the ancient church and the canon that these bishops formed. Because BeDuhn follows Wrede in this matter, he agrees with the following comment of Wrede as well:

> The first thing which must be required of anyone who wishes to engage scientifically in New Testament theology is . . . that he be capable of an interest in historical research. . . . He must be able to keep his own viewpoint, however precious, quite separate from the object of his research and hold it in suspense. . . . One might say that this account of New Testament theology entirely surrenders its specifically theological character. It is no longer treated any differently from any other branch of intellectual history. . . .[2]

BeDuhn says, for instance, that New Testament study for him is a fully historical endeavor. He is, thus, completely consistent on this core question, and my only response to the central issues of this volume is that his essay is the polar opposite of the Orthodox position on the canon. One other critique regarding the details of his historical reconstruction will occupy my comments below, and I will return to the work of BeDuhn below for further discussion. It is enough now to say about

---

2.   Wrede, "The Task and Methods," 70.

the primary concern of this volume that he follows Wrede in rejecting both the authority of the church and the canonical Scripture whose development the church oversaw.

Equally in tune with the position expressed by Wrede is the essay that articulates the Roman Catholic position written by Boxall, who has produced a clearly articulated, carefully wrought essay on the Roman Catholic view of the New Testament canon. Boxall accepts both the authority of the ancient church and church tradition, and the authority of the New Testament canon. He is in accord with Wrede in recognizing that the canon and the church go hand in hand.

Somewhat different are the essays by the evangelical scholars. The conservative evangelical essay written by Lockett becomes quickly stuck on the horns of the dilemma that Wrede identifies. While rejecting any authority for hierarchs or church figures of any kind, he seeks to ground the authority of the New Testament canon upon unclear foundations. He leaps back and forth between modern authors and the New Testament authors as if the intervening work of the ancient church did not occur, even as he insists theologically on the central place of the canon in New Testament interpretation. Because he does not allow church authorities to speak, it is easier for him to suggest that they did not act. His essay will receive further treatment in a moment.

The essay by Nienhuis, representing the progressive evangelical perspective, precisely addresses the problems that the essay by Lockett leaves unresolved. To my mind, Nienhuis has written the most theologically rich essay in this collection. It is certainly the essay that I read with the greatest profit. He articulated with enviable clarity and insight the way in which all New Testament interpretation, including the purpose and the role of the New Testament canon, must be understood against the backdrop of all of God's work in history. He may not completely accept the authority of ancient church officials but he endeavors to explain how their work cannot be separated from the fact of the canon and from the role that the canon plays in New Testament interpretation. Having provided this brief overview of the contents of this volume with reference to the insights of Wrede, I would like to look more closely at each essay individually, beginning with the essay of Lockett.

Response to Darian Lockett

Lockett offers a conservative evangelical perspective on the New Testament canon, and several of his core principles agree with the views on the New Testament held by the Orthodox Church. Chief among these points of agreement are the need to hold together the Old Testament and New Testament in a single Bible and the insistence that the canonical New Testament provides the single authorized view on the purpose and significance of Jesus. Texts like the *Gospel of Thomas* or other purported witnesses to early Christian faith are excluded. Despite these broad points of agreement with the Orthodox view of Scripture, the conservative evangelical position articulated by Lockett struggles because at every turn it seeks to give as little significance as possible to the work of the early church. Lockett, for example, insists that the authority and inspiration of the New Testament texts were "recognized (rather than created) by the church." For Lockett, to say that the church acted in any positive way would be to say that human motivations and concerns were involved in the production of the canon. He writes,

> As suggested above, the development of the New Testament canon was not due to an external force imposed by institutional pressures, nor was it motivated by political or apologetic concerns. . . . Put simply, the recognized authority and inspiration of the texts that were eventually collected into the New Testament was not something that was granted by the church, but was, rather, an intrinsic property of those texts that was recognized by the church.

This language is not problematic, *per se*, since it is founded on the principle that the books of the New Testament are to be given the highest regard, and that their selection was not merely a human political act that can be explained solely on the basis of human decisions. The texts themselves are sacred witnesses to the work of Christ. But where the position seems to become problematic is in statements such as this:

> Though the exact place and time cannot be fixed, the writings that eventually became the New Testament were "spontaneously" (Zahn's word) and "automatically" (Herman Bavinck's word) received as Scripture without any formal or institutional judgment needed.

How this spontaneous and automatic process unfolds is dealt with abstractly and never as a process in social history. If the church just "received" the Scripture, and did so spontaneously and automatically, why was the whole Scripture not received all at once as canonical, Old and New Testaments together? There is clearly a process unfolding in history, with some books being rejected and others accepted. Lockett even stresses the "recontextualization" of the scriptural books that is involved in the canonical process, but the process of recontextualization seems to be a completely disembodied effort. No real people performed any real work. The process unfolds at an abstract level in the history of ideas. But there was nothing spontaneous or automatic about the work of Bishop Serapion (described by Eusebius) when he discerns the character of the docetic *Gospel of Peter* (Eusebius, *Hist. eccl.* 6.12.2). Serapion had heard that the *Gospel of Peter* had caused debate and dissension in his flock, and he urged its reading because it was attributed to Peter the apostle. But after realizing upon further study that the book was inspired by a docetic view of Christ, he forbade its reading. This is an act of pastoral care, and the episode provides a glimpse into the process of canonical formation that is largely concealed by the vicissitudes of history. The Orthodox position would view the work of the Bishop Serapion as an extension of the work of Paul the apostle, who wrote, "I delivered to you as

of first importance what I also received" (1 Cor. 15:3). Transmitting the gospel was so important because there is no other
gospel (Gal. 1:6–9). The apostles and their disciples produced
the books of Scripture in order that people might "believe that
Jesus is the Christ, the Son of God," and that by believing they
might "have life in his name" (John 20:31). The same pastoral
and evangelical effort was continued in the work of later Christian shepherds, as they guided their own followers to true faith,
passed on what they had received, and avoided false teaching.
To the Orthodox, both efforts were guided by one and the
same Holy Spirit.

Even though he mentions the "divine-human" nature of
what he calls "canon-making," Lockett discusses it in a way
that makes it seem abstract and disembodied, and not something carried out by real people making real decisions, all the
while under the inspiration of the Holy Spirit.

The content of Lockett's argument is mirrored by the style
in which he argues. Lockett rarely and only in passing refers to
the various church fathers of the first centuries who engaged in
the process of discerning the canonical Scripture. He relies on
secondary literature, not primary texts, to discuss the history of
the early church. He refers regularly and often to the Bible and
regularly and often to modern scholars but passes over almost
completely the people who performed the work he is discussing. By ignoring their writing, he is the more able to ignore
their work. By not allowing them to speak, he can more easily
claim that they played no role in the process being explored at
the heart of this volume.

Response to David Nienhuis

Nienhuis eloquently confronts precisely this issue when he
offers a progressive evangelical position on the New Testament
canon, and it will be helpful now to turn to his fine essay. Nienhuis places his finger precisely on the problem when he says with
enviable clarity, "one must articulate how the human history
played out 'from below' *while* making a coherent theological

case for understanding God's involvement 'from above.'" First, this statement accords perfectly with what is called "synergy" in Orthodox theology. The term "synergy" expresses the belief that we are saved by the grace of God and by no human effort or initiative, and yet we must respond to that divine grace with faith and obedience. Second, it is as though Nienhuis is responding precisely to the issues raised by the essay of Lockett. While he avoids following Wrede down the path of viewing the evolution of the canon from a purely human level, he also seeks to avoid the mistake of viewing the process as a merely divine activity with no human synergy.

Further, Nienhuis seeks to understand how the development of the canon of Scripture fits into God's work of creating the world and saving it from death and corruption. In the words of Nienhuis, "what is needed is a theology of canonization, one that enables those who approach the Bible as Scripture to understand the Bible's past, present, and future within the much larger scope of God's salvific work." Nienhuis is fully in accord with Orthodox theology in all of this, especially when he adds that the New Testament canon not only provides an authoritative list of books but also the authoritative context within which those books are interpreted. He insists that the books can be misread if read in isolation when he says,

> We can guard against this dangerous tendency when we recognize that the Spirit did not bequeath to the church individual "Scriptures" to be treated in isolation or mixed and matched at our pleasure, because they are not in fact Scripture on their own: the proto–New Testament texts were not *written* as Scripture *per se* but *became* Scripture as they were gathered together into fruitful relationships with other texts. This process of Scripture's becoming took place over generations of use, as churches worked with texts, under the tutelage of God's Spirit, in a variety of configurations, until a particular set of writings in a particular sequence slowly emerged which proved over time to be the arrangement that produced the greatest utility in

the Spirit's work of training God's people in righteousness and equipping them for good works.

Nienhuis develops this further when he writes,

> As the church spread and grew and diversified, authoritative confessional elements developed organically alongside the recognition of authoritative scriptural texts, not to displace them but to provide believers with a set of basic agreements about Scripture's message and import. These confessional elements, often collectively called "the Rule of Faith," developed as an analogy of the canon of Scripture to function as a kind of interpretive lens—in the form of creed and doctrine and song and sacrament—through which the unity of Scripture's message might be profitably communicated to God's people.

From an Orthodox perspective, this is all beautifully articulated. The Orthodox, however, would say this differently in some places and would augment it in others. For instance, the life of the church, which Nienhuis here summarizes as "creed and doctrine and song and sacrament," is not solely designed as an interpretive lens for Scripture. The life of the church is designed to bring one into living communion with the Living God. Creed and doctrine and song and sacrament are tools to lead us to the God whom Scripture describes. But these tools are not quite so optional or secondary as Nienhuis' presentation suggests. The sacraments of the Christian life and the role of things like holy icons in the life of faith are not helpful additions to our faith but essential elements of it. Chronologically speaking, these sacred tools even have a priority over the canonical Scriptures. The sacraments were drawing people into communion with God even as the texts of the New Testament were being written and as they were later being assembled into a canon. The ascetical and sacramental life of the Church, then, is not so much an interpretive lens for Scripture as it is the means by which we are united to the God whom Scripture proclaims.

Nienhuis centers his discussion of the New Testament on the work of the Triune God in history and sees the development of a New Testament canon as an essential element in God's work. He articulates this position with theological precision and in a way that is convicting and inspiring. I read this essay with great profit. To the extent that he articulates this position so well, there is little to criticize from an Orthodox perspective. The Orthodox position would only augment what Nienhuis says by elaborating, sometimes in fuller ways and sometimes in different ways, how the New Testament canon relates to the ascetical, liturgical, and sacramental aspects of God's work in history.

Response to Jason BeDuhn

The liberal Protestant view has been enthusiastically articulated in this volume by BeDuhn. Because BeDuhn is the author most aligned with Wrede in the foregoing volume, he is simultaneously the author who is least in accord with the Orthodox approach to the canon. Like Wrede, he views not only the development of the New Testament canon but also the original production of the New Testament texts themselves as artifacts to be studied and understood from a strictly historical perspective. Because the decisions about exclusion or inclusion in the canon were strictly human decisions, other people living later can make different decisions about what texts are most valuable for the study of early Christianity. BeDuhn is consistent in this point even up to the point of saying that texts long excluded from canonical Christian Scripture, like the *Gospel of Thomas*, can be included in Christian worship and theological reflection. In all of this, he is thoroughly consistent with his core belief that critical history, and not theology, is the lens through which to view the production of the New Testament documents and their inclusion in the New Testament canon.

My critique of BeDuhn comes from a closer look at the details of his historical reconstruction. He seems invested in the idea that early Christianity from the beginning had no theological center, and this lack of a theological center in the beginning justifies the liberal Protestant insistence that there need be no theological center today. His historical survey of the evolution of the canon seems designed to serve this effort. He writes,

> The abundant signs of slowness, resistance, and indetermi-
> nacy in defining the canon in earlier eras serves as a caution
> against anachronistic views of the role of the New Testament
> at the historical foundations of Christianity. Consequently, the
> authority of the writings of the New Testament may come to be
> seen in a different light, inviting interpretive stances that allow
> modern readers to engage them in a more dialogic manner.

In the service of this effort, he argues for the social location of early Christian epistolography which is both incomplete and incorrect, and which seems to support the overall theme of his essay, so it needs to be addressed. BeDuhn defines and explains the importance of letters in ancient Christianity by comparison with the use of letters in ancient voluntary associations. This is an impoverished way to view the social location of early Christian epistolography. BeDuhn writes,

> Unlike the easily understandable place of Gospel narratives and
> apocalypses among early Christian writings, the prominent
> place of letters ("epistles") in the New Testament canon requires
> further explanation as nothing in prior Jewish tradition prepares
> the ground for this genre of Scripture. Instead, we must look to
> the practices of Greco-Roman associations and organizations,
> and the key role that correspondence played in their formation
> and operation.

This is both true and profoundly not true. It is obviously true that no analogy exists in the Scriptures of Israel for explaining the epistolary impulse in early Christianity, but it is simply wrong to say that early Christian epistolography is most completely understood by comparing it with the use of letters in voluntary associations. BeDuhn supports this claim by citing a volume edited by Kloppenborg et al. on voluntary associations, and that volume contains useful comparative material, to be sure. But voluntary associations are only one of the social institutions that provide comparative material for understanding early Christian communities, and they are hardly the primary one, especially when it comes to letter writing.[3] Philosophical schools are a much closer place to look for comparative material. As Stowers writes, "The kinds of letters that figure most prominently in early Christianity were types used especially by those who pursued the philosophical life."[4] About 100 pseudepigraphic Cynic epistles were circulated in the early Roman Empire as tools of defense and propaganda, and Epicurus used letters much earlier to shepherd his disciples. Diogenes Laertius (Book 10) cites three of Epicurus' letters (as well as letters of other philosophers in other places) and he lists various figures who slander Epicurus by writing pseudepigraphic letters in his name, so renowned was Epicurus as a letter writer (Diogenes Laertius 10.2–4). Seneca and other Pauline contemporaries cite these letters, often as they craft their own epistolary philosophical works. This list of epistolary philosophers could be extended considerably, as could the connections between early Christian letters and philosophical letters.[5]

This point requires stress because, in the first place, it is important to be correct when writing history, and, in the second place, the letters of voluntary associations are much

---

3. Meeks famously proposes four social groups most useful for understanding the social location of early Christian groups, in which he includes the household, synagogues, voluntary associations, and philosophical/rhetorical schools. See Wayne A. Meeks, *The First Urban Christians*, rev. ed. (New Haven, CT: Yale University Press, 2003), 75–84. Each has arguments "for" and "against" when it comes to explaining early Christianity's shape in the Roman world.

4. Stanley Stowers, *Letter Writing in Greco Roman Antiquity* (Philadelphia: Westminster John Knox, 2004), 36.

5. The list of primary and secondary literature is endless. It is enough to cite certain handbooks, as follows: David E. Aune, *The New Testament in Its Literary Environment* (Philadelphia: Westminster, 1987), 167–68; Abraham J. Malherbe, *Moral Exhortation: A Greco-Roman Sourcebook* (Philadelphia: Westminster, 1986), 79–85.

more casual and far less intellectually weighty documents than those of the philosophers of the Roman Empire. One should not overstate the connections that early Christian epistolography has with ancient philosophical letters, but BeDuhn severely understates—and actually ignores—these connections. Because BeDuhn argues that the canon should not have a central place in Christian theology, he seems to be cherry-picking the most suitable social comparison in the ancient environment to support this case. To argue that moral formation and philosophy is the social location of ancient letters has a different ring to it. If nothing else, it is a more serious intellectual ring. Other concerns arise from his essay, but the limits of space prevent further discussion.

Response to Ian Boxall

Finally, the essay by Ian Boxall on the Roman Catholic view of the canon is largely consistent with the Orthodox view, where the development of the canon is seen as an effort to preserve the apostolic faith. Boxall writes,

> Ultimately, then, Christianity is understood not as a religion of the book, but as a religion of a person. The climax of revelation is found in the person of Jesus Christ, his teaching and his story, especially his passion, death, and resurrection, proclaimed by the first witnesses and preserved in authoritative writings from the first generations.

This quotation also locates the development of a canonical scripture within the larger sweep of Christian life and union with God. If one is to commune correctly with God, one must have the correct image of God, founded on the proper interpretation of the proper books. This is fully consistent with the Orthodox position.

Finally, Boxall views the development of the canon as a gradual process of discernment in the life of the church, which is also a position shared by the Orthodox Church. Boxall writes,

> In summary, the formation of the New Testament canon as a widely accepted, closed list of authoritative and normative early Christian writings was a long and complex process of community discernment.

The largest difference, of course, from the Orthodox position is that the Roman Catholic Church codified the canonical body of Scripture at the Council of Trent in 1546. For the most part, however, the Orthodox and Catholic views on the development and significance of the canon are very similar.

Conclusion

By way of very brief conclusion, I will return to the comments of Wrede cited above. Wrede argued that the twenty-seven-book New Testament canon is a product of discernment by the church over time. Those who accept the authority of that canon, therefore, implicitly accept the authority of the bishops and church leaders who authorized the canon. Each of the essays in this collection wrestles with this insight of Wrede in various ways, and each of them can be read most clearly in the light of Wrede's insights.

CONCLUSION TO THIS DISCUSSION OF THE NEW TESTAMENT CANON

Stanley E. Porter and Benjamin P. Laird

The origin, formation, and recognition of the New Testament canon remains a topic of interest and diverse opinion. Our goal for this volume has been to expose interested readers to several of the dimensions of the question of the New Testament canon. As a result, we have used this multiple-view approach, so that confirmed proponents in the various positions represent their beliefs and then respond to the viewpoints of others. We believe that, by isolating the points of agreement and disagreement, one is able to formulate a better-informed understanding of how the canon came into being and to develop a more nuanced perspective on its theological and hermeneutical implications. We recognize that the five positions that we have included in this volume do not encompass all the possible viewpoints, and even within these viewpoints there is diversity of opinion. Nevertheless, we believe that these five viewpoints capture varied and important perspectives that are currently at play within the scholarly discussion. As we bring our discussion to a conclusion, we think it

helpful to examine and evaluate the notable points of agreement
and disagreement that have emerged throughout the volume.
Our hope is that the dialogue contained in this volume will elicit
among our readers interest in further research and thought. For
those inclined to explore in greater detail the historical questions
relating to the canon, the final section in this chapter provides a
survey of the primary historical sources for the study of the New
Testament's formation, development, and early reception.

Common Ground in Discussion of the New Testament Canon

Since the 1980s there has been, as already adumbrated in
the introduction, a continual interest in studies of the New
Testament canon, far too many to note here. We trust that
this volume, and in particular the major essays within it, will
become a part of this continuing discussion and contribute
to it. Worth noting here instead—especially in relation to the
five essays in this volume—are the elements commonly agreed
upon within study of the New Testament canon. It is unnecessary to treat in detail these points of agreement, because they
are more than adequately noted by our contributors, but they
are nevertheless worth mentioning because it is in the agreement of these details that several of the challenges related to the
study of canon become evident.

All five of the positions presented within this volume—
so far as they represent the range of possible opinions on the
formation of the New Testament canon—agree that there is
a New Testament canon that consists of twenty-seven books.
The process of recognition may or may not have been formally
established, but so far as these ecclesial traditions are concerned,
there is a New Testament canon. Some of the books within this
canon may have taken longer amounts of time to become recognized, and they have been variously ordered at times within the
tradition of their transmission, based upon a range of possible
factors. It would also seem highly likely that these books were
first grouped together into sub-corpora or subcollections before

they came to be joined together as what we now recognize as the canon of authoritative writings. We may not know precisely how and when they emerged or even what constituted each of these sub-corpora during the earliest period of their transmission, but they seem to have existed and been part of the canonical formation process. The process by which the recognition of this canon occurred involves a variety of factors. The range of posited variables includes historical, theological, and circumstantial factors, with much of the discussion involving debate over the relationship between human and divine agency. All are agreed that human involvement occurred at some stage in the process, although the amount and type of human involvement is debated. Finally, all the positions represented here agree that the New Testament canon has some form of abiding and normative value and function within the Christian church, although the source and type of this normativity often varies from tradition to tradition.

One might legitimately think that such an amount of agreement is sufficient to render the question of canon relatively settled. However, the essays in this volume reveal that this is far from the case. The five positions align themselves with each other in various ways depending upon the issue at hand. The kinds of alliances and disjunctions that are formed among our contributors to this volume are well laid out in their major essays and in their responses. One is probably not too surprised to see that the Roman Catholic and Orthodox positions have numerous similarities, even if one position can point to a date of canonical finality while the other cannot. Nevertheless, one might be surprised to see that the conservative evangelical position and the progressive evangelical position have several major differences in approach and orientation. As a result, the conservative evangelical position has some striking similarities with the liberal Protestant view concerning the historical process, while the progressive evangelical view has several similarities with the Roman Catholic and Orthodox positions regarding the role and influence of tradition. We do not need to recount these points of overlap and distinction in more detail here when fuller statements by the various proponents are available and worth extended consideration.

There is merit in dwelling upon the points of agreement among the proponents within this volume because there is much that unites their positions despite their ostensive disagreement. However, there are also points of disagreement that we should note.

Points of Contention

As the concluding statements to several of the responses indicate, the various proponents have benefited from reading the proposals of their colleagues as they have attempted to refine their own positions. Nevertheless, despite the amount of agreement, there remain points of unresolved contention. Although various positional alliances may have been formed, at the end of the day each of the views retains its distinctive integrity, not because one view is like the other but because each view remains distinct and is not exactly like any other. We think that it is not just interesting but important to note some of the issues at stake regarding the origin, formation, and acceptance of the canon that remain points of disagreement.

One of the recent advances in textual studies is a more nuanced understanding of the very notion of text. We traditionally think of a text as a stable entity of some length, consisting of words and usually, though not always, written rather than spoken. There is a sense in which such an entity, what we call a text, is a fixed object and is therefore subject to evident and agreed upon means of interpretation. The literary scholar Stanley Fish tells the story of how an interested student once asked a fellow professor, "Is there a text in this class?"[1] Those familiar with Fish's book by this name will know that the question was anything but a simple one. The professor assumed the

---

1.   Stanley Fish, *Is There a Text in This Class? The Authority of Interpretive Communities* (Cambridge, MA: Harvard University Press, 1980), 305.

student's question related to a specific printed text, in which case one could go to the bookstore and purchase it, whether it was a collection of poems or a play by Shakespeare. The student, however, had taken a course from Fish. For Fish, the problem was far more complex, because it raised questions about the very nature of a text. Rather than focusing upon its mere physical properties, he was concerned with a host of other debatable characteristics regarding its status, interpretation, meaning, and the like. In his book on textuality the philosopher Jorge Gracia offers several different statements that reveal that, even in common parlance, we speak of a text in a variety of ways.[2] Sometimes we speak of a physical object, but we often speak of a variety of other things, including texts as conceptual entities, such as a novel or a logical or grammatical argument.

The result of such semantic ambiguity is the definition of a variety of texts. In relation to New Testament studies, we might well posit that there are a variety of texts that we study, even if we study one New Testament. These texts may be identified as the text-critical text, philological text, literary text, linguistic text, phenomenological text, ontological text, and theological text. Although some of these texts may overlap, each of them is recognizably and identifiably different. A text-critical text is the text used in textual criticism, in which textual data are mined for variant readings of an idealized or notional text. A philological text is the expression also of an idealized text but one mined not for text-critical data but for appreciation of the best representation of the literary and linguistic accomplishments

---

2.   Jorge J. E. Gracia, *A Theory of Textuality: The Logic and Epistemology* (Albany: SUNY Press, 1995), xx. See also John Mowitt, *Text: The Genealogy of an Antidisciplinary Object* (Durham, NC: Duke University Press, 1992), who also helps inform this discussion. Previous exploration of the topic of textuality in New Testament studies occurs in Stanley E. Porter, "Text as Artifact: An Introduction," in *Scribes and Their Remains*, eds. Craig A. Evans and Jeremiah J. Johnston, LSTS 94 (London: T&T Clark, 2020), 1–14; Porter, "What Is a Text? The Linguistic Turn and Its Implications for New Testament Studies," in *Studies on the Intersection of Text, Paratext, and Reception: A Festschrift in Honor of Charles E. Hill*, eds. Gregory R. Lanier and J. Nicholas Reid, TENT 15 (Leiden: Brill, 2021), 175–98.

of a writer. A literary text is much like a philological text, but it is not necessarily valued for its philological contribution but for its literary features as a work such as a novel or drama. A phenomenological text is a form of philosophical and literary text such as was conceived by the Roman Formalists and later the New Critics, characterized by attention to the thing itself. An ontological text is a philosophical text construed according to the individual philosophical school of thought concerned with questions of being. Finally, a theological text is a text concerned with addressing and answering questions of a particular sort regarding the divine. These all-too-brief definitions of at least some categories of texts make clear that in fact there is a wide variety of texts. The definitions provided above tend to move from the more concrete to the more abstract concerns of the texts involved, as we move from text-critical to theological texts, with others mediating this cline along the way. The closer these texts are to each other along the cline, the more the questions that one asks of each text begin to overlap. However, the further these texts are from each other along the cline, the more distinct are the questions that one asks of each. The kinds of questions one asks of a text-critical text, for example, are significantly different from those asked of an ontological or theological text, and to confuse the two is probably to engage in what the philosopher Gilbert Ryle calls a "category mistake."[3]

Having observed that there are various types of text, we may also observe that a text may not just have its own properties, according to which it is created by and then used within various intellectual disciplines, but texts may themselves move among these categories, as these categories are not hard and fast divisions but ways of addressing the question of what constitutes a text. As a result, the kinds of texts that are examined within textual criticism thereby become text-critical texts, and those that are examined by literary scholars become literary texts, etc. These characterizations and functional uses of

---

3.   Gilbert Ryle, *The Concept of Mind* (London: Hutchinson's, 1949), esp. 15–23.

the texts are not determined based upon intrinsic properties of the texts so much as on their functional properties, that is, the functions that these texts perform within the academic discipline (or other venue) in which they are used. Consequently, different sets of questions are asked of these texts because of how they function within these disciplines. The kinds of questions that are asked of a text by a philologian—by which this text functions as a philological text—concern such things as the characteristics of the language of the text, especially with attention to it as preserving the best examples of instances of this kind of language. These kinds of questions vary significantly from the questions that might be asked of a phenomenological text, in which major interests are the constituency and being-ness of the text. A text-critical text is used in a very different way than is a theological text, or at least it should be.

Texts can be asked a wide variety of questions, but the nature of the discipline involved and one's view of a text will affect the kinds of questions asked. The issue becomes a problem when one type of text is treated as if it were a different kind of text. For example, one would be committing a form of category mistake if one were asking theological questions of a historical text. One of the issues that this book on canon has uncovered is that there is a fundamental difference of opinion on the nature of the New Testament, that is, what kind of text it is. There are implicit (and sometimes explicit) differences of opinion held by our contributors as to the nature of the text of the New Testament and the individual texts that are identified within it. If we use this framework to discuss the points of disagreement among our contributors, we can account not only for much of their agreement but possibly also for much of their abiding disagreement. One of the reasons that they disagree is that they have different views of text, and because of this they are asking different questions of the text and expecting different answers. For our discussion of canon, we may utilize any number of different types of text. For the sake of convenience in this conclusion, we may posit that there are three types of text of relevance. The first is theological texts, and this is a category that is clearly operative in our discussion of the canon in this volume. However, we may also posit that there are historical texts and canonical texts. A historical text is a text that is defined by its purporting to represent and depict a historical process and it is mostly used by those interested in questions of historical reconstruction and determining historical knowledge. A canonical text is a text that is defined as a text recognized for being authoritative within its respective sphere of functionality. We may use these three categories—while also acknowledging that others may be pertinent as well, which only adds to the complexity of our discussion—as a means of examining the contributions to this volume and the remaining areas of disagreement.

We will treat the five positions in the order in which they are presented within the volume. Before we do so, it will be helpful to preface our recapitulation and assessment by noting that each of the contributors has attempted to define the means by which we are able to speak about the origins and development of a defined canonical text known today as the New Testament. Each contributor agrees that there is in fact a canonical collection of New Testament writings and has not disputed that their respective tradition accepts such a text. Even the liberal Protestant view, so far as it speaks for a secular historical viewpoint, recognizes that the Christian church at some point came to accept a canonical text. This is, in fact, the presumption of this volume that provides its rationale. Each of the major traditions represented in this volume affirms that there is a canonical New Testament text, even though there are a variety of opinions on fundamental matters such as the impetus for the canon's creation, the process that led to its formation, the basis of its authority, its role in the life of the church, and the manner in which the structure and content of the canon is to inform the manner in which we interpret the individual writings.

At this point, however, there is significant disagreement over a variety of factors. This disagreement includes the date at which such a canonical text can be said to exist, how this recognition occurred, and the implications of these conclusions. Here the range of disagreement is large. The conservative evangelical view posits the individual books that make up such a canon as having from the outset what would eventuate in canonical status, and thus such a position places the canonical text at the beginning of the process of canonical formation. The result is that canonical formation becomes a process of discovery and discernment of what is already the case, canonical authentication and recognition, rather than a process of emergence and development and then recognition. At the opposite end, the Orthodox view is that there is a canonical text even if one cannot point to any specific date, event, or act that indicates when this process occurred. The canon is an implicit recognition by church tradition. The other views have varying temporal locations along the continuum of the last two millennia. All the positions, apart possibly from the conservative evangelical view, believe that the process by which the canonical text came to be was one that involved noncanonical criteria, for the most part revolving around a variety of historical factors within the life of the Christian church. In other words, most of the positions, and even the conservative evangelical view in that it sees the two as in harmony, argue that one can arrive at a canonical text by means of discussing it as a historical text.

This approach to texts raises a question that we will return to below, and that is what the relationship is between a historical text and a canonical text. It is not self-evident that one can be equated with the other, without making a category mistake. This also reveals the question of what place a theological text has in relationship to this tension between a historical and a canonical text, when appeal is frequently made to historical criteria, such as questions of authorship, dates of composition, generic questions, tensions within the early church, competing theologies, subcollections of texts, and the emergence of various witnesses to formation of groups or a group of authoritative texts.

Finally, we see that all the positions in this volume, with most reservations held perhaps by the liberal Protestant view so far as it represents secular historians, accept that a canonical text provides the basis for some form of ecclesial normativity within the church. In that sense, the canonical text in effect becomes a theological text in so far as it reflects, even in an abstract and interpreted way, the theological norms or at least the norming point for the ecclesial tradition concerned. In some of the discussions, this authority seems to be placed upon or recognized within the canonical text regardless of the historical processes that accompanied such recognition. In other words, regardless of the historical process, the canonical text appears to exercise a role within the ecclesial tradition that is in some ways distinct from its other textual functions.

When we turn to the individual traditions, we see some further points of potential tension and disagreement. The conservative evangelical position seems to equate a historical, theological, and canonical text, or at least an incipient canonical text, as coterminous with the authorial text, that is, the text as authored by the biblical writer. This position is taken by no other within the five views under discussion, where, as we shall discuss below, there is at least some distinction or separation among these kinds of texts. Several of these positions criticize the conservative evangelical view for this very reason. The result for this position is that the canonical text is associated with a particular view of historicity and theological relevance that the other positions do not necessarily share, but that is necessarily insisted upon by this position.

The progressive evangelical position, despite its ostensibly having much in common with the conservative viewpoint, takes a significantly different approach to the matter of text. The progressive evangelical position treats the New Testament as a historical text but subordinates this estimation and the results of it to its treatment as a theological text that is then equated with the canonical text. The separation of history and theology and canon in the progressive evangelical approach is very similar to the canonical approach of Brevard Childs, who is invoked in this discussion.[4] One of the major observations we might make about Childs' approach is that he recognizes the Bible, both Old and New Testaments, as both a historical text and a canonical and theological text, but he also does not fully explore the implications of this bifurcation, so that the answers to historical questions are seen to be separate from canonical issues. Thus, for the progressive evangelical position, the treatment of the Bible as a historical text does not seriously impinge upon its being a canonical text, one that seems to have become canonical relatively early in church history, with direct implications therefore as a theological text. As we shall see, in some ways this makes the progressive evangelical position very similar to the Roman Catholic and the Orthodox positions. However, in many respects because of their postponement of recognition of a canonical text, the Roman Catholic and the Orthodox positions are more fully able to integrate the conclusions to investigation of the New Testament as a historical text regarding such issues as authorship, date, and origins.

The Roman Catholic position is less concerned with the New Testament as a historical text in relation to its being a canonical text, because of the importance of the Council of Trent that fixed the canonical status of the Bible. The Roman Catholic viewpoint is the only one within our discussion that can point to such a defining moment, in which historical text and canonical text converge at a singular point of decision that validates the already existing use and function of the New Testament as a theological text. The urgency of the canonical approach so prevalent in the progressive evangelical viewpoint is mitigated in the Roman Catholic position by means of the fact that the recognition of a canonical text in the sixteenth

---

4. Childs himself presents an interesting case of a scholar who began his career focused upon the historical text and then became more fully occupied with the canonical text. He wrote numerous works on how his canonical approach might influence interpretation, especially as envisioned within the canon. As examples, see Brevard S. Childs, *Introduction to the Old Testament as Scripture* (Philadelphia: Fortress, 1979); Childs, *The New Testament as Canon: An Introduction* (Valley Forge, PA: Trinity Press International, 1994 [1984]).

century avoids most of the historical issues raised in several of the other viewpoints.

The Orthodox Church position is, in many respects, like that of the Roman Catholic, but with two major distinctions. One of these is that the Orthodox Church never had its defining moment as did the Roman Catholic position with its Council of Trent. In that regard, the Orthodox position is like all the others in not having a fixed date for the New Testament becoming a canonical text. However, the Orthodox Church has a more overt and continuous recognition of the New Testament as a theological text, in that it has not just a traditional advocacy for its canonical text but a theological one in which the Holy Spirit has guided the process by which the historical text becomes a canonical text. The question of the relationship between the historical text and the canonical text and the theological text remains, even if the canonical and theological texts are ultimately triumphant.

The final position is the liberal Protestant viewpoint. The liberal Protestant viewpoint places its greatest emphasis upon the New Testament as a historical text. In fact, one might even wonder what the basis of the canonical text is in light of the New Testament as a historical text. The liberal Protestant viewpoint probably has the most malleable view of what constitutes a canonical text, as that text is the direct result of not just historical processes of the past but ongoing historical debate, to the point that one might well consider the canonical text itself a historical text that is subject to further historical discussion. Nevertheless, this does not prohibit the liberal Protestant perspective from also seeing the canonical text as a theological text. However, because of this view of the canonical text, one might wonder about the strength of the lines of connection between the canonical and theological texts and the resultant normativity of theological conclusions determined on that basis. In this regard, the liberal Protestant viewpoint is probably the most divergent from the other four traditions, in which the canonical text has a more historically based status and hence exercises a stronger regulative position as a theological text.

The Primary Historical Sources for the Study of the New Testament Canon

Now that we have suggested several areas of agreement and disagreement in the study of the New Testament canon, it is helpful to briefly survey the primary historical sources that provide insight into the canon's formation and early reception. While the study of the canon necessarily involves an array of theological and hermeneutical considerations, historical questions relating to the formation of the canon merit special attention given their complexity and fundamental nature. As noted above, our desire is that the issues explored throughout this volume will encourage readers to examine the formation of the New Testament in greater detail. To do this, of course, one must first become familiar with the basic types of historical evidence and what and how they contribute to our understanding of the canon's emergence. Some readers may wish to begin evaluating these sources for themselves in order to gain a better-informed perspective on various aspects of the canon's development. At the very least, a familiarity with the primary sources will take away some of the mystery concerning the types of evidence that often serves as the basis for modern theories on the canon's origin. Although space will not permit a full treatment of the many witnesses to the early state of the canon, we may conclude our volume with a brief treatment of three broad types of historical evidence pertaining to the canon: patristic writings, biblical manuscripts, and canonical lists.

Patristic Writings and the Study of the New Testament Canon

One of the most valuable witnesses to the early state of the canon is the extant writings of early Christian writers. Throughout the early centuries of the Christian era, a large body of writings was produced, most of which was composed in either Greek or Latin. This patristic literature, as it is often described, includes both a relatively small collection of late-first and early-second-century works known as the Apostolic

Fathers (e.g., *1* and *2 Clement*, the letters of Ignatius, the *Didache*, the *Epistle of Barnabas*, and the *Shepherd of Hermas*) and a large and diverse body of later Christian writings by a variety of authors—theological treatises, sermons, catechetical instruction, letters, apologetic works, and other types of literature. Many of these works were composed by prominent theologians and bishops in the early centuries of the church's existence (e.g., Clement of Alexandria, Origen, John Chrysostom, Augustine, and Jerome), though the authorship of several writings is disputed or unknown (e.g., *2 Clement*, the *Epistle of Barnabas*, and the *Epistle of Diognetus*).

In addition to what these writings reveal about the development of Christian doctrine and the challenges facing the early church, they also serve as a valuable witness to the early state of the canon. One of the more helpful features of these writings is the numerous references to the canonical texts. Several patristic writings contain a significant number of direct quotations, allusions, or paraphrases from one or more writings contained in the New Testament. This mere fact would indicate that the writings that came to be recognized as canonical were very popular during the early centuries of the Christian era and that they did not begin to be read only in subsequent centuries after some decisive event. Some of the canonical writings (e.g., James, 2 Peter, and 1–3 John) admittedly do not appear to have circulated as extensively as others, but, taken as a whole, the patristic authors demonstrate that the writings that now comprise the New Testament were highly revered and well known in early Christianity.

The patristic literature often provides invaluable insight into the literary world of early Christians and the role of the canonical writings in shaping the thought of early Christian writers. However, ascertaining what they reveal specifically about the early development of the New Testament can be a significant challenge for several reasons. First, for those who are not patristic scholars or church historians, it can be overwhelming to wade through large amounts of unfamiliar material (it is

admittedly difficult for everyone). Some may even find it difficult to access the relevant sources.[5] Fortunately, it has never
been more convenient to access patristic material. One of the
best sources for the study of the early writings of the Apostolic
Fathers is the single volume produced by Michael Holmes.
Now in its third edition, the volume contains helpful introductions to each writing, the original Greek text, and an English
translation.[6] Holmes includes notes throughout the text of each
writing, many of which indicate possible parallels between the
writing and a New Testament passage. In addition to Holmes'
volume, English translations of the Apostolic Fathers and a
number of later Christian writings can be accessed in the older
ten-volume set, *The Ante-Nicene Fathers (ANF)*[7] and the larger
series known as *The Nicene and Post-Nicene Fathers (NPNF)*,[8] the
latter of which is divided into two series. A more modern and
rapidly expanding series of English translations of Christian
literature is the series produced by the Catholic University of

5. For an introduction to the writings of the Apostolic Fathers, readers are
    encouraged to consult one or more of the following volumes: Wilhelm Pratscher,
    ed., *The Apostolic Fathers: An Introduction* (Waco, TX: Baylor University Press,
    2010); Clayton Jefford, ed., *The Apostolic Fathers and the New Testament* (Grand
    Rapids: Baker, 2006); Paul Foster, ed., *The Writings of the Apostolic Fathers* (London:
    T&T Clark, 2007). For a basic introduction to Christian writings through the
    fifth century, see Justo González, *A History of Early Christian Literature* (Louisville:
    Westminster John Knox, 2019).

6. Michael Holmes, ed., *The Apostolic Fathers: Greek Texts and English Translations*,
    3rd ed. (Grand Rapids: Baker, 2007). This volume is a further revision of and
    originally based upon J. B. Lightfoot, *The Apostolic Fathers*, ed. J. R. Harmer
    (London: Macmillan, 1891).

7. Alexander Roberts and James Donaldson, eds., *The Ante-Nicene Fathers:
    Translations of the Writings of the Fathers Down to A.D. 325*, 10 vols. (repr., Peabody,
    MA: Hendrickson, 2004). The series was originally published in 1886 by the
    Christian Literature Publishing Company. While the translations contained in
    these volumes are now quite dated, they remain valuable resources for the study
    of Christian literature.

8. Philip Schaff and Henry Wace, eds., *A Select Library of Nicene and Post-Nicene Fathers
    of the Christian Church,* 28 vols. (repr., Peabody, MA: Hendrickson, 2004). The
    original volumes were published between 1886–1889 by the Christian Literature
    Publishing Company. In addition to the printed volumes, both the *ANF* and
    NPNF series are freely accessible online through the website of the Christian
    Classics Ethereal Library.

America Press known as *The Fathers of the Church*. There are now well over 100 volumes in the series with additional works continuously being added.[9] Finally, *Patrologia Latina* (PL) and *Patrologia Graeca* (PG), two series containing a large body of early Christian writings in the original languages, were produced in the nineteenth century by the French cleric Jacques Paul Migne (although these are not considered critical editions for those doing scholarly research, for some authors they are still the only editions available). With the publication of such a large body of primary sources, there has never been so many accessible sources for the study of early Christian literature. Many of the extant writings can even be conveniently accessed on one or more internet websites.[10]

But with such a vast amount of existing early Christian literature, where is one to begin? With hundreds of translated works now available either in print or online, and with new works continuously being translated and published, the study of early Christian writings can certainly seem overwhelming. As it relates to the study of canon, it should be kept in mind that the most important writings are those that were composed during the first several centuries of the Christian era. Scholars continue to debate the state of the canon even into the fifth century and beyond, but there is widespread agreement that the canon was, for most intents and purposes, relatively settled and recognized by the late fourth century. Consequently, the patristic literature composed during the first four centuries or so of the Christian era remains the most relevant and valuable

---

9. *The Fathers of the Church*, 127 vols. (Washington, DC: Catholic University of America Press, 1947–present). Like the volumes in the *ANF* and *NPNF* series, the volumes in this series contain introductions to each writing and footnotes containing references to possible citations of or allusions to the New Testament.

10. Online websites containing the full text of patristic literature include Early Christian Writings (http://www.earlychristianwritings.com), Christian Classics Ethereal Library (https://ccel.org), and New Advent (https://www.newadvent. org). One must be cautious with use of websites, as they often contain only an English translation and are sometimes unclear as to the translation used (or original text if available).

sources for the study of the early state of the canon and the early reception of specific canonical writings.

Not all writings produced during the early centuries of the Christian era provide significant insight that is useful in establishing the development of the New Testament canon, of course, but several writings from this period offer valuable information regarding the early reception of the individual canonical works or the state of the canon considered as a whole.[11] On many occasions, writers quote extensively from one or more of the canonical writings or appeal to them as an authoritative source. At times they may even refer to them directly as Scripture or identify them as the work of a particular individual. Early writings such as *1* and *2 Clement*, for example, and the writings of notable figures such as Ignatius, Polycarp, Justin Martyr, Irenaeus, and Origen include multiple references to the New Testament writings and often treat these writings as authoritative Scripture.

As noted above, many of the published translations of these writings include footnotes that provide citations of possible references to the New Testament writings. The most effective means of locating the possible references to the canonical writings in early Christian writings, however, are electronic databases. One of the more helpful electronic tools is the *Thesaurus Linguae Graecae* (TLG).[12] Although it is limited to Greek literature, the database allows users to perform searches of a vast library of Greek works. Another helpful electronic resource is *BiblIndex*, an online searchable database of the content contained in the multivolume *Biblia Patristica*.[13]

One of the difficult challenges of dealing with patristic literature is ascertaining exactly where the canonical writings

---

11. For a helpful summary of the most notable patristic sources relevant to the study of the formation of the New Testament canon, see Lee Martin McDonald, "Appendix B: Primary Sources for the Study of the New Testament Canon," in *The Canon Debate*, eds. Lee Martin McDonald and James A. Sanders (Peabody, MA: Hendrickson, 2002), 583–84.

12. The *TLG* database may be accessed at http://stephanus.tlg.uci.edu.

13. The *BiblIndex* database may be accessed at https://www.biblindex.org/en.

are cited and what these possible references may reveal about the author's perception of a given work. In some cases, it is abundantly clear that the author is referring to a specific New Testament writing and that the writing is cited because it is viewed as an authoritative source. There may be a lengthy or unambiguous reference to a specific New Testament passage, for example, and the work may refer to the biblical writing by name, cite the author, or include a prefatory remark such as "according to the apostle . . .". On other occasions, however, it may not be entirely clear whether the work is directly quoting from a particular canonical writing or simply alluding or making passing reference to it. Discerning which of the canonical writings were familiar to early Christian writers and what these possible references reveal about the early state of the New Testament and the reception of individual works has received significant scholarly attention for over a century. This attention includes several doctoral dissertations and theses as well as several edited volumes and scholarly articles. The first major modern study to take up this subject was published in 1905 by the Oxford Society of Historical Theology.[14] More recently, Andrew Gregory and Christopher Tuckett have produced an updated study which, like the earlier Oxford study, identifies possible references to the canonical writings in the writings of the Apostolic Fathers and seeks to determine what these references may reveal about the early reception of the New Testament writings.[15] In addition to this volume, a number of studies have been published in recent decades that focus specifically on the reception of one writing of the New Testament or perhaps on a smaller body of writings such as the Gospels or the Pauline Epistles.[16]

---

14. Oxford Society of Historical Theology, *The New Testament in the Apostolic Fathers* (Oxford: Clarendon, 1905).

15. Andrew Gregory and Christopher Tuckett, eds., *The Reception of the New Testament in the Apostolic Fathers* (Oxford: Oxford University Press, 2005).

16. With regard to the Pauline Epistles, helpful studies include Jennifer Strawbridge, *The Pauline Effect: The Use of the Pauline Epistles by Early Christian Writers*, SBR

Biblical Manuscripts and the Study of the New Testament Canon

The second major type of witness to the early state of the New Testament canon is biblical manuscripts. This would include the manuscripts containing the Greek text of one or more of the New Testament writings and those that contain a translation of the Greek text into an ancient language such as Latin, Coptic, or Syriac. Over a span of some sixteen hundred years, a large body of handwritten copies of the New Testament was produced, many of which have survived. Scholars have scrutinized these manuscripts for insight useful in discerning the earliest distinguishable form of the text of the New Testament and the state of the text during various periods of its transmission. While the importance of the manuscripts for the discipline known as textual criticism is widely recognized, the value they serve for the study of canon has often been overlooked. These witnesses often indicate which works circulated as Scripture during a particular time and in a particular place, offer insight regarding the development and circulation of the various subcollections of canonical writings (e.g., the Gospels or Pauline Epistles), and reveal how the canonical writings were arranged and presented.[17]

It is helpful to note that the content included in the earliest collections of the canonical writings and the way the material was arranged and presented would have been carefully considered by the original editors of the canonical collections as well as by the large number of scribes who later took part in their reproduction. Scholars are now more aware that significant thought went into the design of ancient letter collections and other bodies of literature. Whether it was the author of a collection of

---

5 (Berlin: de Gruyter, 2015); Todd Still and David Wilhite, eds., *The Apostolic Fathers and Paul*, PPSD 2 (New York: T&T Clark, 2018).

17. For recent studies on early Christian literary collections, see Bronwen Neil and Pauline Allen, eds., *Collecting Early Christian Letters: From the Apostle Paul to Late Antiquity* (Cambridge: Cambridge University Press, 2015); Christiana Sogno, Bradley Storin, and Edward Watts, eds., *Late Antique Letter Collections: A Critical Introduction and Reference Guide* (Oakland: University of California Press, 2017); Roy Gibson, "On the Nature of Ancient Letter Collection," *JRS* 102 (2012): 56–78.

works, one of his associates, or a later scribe, neither the material that was included in ancient literary collections nor the way
its contents were arranged was arbitrary. This may be observed
in ancient collections of writings by figures such as Pliny the
Younger, Seneca, and Cicero. As the editors of a recent study on
ancient letter collections explain, the individual responsible for
organizing an early collection of writings did

> not simply present whatever letter he could find in his records in
> whatever order they were filed. His goal was self-preservation,
> not comprehensive epistolary inclusion. This means that the
> letters were both selected for inclusion and deliberately orga-
> nized. Whether Greek or Latin, this type of authorship required
> the author to develop a strategy that enabled him to decide
> which letters to include and exclude as well as which features
> within the letters ought to be highlighted or downplayed.[18]

This insight becomes relevant to the study of the New Testament canon when it is recalled that most New Testament writings tended to circulate as part of one of three or possibly four
small subcollections: the fourfold Gospel, the Pauline Epistles,
and the Catholic Epistles, as well as possibly a Johannine collection.[19] Acts and Revelation were the only two writings which
appear to have circulated independently to any significant
degree, though at some point Acts began to circulate, at least
in some instances, alongside the Catholic Epistles, forming a
collection referred to as the *Praxapostolos*. Most of the extant

---

18. Christiana Sogno, Bradley Storin, and Edward Watts, "Introduction: Greek
     and Latin Epistolography and Epistolary Collections in Late Antiquity," in *Late
     Antique Letter Collections: A Critical Introduction and Reference Guide*, eds. Christiana
     Sogno, Bradley Storin, and Edward Watts (Oakland: University of California
     Press, 2017), 1–37 (4).

19. For further background on the canonical development of the subcollections
     of the New Testament, see W. Edward Glenny and Darian R. Lockett, eds.,
     Canon Formation: Tracing the Role of Subcollections in the Biblical Canon (London:
     Bloomsbury, forthcoming); Stanley E. Porter and Benjamin P. Laird, eds.,
     The New Testament Canon in Contemporary Research, TENT (Leiden: Brill,
     forthcoming).

Greek manuscripts appear to have included only one of these subcollections (typically the four Gospels), though a small number included multiple subcollections. Of the nearly six thousand Greek manuscripts that have been catalogued to date, only around sixty may be determined with reasonable certainty to have originally contained the entire New Testament. Because most of these were produced long after the fifth century, earlier manuscripts that include large portions of the New Testament canon, such as the fourth-century majuscule manuscripts Codex Sinaiticus and Codex Vaticanus, are of great importance, not merely for what they reveal regarding the early state of the New Testament text, but for the information they provide regarding the state of the early canonical collections and the way the writings were arranged and presented.

One interesting observation that can be made from the biblical manuscripts is that as the New Testament writings were reproduced over the following centuries, scribes continued to influence the way the canonical writings were presented and arranged, and even which writings were included. Just as a scribe might determine to make changes to a text at some point in church history to "improve" its grammar and syntax (e.g., changes in spelling and word order or the addition or omission of the Greek article) or, on some occasions, even to address a theological concern,[20] so too might a scribe decide to include works not included in his source material (the exemplar), to omit material, or to rearrange the writings. It is well known that many variant readings of the text of the New Testament emerged over the centuries as copies of the writings were produced. In addition to this, the extant manuscripts also indicate that various canonical-level features were introduced and refined. This demonstrates that in addition to several micro-level changes that took place within the text of the individual writings—changes involving individual words and phrases—so

---

20. For example, the omission of the words "nor the Son" from the text of Matthew 24:36.

too did a number of macro-level changes and developments to the biblical writings take place over the centuries. We find that some writings were included in some witnesses but not in others and that the arrangement of the material sometimes differed. This is not to suggest that there were no discernable characteristics of the biblical writings in the early centuries or that there was a lack of consistency or pattern in which writings typically appeared within each subcollection. There were clearly some writings that were consistently included in biblical manuscripts, and we even find common ways in which the material was arranged. The four canonical Gospels consistently appear together, for example (although their order is not always the same), and there is a basic pattern in the ordering of the Pauline Epistles, one that, as was noted earlier, was based primarily upon length. Hebrews is missing, however, in a few later manuscripts.[21] There are also some manuscripts that do not appear to have included certain writings that are part of the Catholic Epistles.[22]

As to the arrangement of the canonical writings, the extant witnesses provide insight relating to the overall structure of the New Testament canon as well as how the material within each subcollection was arranged. Regarding the former, we find that many of the Greek witnesses that include multiple subcollections follow the sequence Gospels—Acts—Catholic Epistles—Pauline Epistles—Revelation.[23] Many English readers are

---

21.   Hebrews is not included in Codex Boernerianus (012), a ninth-century manuscript. The Greek text of Hebrews is also missing from Codex Augiensis (010), although this manuscript includes a Latin version of Hebrews. This may suggest that Hebrews was not present in the original codex or in the exemplar used by the scribe.

22.   Examples include P[72], which omits James and 1–3 John, and Codex Vaticanus Graecus 2061 (048), which omits Jude.

23.   This is the case in important early witnesses such as Codex Alexandrinus, Codex Vaticanus, and Codex Ephraemi Rescriptus. A notable exception to this arrangement in the Greek tradition is Codex Sinaiticus which follows the unusual order of Gospels—Pauline Epistles—Acts—Catholic Epistles—Revelation. Aside from the placement of Acts, this arrangement found in Sinaiticus is most closely aligned with the arrangement found in modern English translations.

surprised to learn that the arrangement of the New Testament writings to which they are accustomed is represented more frequently in Latin manuscripts than in the Greek tradition. In many Latin manuscripts, the Catholic Epistles are often placed between the Pauline Epistles and Revelation, whereas Greek manuscripts tend to place the Catholic Epistles before the Pauline Epistles.

In addition to the more common ways in which the larger codices arrange the smaller units of the New Testament writings, there are also differences in how the material within the individual subcollections is presented. As an illustration, we may briefly consider textual witnesses containing Hebrews. It is clear, for example, that some of the earlier papyri witnesses containing the Pauline letter corpus placed Hebrews near the beginning of the collection. This was the case with the early papyrus manuscript of the Pauline Epistles, P[46], where Hebrews is placed between Romans and 1 Corinthians, and possibly with P[13] and P[126].[24] The placement of Hebrews near the beginning of the corpus was short-lived, however, as scribes eventually began placing it after 2 Thessalonians, that is, at the end of Paul's letters to the churches. This was later followed by its placement at the very end of the collection after Philemon. We find Hebrews placed, for example, after 2 Thessalonians in Greek codices such as Sinaiticus, Alexandrinus, Vaticanus, Ephraemi Rescriptus, and Freerianus. Manuscripts produced after the fifth century, however, consistently placed Hebrews at the end of the Pauline corpus. By examining the textual witnesses to the Pauline corpus, we are thus able to learn something about the canonical status of Hebrews over the centuries. To be sure, the placement of Hebrews was not arbitrary. Because the Pauline Epistles were originally arranged according to length, its relocation to the end of the corpus would have

---

24. While these two manuscripts include only portions of Hebrews, they include pagination that indicates that Hebrews was placed near the beginning of the collection.

communicated to readers that something was unique about its background or relationship to the other writings.

Canonical Lists and the Study of the New Testament Canon

A third category of ancient witness to the early state of the New Testament is ancient lists that enumerate the individual writings of the New Testament. While many of the canonical lists may be found in the writings of Christian writers and in biblical manuscripts, it is perhaps best to treat them as a separate type of witness to the early state of the New Testament canon.[25] In addition to quotations and allusions to the canonical writings, some patristic sources provide specific lists of the individual writings that were received as Scripture. Perhaps the most valuable listing of the canonical writings comes from the fourth-century historian and bishop Eusebius of Caesarea who, in his *Ecclesiastical History*, famously lists the writings received by the church and organizes them into specific categories (see *Hist. eccl.* 3.3 and 3.25). Eusebius not only provides a list of writings regarded by the church as Scripture, he also quotes frequently from earlier writings that are no longer extant, many of which provide valuable insight regarding the background of the New Testament. Within his writings, for example, are lengthy citations of the works of important writers such as Papias (*Hist. eccl.* 3.39.15–16) and Origen (*Hist. eccl.* 6.25.11–14).

Origen's homily on Joshua (*Hom. Jos.* 7.1) provides an exceptionally valuable listing of the canonical writings. The source has been preserved in a Latin translation completed by Rufinus of Aquileia in the early fifth century. Though scholars have long disputed the accuracy of Rufinus' translation, the list provides an important early witness to the state of the canon. Remarkably, Origen's list refers to each major unit of the New Testament, though there is some ambiguity regarding some of

---

25. There is a lack of consensus as to which ancient witnesses may be properly categorized as canonical lists and even the features that might define such a category.

the details. Because he simply refers in a general way to the epistles of John, it is not entirely clear that he was familiar with all three epistles. There is also dispute regarding his viewpoint on Revelation. While some witnesses to this list do not refer to Revelation, it is clear from Origen's other writings that he regarded Revelation as canonical. Hence, while Origen does not refer explicitly to each writing in the New Testament by name, a plausible case could be made that he recognized the same twenty-seven writings that are now affirmed as canonical.

In addition to the notable lists contained in the writings of Origen and Eusebius, canonical lists appear in one of Cyril of Jerusalem's *Catechetical Lectures* (4.36), in Athanasius' famous Festal Letter of 367 CE, in Epiphanius' *Panarion* (*Pan.* 76.5), in Gregory of Nazianzus' poetic work *Carmina Theologica* (*Carmen* 12.31), in Canon 85 of the so-called *Apostolic Canons*, a writing that appears in a larger body of works known as the *Apostolic Constitutions*, and in Amphilochius of Iconium's poetic piece *Iambics for Seleucus*.[26]

Several canonical lists have also been discovered in biblical manuscripts and other sources that are difficult to categorize. For example, some manuscripts include what is referred to as a stichometric list, that is, a list in which a scribe recorded the number of lines (*stichoi*) of each writing contained in the manuscript. Since scribes were typically paid by the number of lines completed, they would sometimes place a list of the works completed at the end of their manuscript with the number of *stichoi* that corresponds to each writing. Notable examples of this include a stichometric list found in the middle of the mid-sixth century manuscript Codex Claromontanus, the so-called Cheltenham Canon, a list of the biblical writings discovered by Theodor Mommsen in the nineteenth century, and a list

---

26. For a treatment of the early canonical lists, see Edmon L. Gallagher and John D. Meade, *The Biblical Canon Lists from Early Christianity: Texts and Analysis* (New York: Oxford University Press, 2017), which includes the texts in both the original languages and translation, along with explanation.

composed in Syriac that was discovered in St. Catherine's Monastery that has been classified as Syriac Manuscript 10.

Scholars have also analyzed the decrees rendered by various ecclesiastical councils during the late fourth century and in later periods of church history. These "canons," as they are often described, occasionally refer to the individual works contained in the New Testament. The earliest council to which a canonical list is attributed was the regional gathering of bishops in Asia Minor known as the Synod of Laodicea, a local gathering which took place around 363 CE. Fifty-nine canons from this gathering have been preserved, with the final canon stating that only the writings from the Old and New Testaments are to be read in the church. In some later witnesses, a Canon 60 is included that lists each of the New Testament writings with the exception of Revelation by name. It is unclear if this canon was original or if the list it contains emerged at some point after the synod convened. In either case, the list provides an early witness to the scope of the New Testament. Another important list associated with an ecclesiastical council is Canon 24 of the Council of Carthage, a larger gathering which convened in 397 CE. In stating its approval of various decrees made some four years prior at the Synod of Hippo, this canon cites by name each of the twenty-seven New Testament writings.

Perhaps the most notable early canonical list is contained in the so-called Muratorian Fragment.[27] Discovered during the eighteenth century in the Ambrosian Library of Milan, Italy, the Fragment contains an ancient eighty-five-line description of early Christian writings often referred to as the Muratorian Canon. The author lists the writings that have been received as Scripture, as well as a small number of additional writings

---

27. For an overview of research relating to the Fragment, see Geoffrey Mark Hahneman, *The Muratorian Fragment and the Development of the Canon* (Oxford: Clarendon, 1992); Joseph Verheyden, "The Canon Muratori: A Matter of Dispute," in *Biblical Canons*, eds. Jean-Marie Auwers and Henk Jan de Jonge, BETL 163 (Leuven: Leuven University Press, 2003), 487–556; Eckhard J. Schnabel, "The Muratorian Fragment: The State of Research," *JETS* 57 (2014): 231–64; Gallagher and Meade, *The Biblical Canon Lists*, 175–83.

outside of the New Testament. The Fragment is written in Latin, though it is often thought to be a translation from an earlier Greek source. Of dispute is the likely date in which the Fragment originated. The traditional viewpoint is that the list was compiled during the second half of the second century, a date consistent with its claim that the *Shepherd of Hermas* was written "in our times." This has been challenged, however, by those persuaded that such a developed list is not likely to have existed until the fourth century. Though the initial portion of the Muratorian Canon has not survived, it appears to assume the canonical status of the four Gospels (the surviving portion of the manuscript begins by referring to Luke as the third Gospel). In addition to the Gospels, the Canon refers to Acts, thirteen epistles of Paul (Hebrews excluded), what appears to be two epistles of John, Jude, and Revelation. Regardless of whether the list originated during the second century or during a later period, it provides a valuable window into the early state of the canon, at least as it was known in the West. The omission of Hebrews and some of the Catholic Epistles would seem to indicate that these writings were slower in gaining recognition than the other portions of the New Testament.

Conclusion

Neither our survey of the primary sources for the study of the New Testament canon nor our discussion of the major points of agreement and disagreement among canon scholars is designed to be the final word on these subjects. No doubt there are many more observations and insights that could be offered about the various positions relating to the New Testament canon and the relevant primary sources. We have not attempted here to dissect and exegete the essays themselves or their responses, because we do not wish to preclude the active engagement of our readers with these essays and their responses. As editors, we have found each of the major proposals to be a substantial articulation of the respective position, in which the authors have taken seriously their task of engaging discussion of their respective tradition's view of the origin, formation, and purpose of the New Testament canon. The authors have addressed the major questions that we posed to them and have marshaled a variety of evidence to answer the questions and make clear the substance of their respective positions. The substantial quality of these essays is reflected in the fact that the responses by each contributor make their own unique and worthy contribution to the further debate. The responses have moved beyond simply picking at small points and have engaged the larger and substantial issues that are raised in the major proposals, so that, in the end, we as readers are left with clear indications of the strengths and weaknesses of each position. More than that, however, we are left with a greater appreciation of the individual positions—some of which may be relatively lesser known to us—to the point that we may wish to explore each of them more fully. We thank our contributors for presenting this challenge and providing guidance for us.

NAME INDEX

SCRIPTURE AND ANCIENT SOURCES INDEX